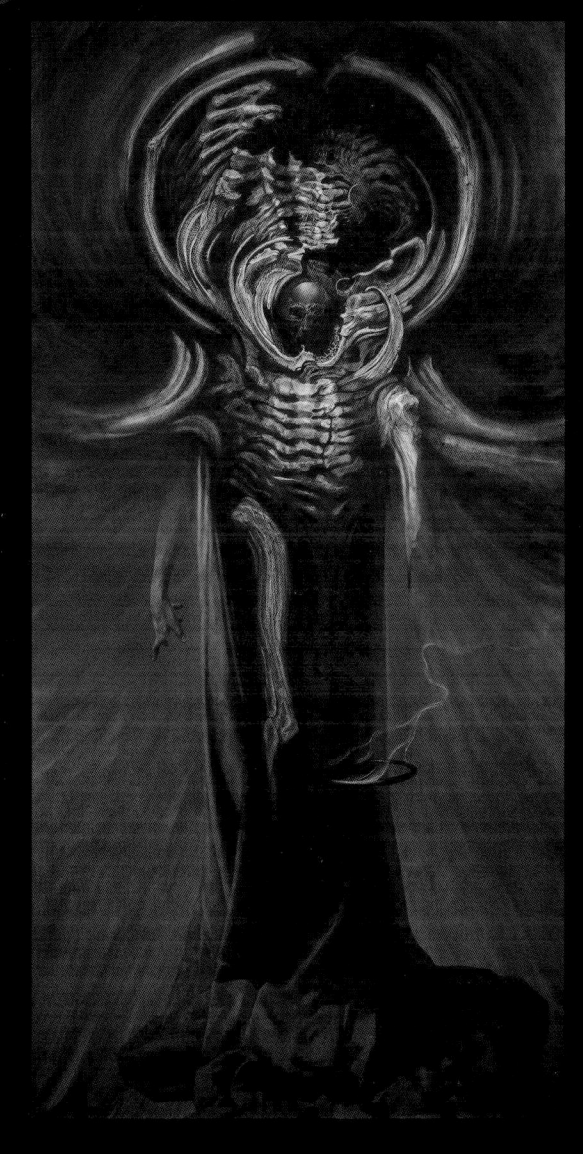

COVENANT

THE ART OF ALLEN WILLIAMS

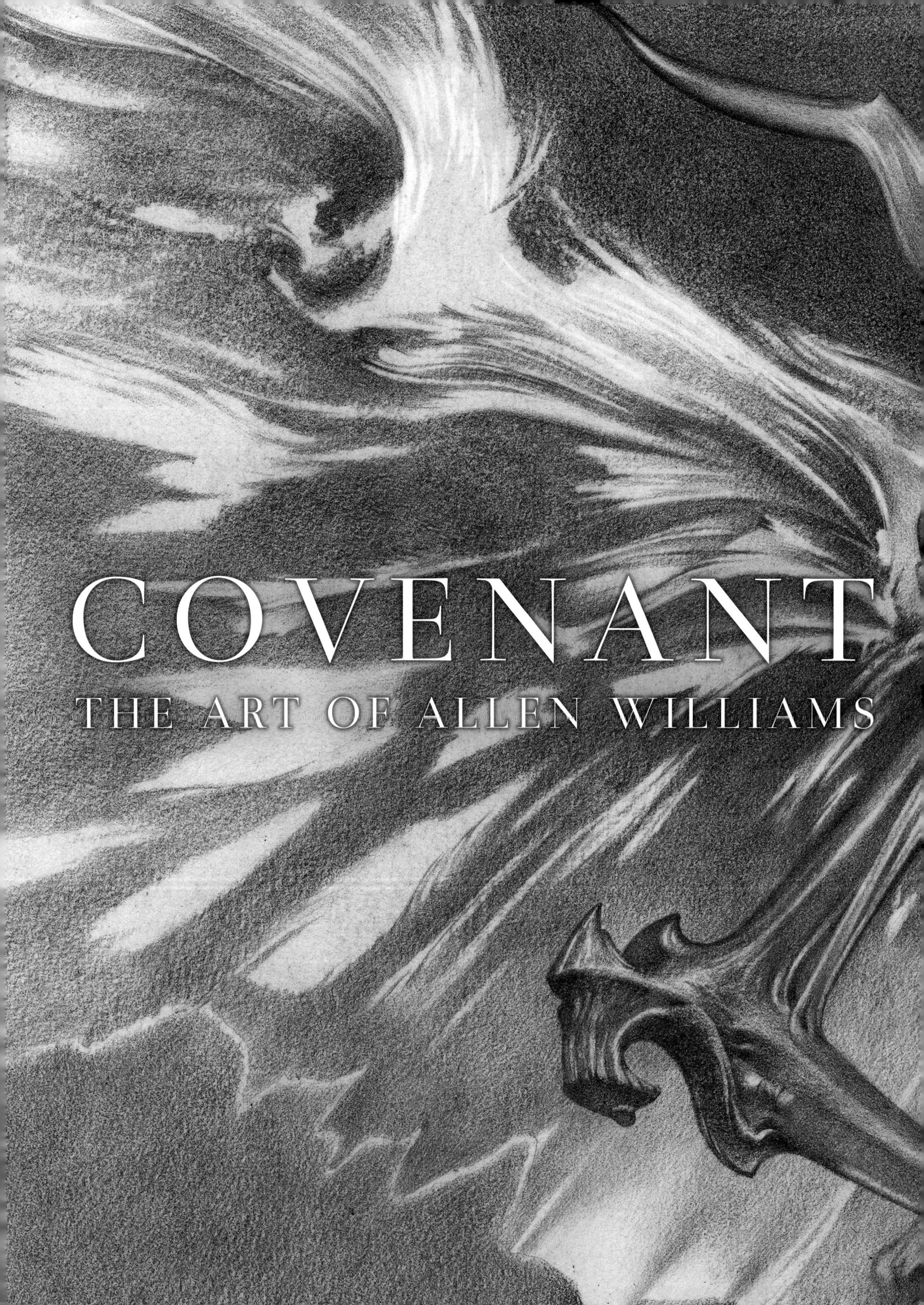

COVENANT

THE ART OF ALLEN WILLIAMS

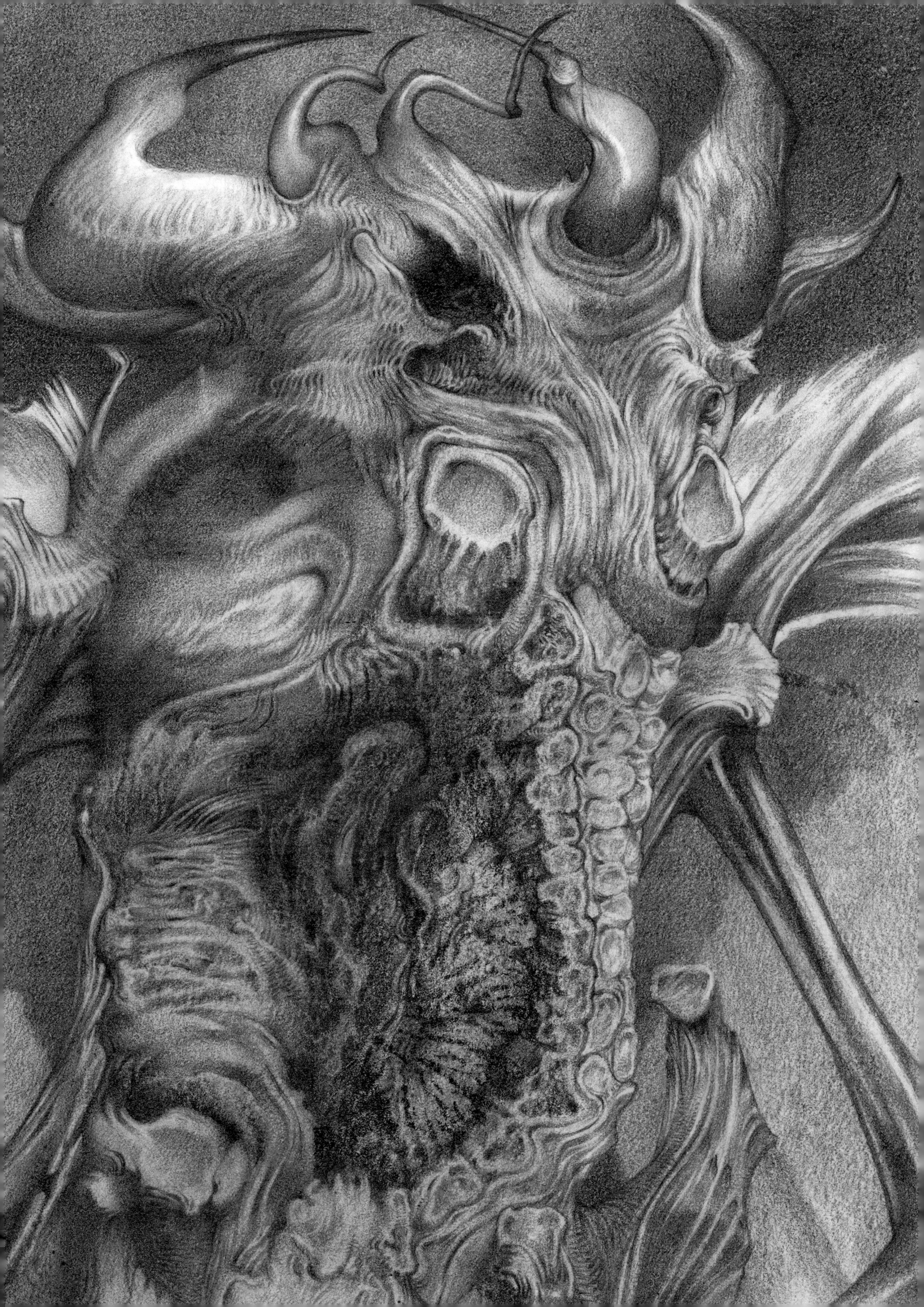

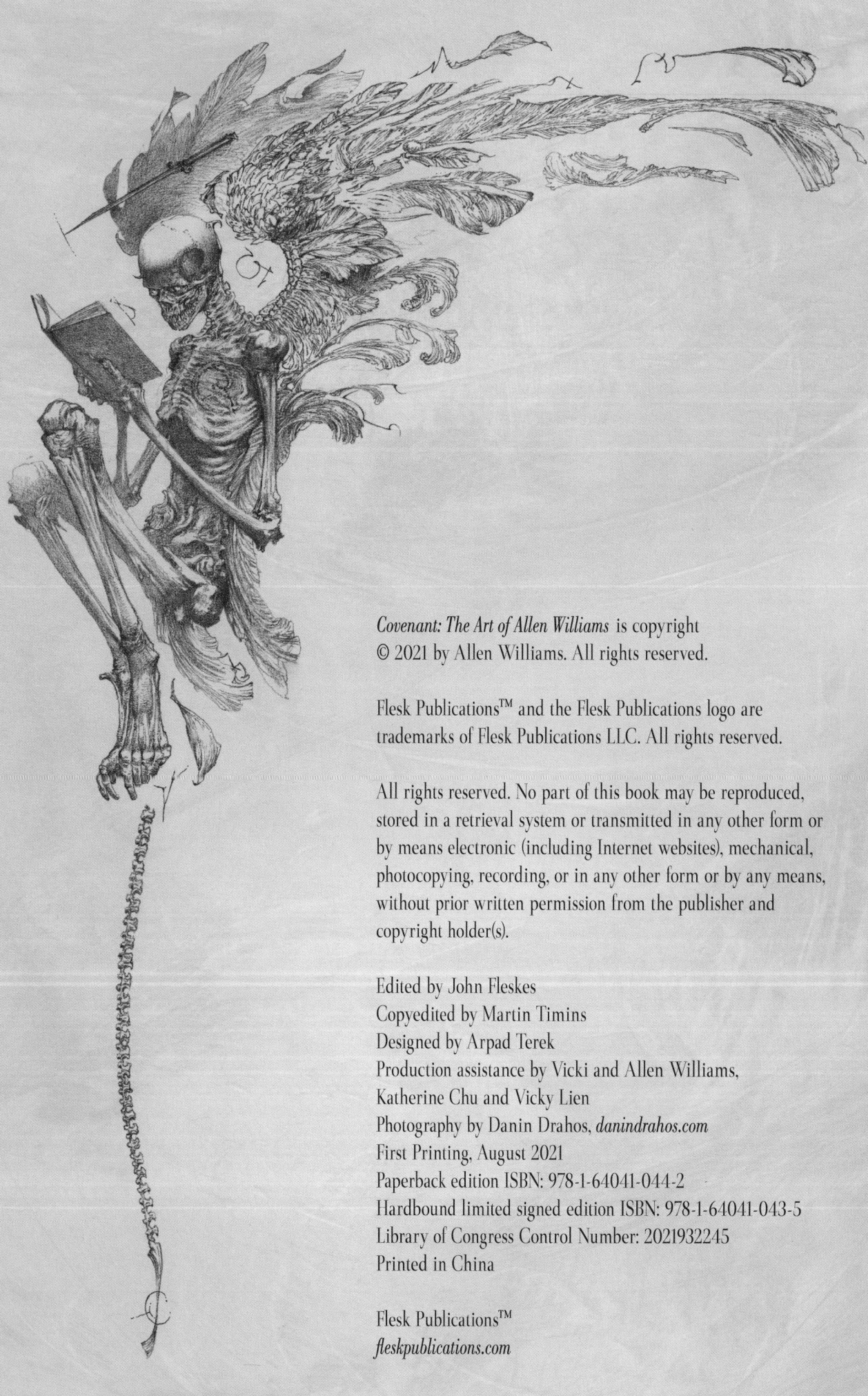

Edited by John Fleskes
Copyedited by Martin Timins
Designed by Arpad Terek
Production assistance by Vicki and Allen Williams,
Katherine Chu and Vicky Lien
Photography by Danin Drahos, *danindrahos.com*
First Printing, August 2021
Paperback edition ISBN: 978-1-64041-044-2
Hardbound limited signed edition ISBN: 978-1-64041-043-5
Library of Congress Control Number: 2021932245
Printed in China

Flesk Publications™
fleskpublications.com

Introduction

This book, *The Covenant*, is begun. It represents a petition of sorts—to the manifestations of metaphor contained within, a representation of a thematic approach to the summoning of guardians, and in and of itself a sigil. I am often asked if I believe in what I make, and my answer is: I believe in willful, purposeful creation. I believe the things we make can have meaning, and whether that meaning is concrete or philosophical doesn't really change the fact that the creation *is*.

Is this real? It is as I am. A collection of ideas, faults, desires and in general, humanity, constructed in unusual ways.

A great deal of the work that I do for myself is explorational, which is to say, in regards to will, sometimes it feels like I am led by the will of the piece. This is a romantic way of saying that I allow some chaos into the piece and then respond to its subconscious suggestion. Much of the narrative that I have written here comes from a similar place, at times seeming to self-assemble from a few words that pop into my mind as I work. At other times, the narrative leads the piece and comes fully formed.

The guardian theme is evident and has been a part of my work for a great while—maybe even from the beginning—and certainly born out of my own life and experiences. When I was a child, very young and still afraid of the dark, I would close my eyes and envision a being, bright and shining that would stand in front of an enormous door, barring any frightful beast or thought from entering. As I grew older, I came upon the realization that most of the *beasts* of the world were not at all frightful looking (and my thoughts were nothing to fear), that the danger was in believing the look of a thing was a window to its nature.

I came to a similar conclusion about night and day when I realized that as many (if not more) wretched things were perpetrated in the light of day, in full view, as were in the shadows of night and that to believe one more fearful than the other would be incorrect. But rather than say to fear them equally, let me say that I came to see as much wonder in the night as in the day. And, to this day, I tend to be nocturnal and enjoy walking by myself at night.

My hope is that you will see my work for what it is: a desire to create and, in a way, to be a guardian of those aspects of humanity that so often fall under attack or are left in disregard.

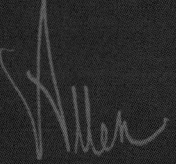

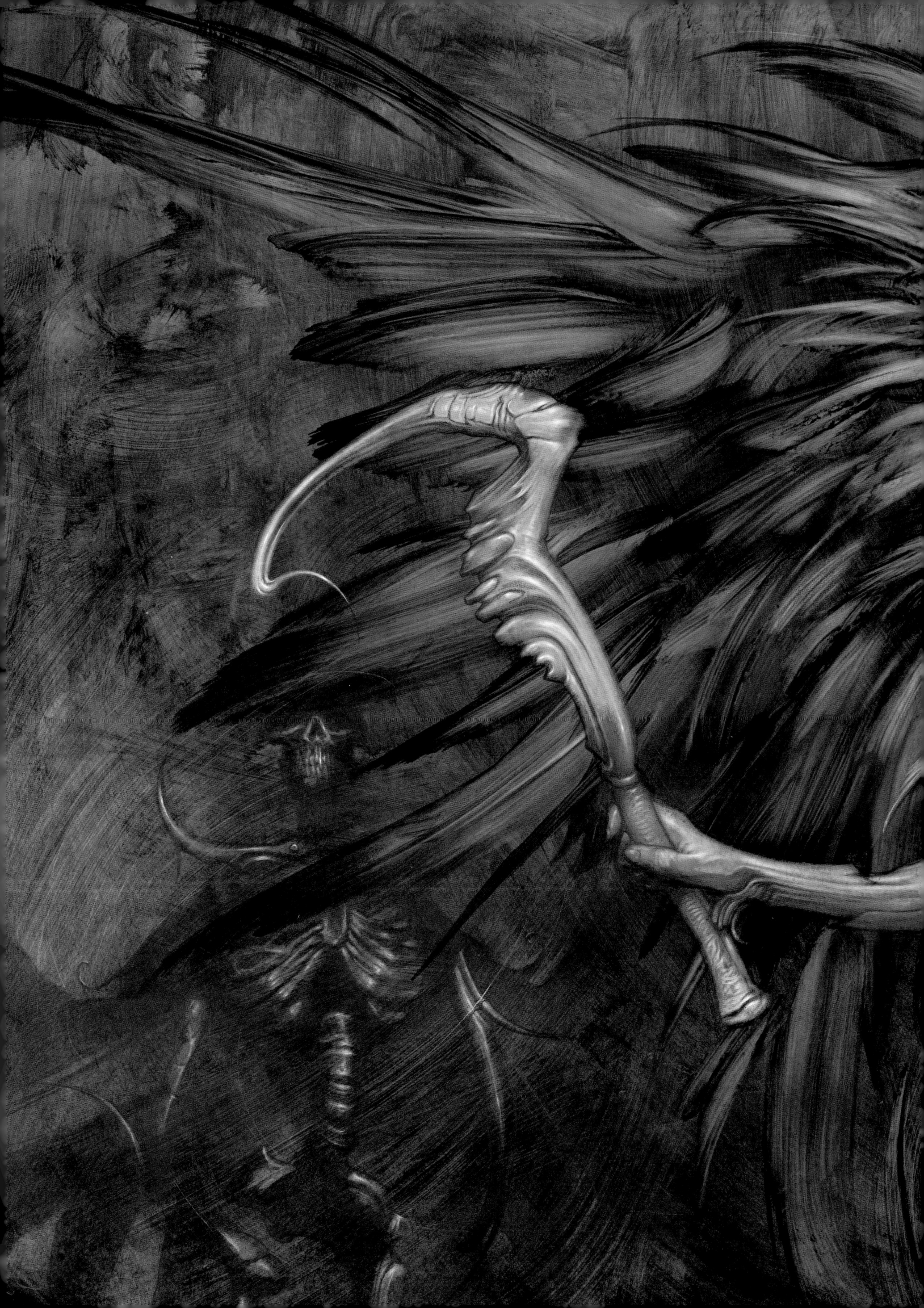

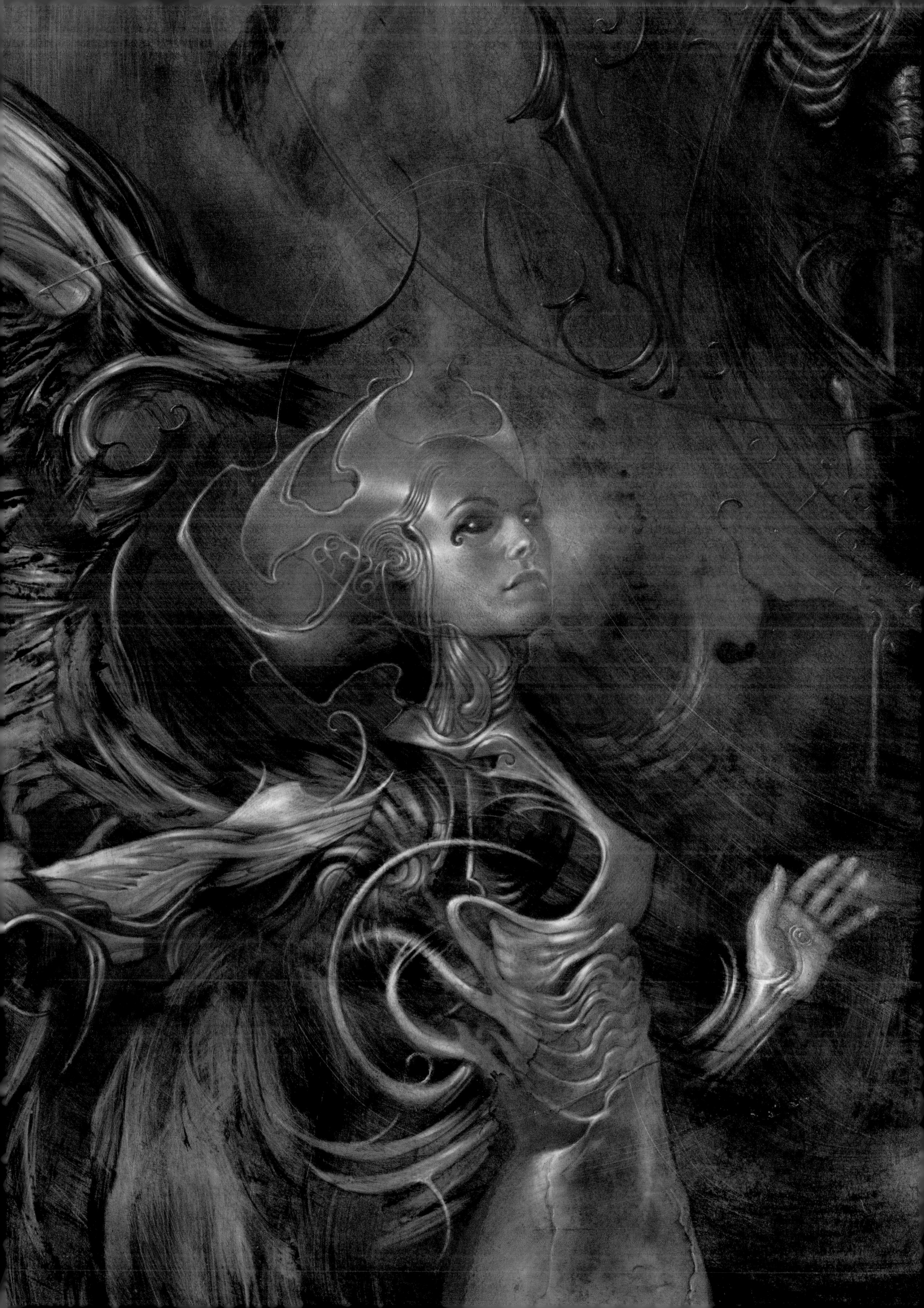

Heru:
The Distant One

The Sky, the many-shaped.
She is anything she wishes to be...
but keeps her human face
to commune with humankind.
"Know her by the passing
of the shadow of a great
winged creature
upon the ground."

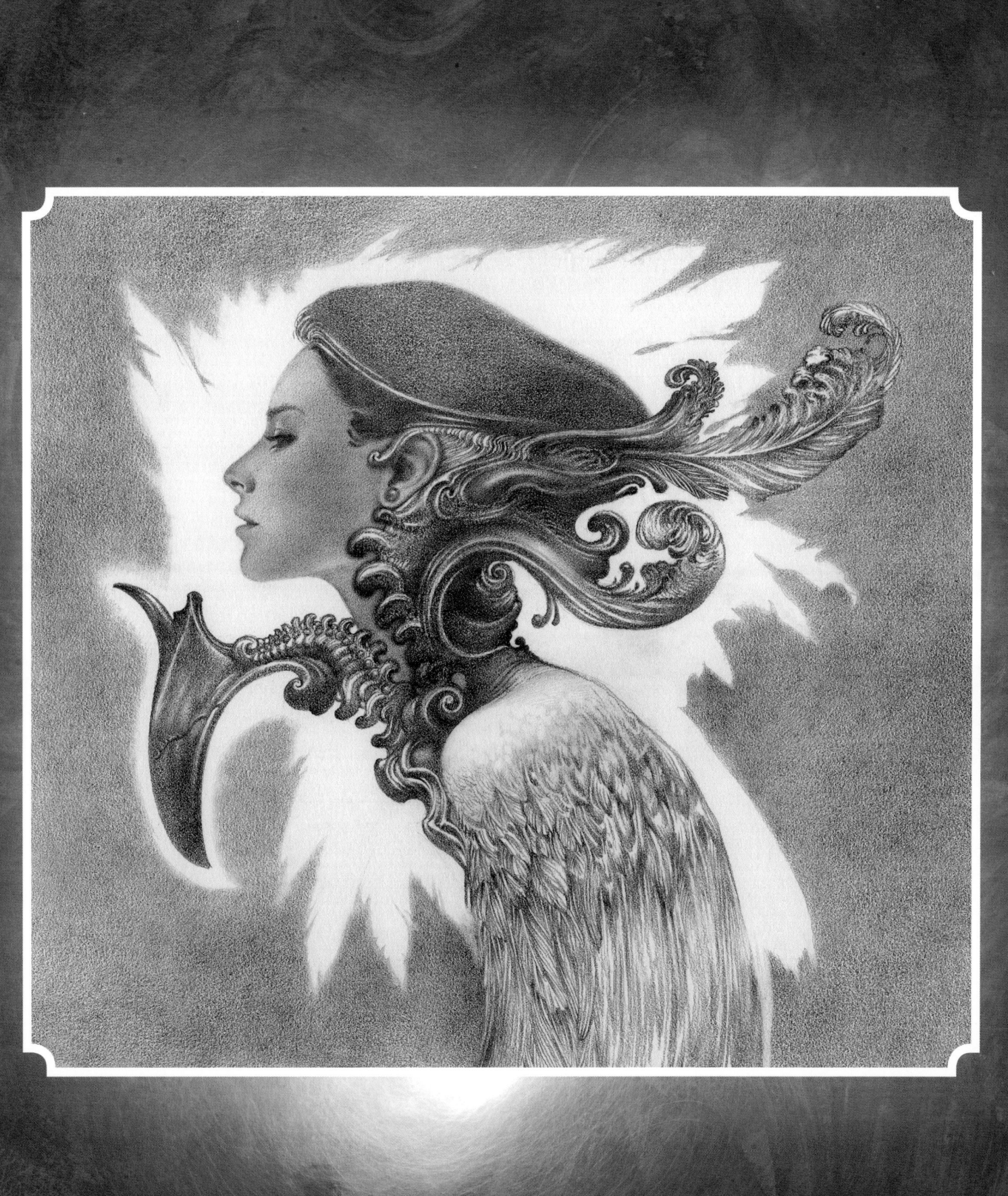

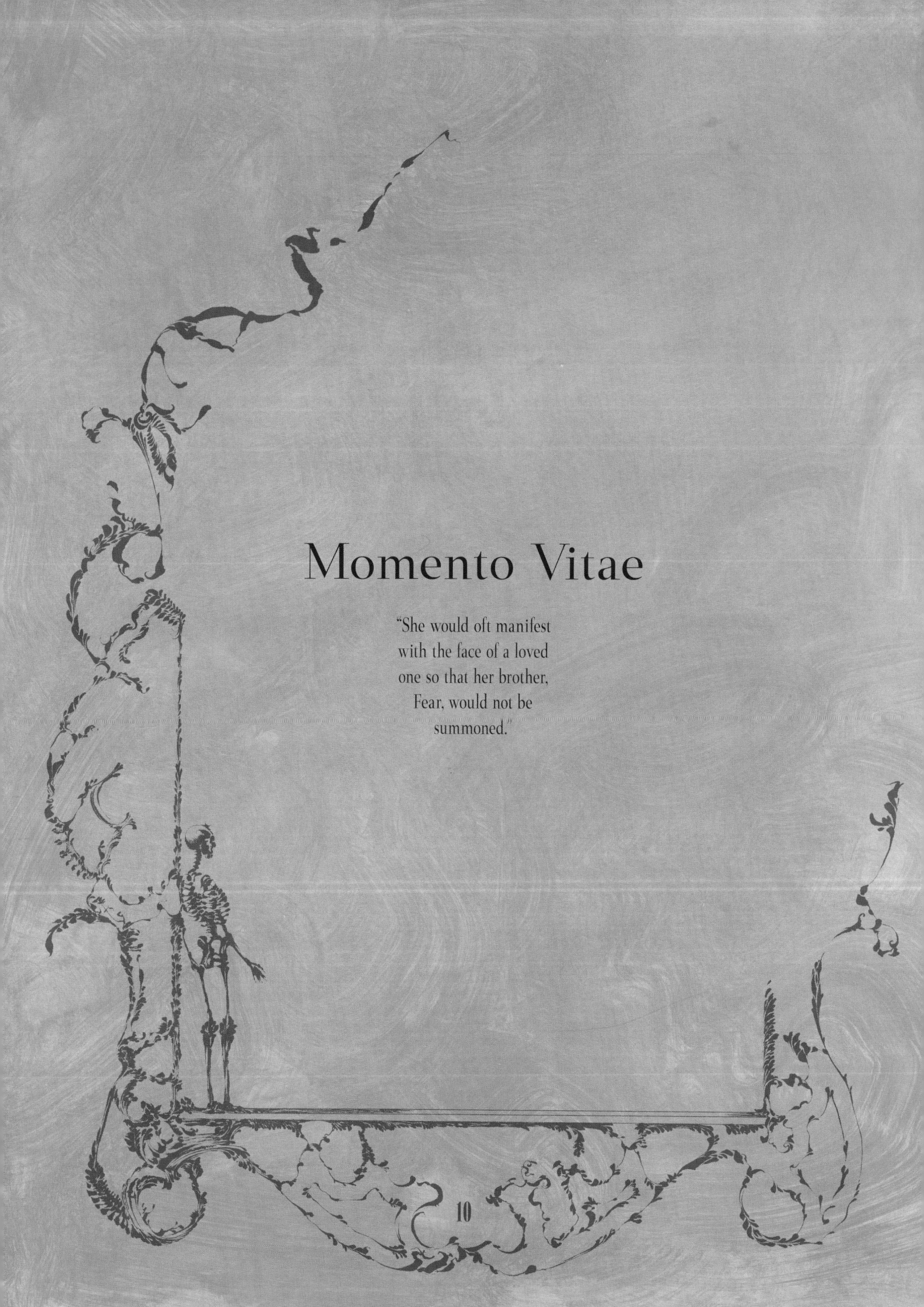

Momento Vitae

"She would oft manifest
with the face of a loved
one so that her brother,
Fear, would not be
summoned."

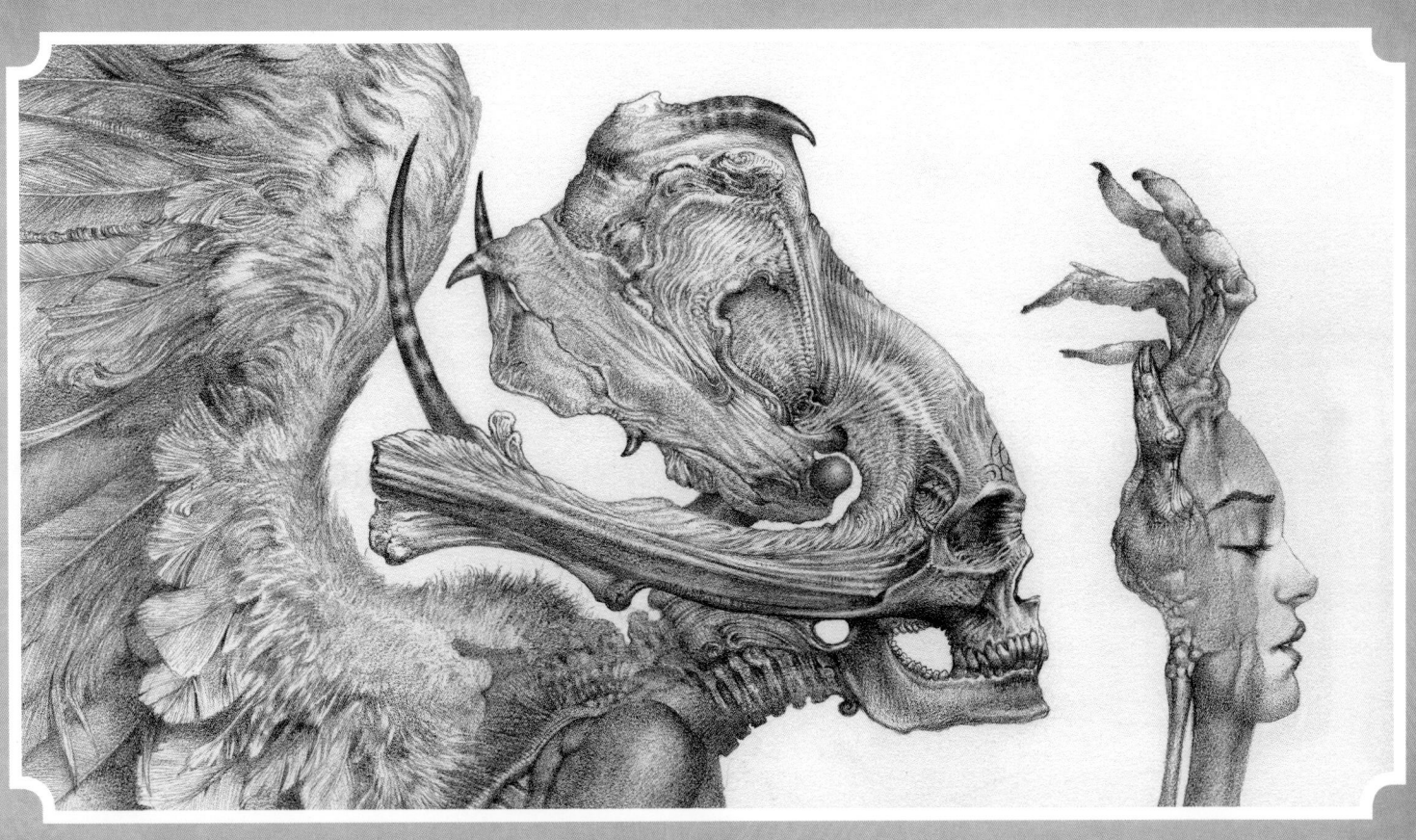

The Eye Thief

"I found her lying upon my path.
She had no eyes of her own,
so I lent her one of mine.
She never returned it...
But now when I dream,
I always dream of flying."

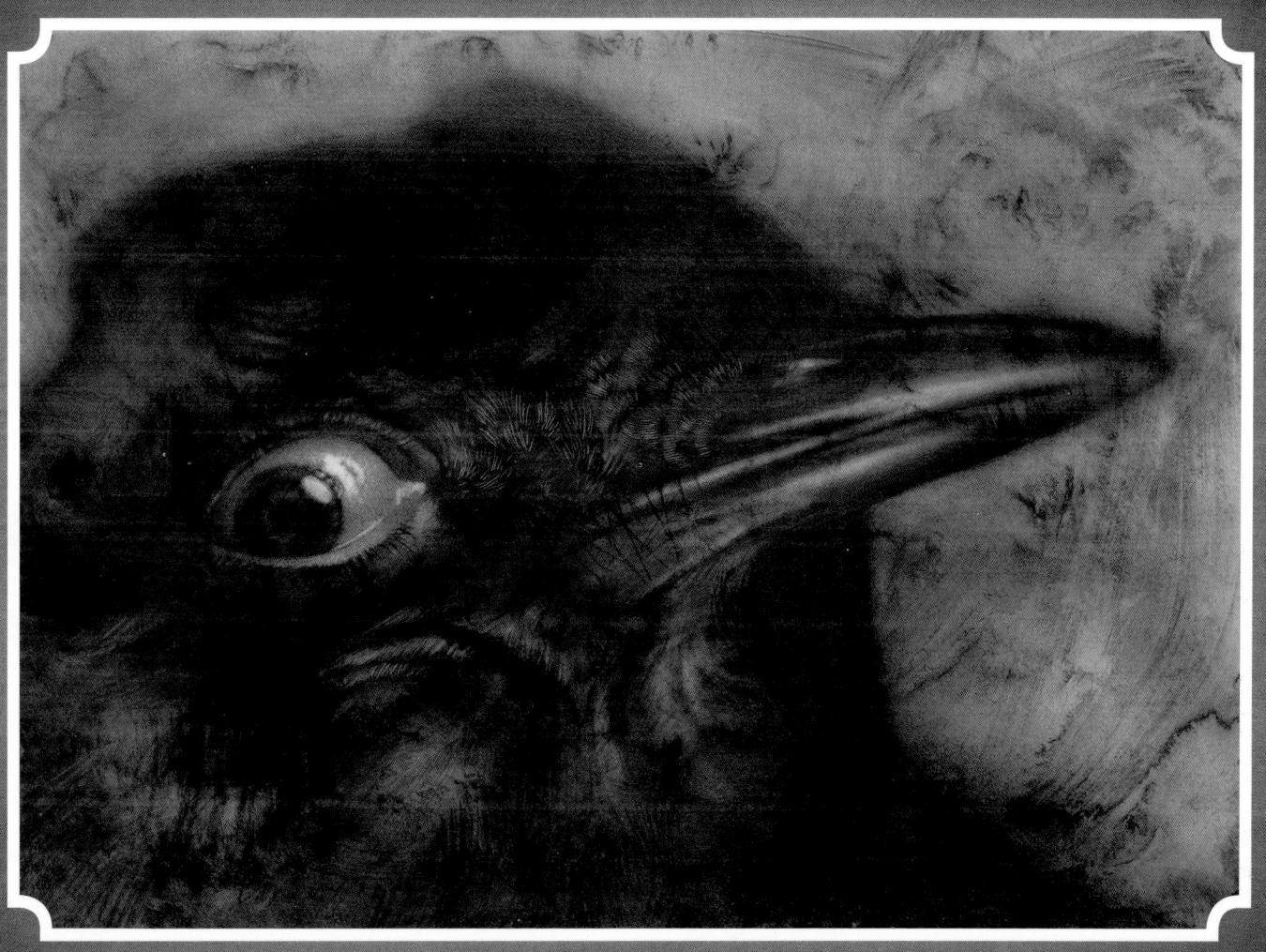

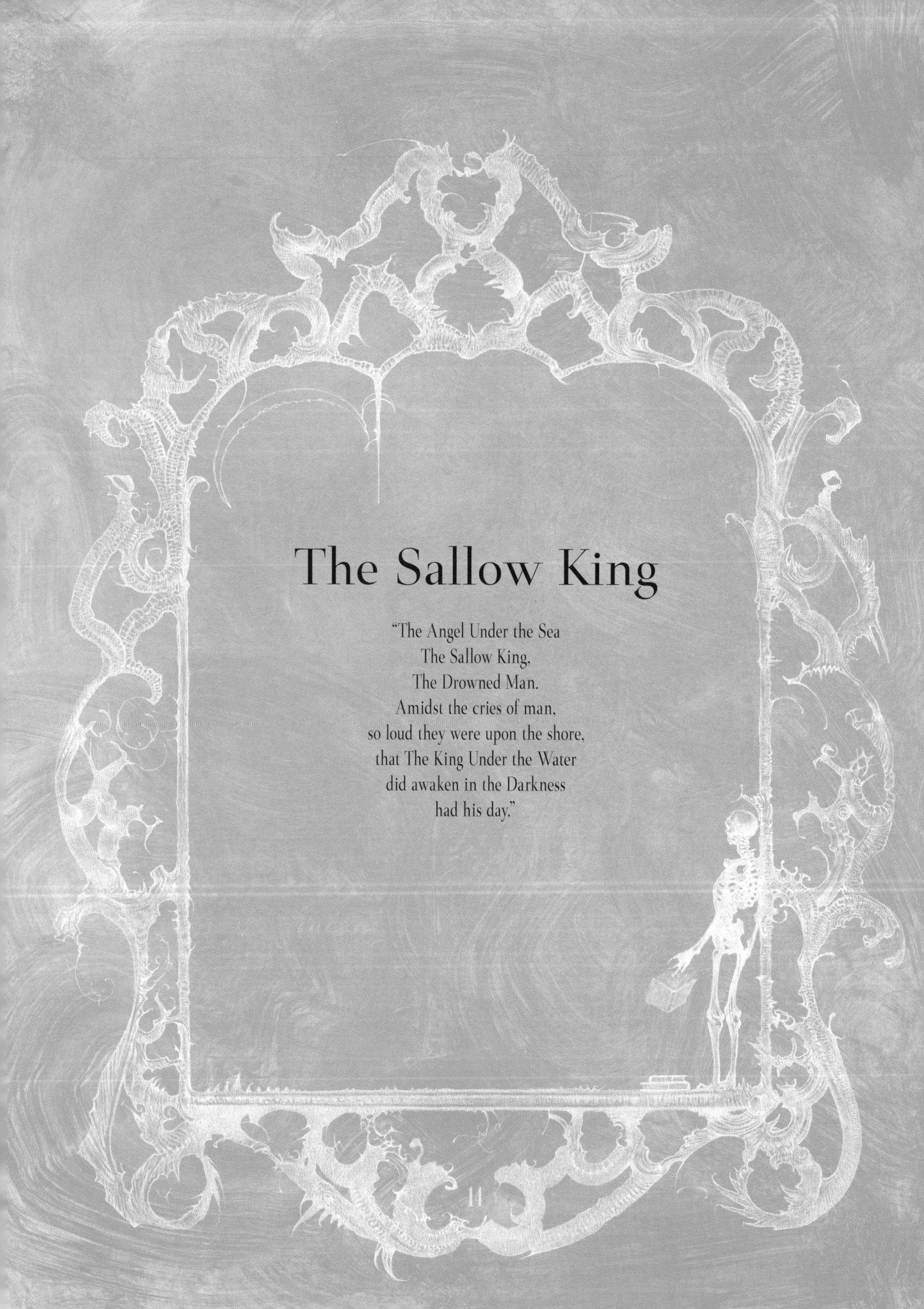

The Sallow King

"The Angel Under the Sea
The Sallow King,
The Drowned Man.
Amidst the cries of man,
so loud they were upon the shore,
that The King Under the Water
did awaken in the Darkness
had his day."

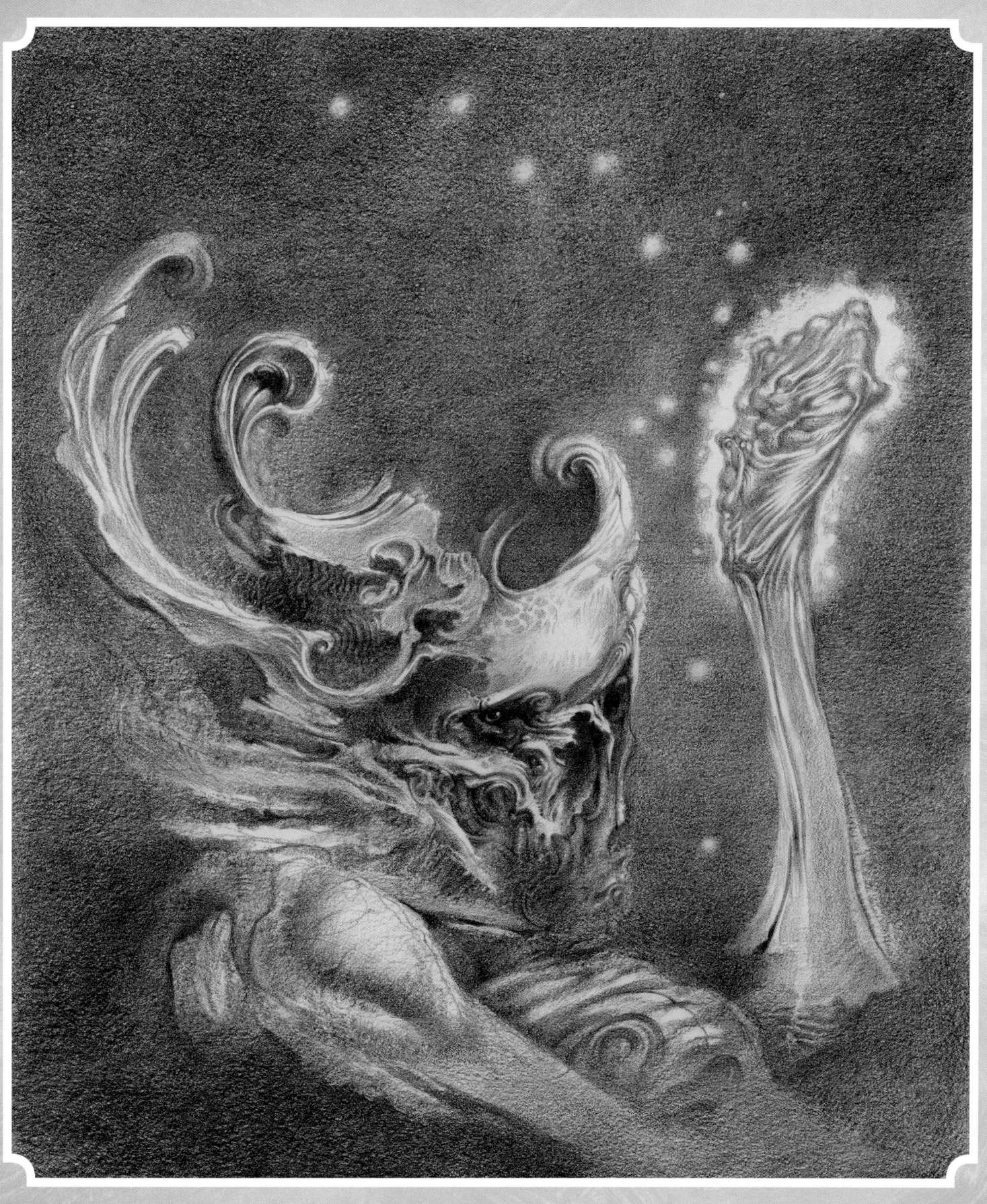

The Marker

"Beware," it said.
"The golden things
of the world
do not glitter
but salivate."

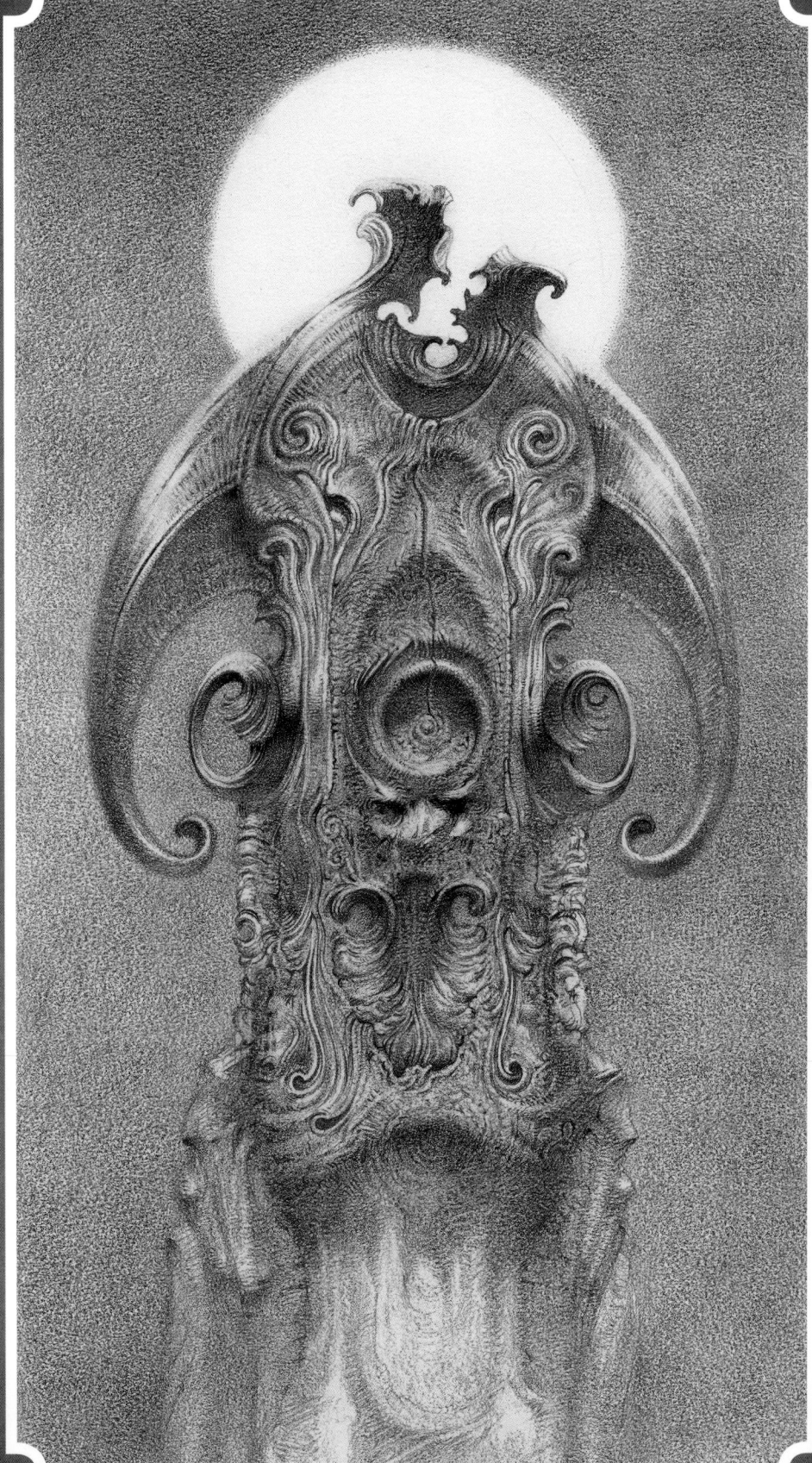

The Gaunt
Queen

The Gaunt Queen
bore a wreath
of tempestuous storms.
The three blind kings
sought her counsel
and with them came
their offering
of dreamers.

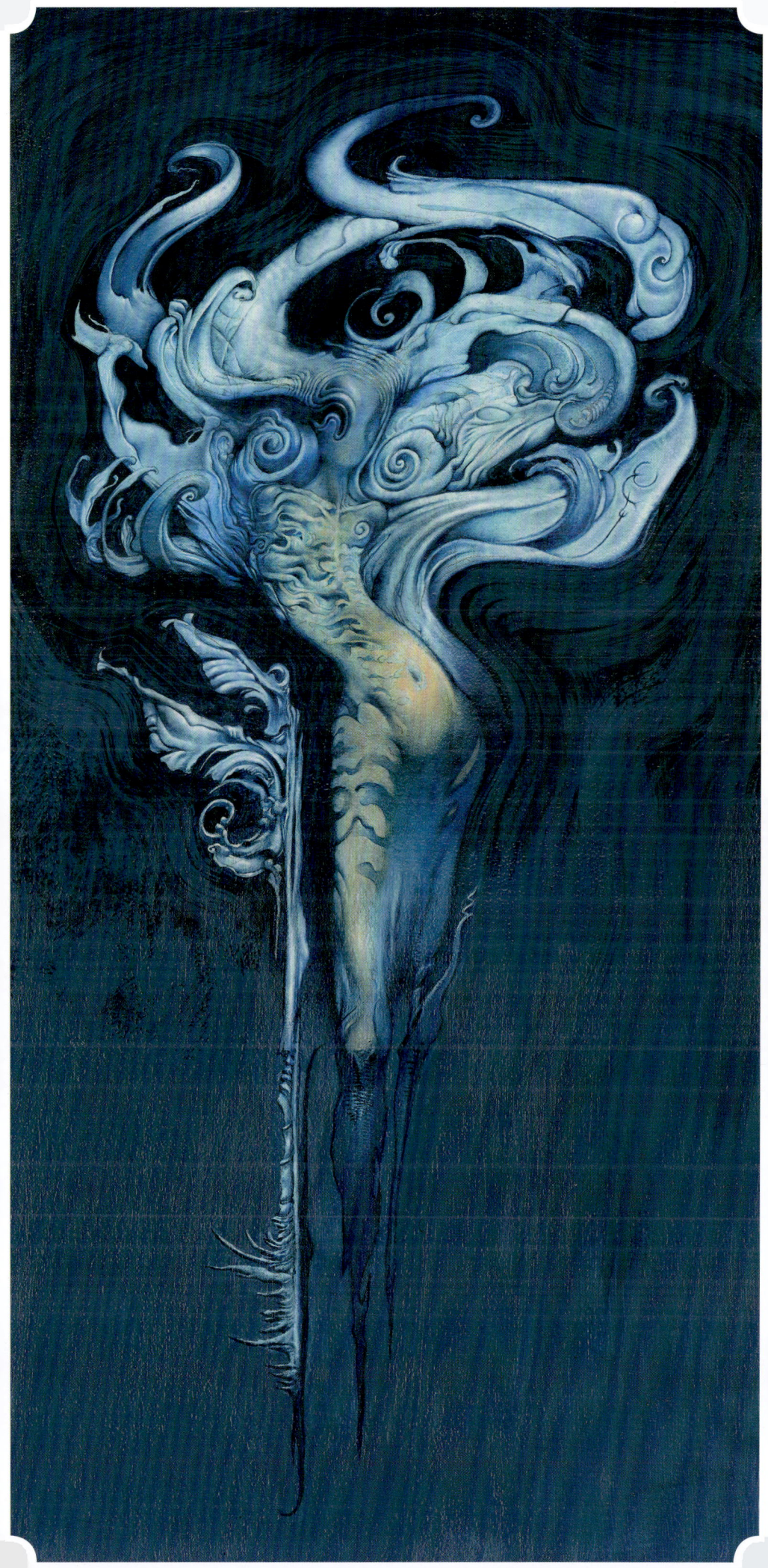

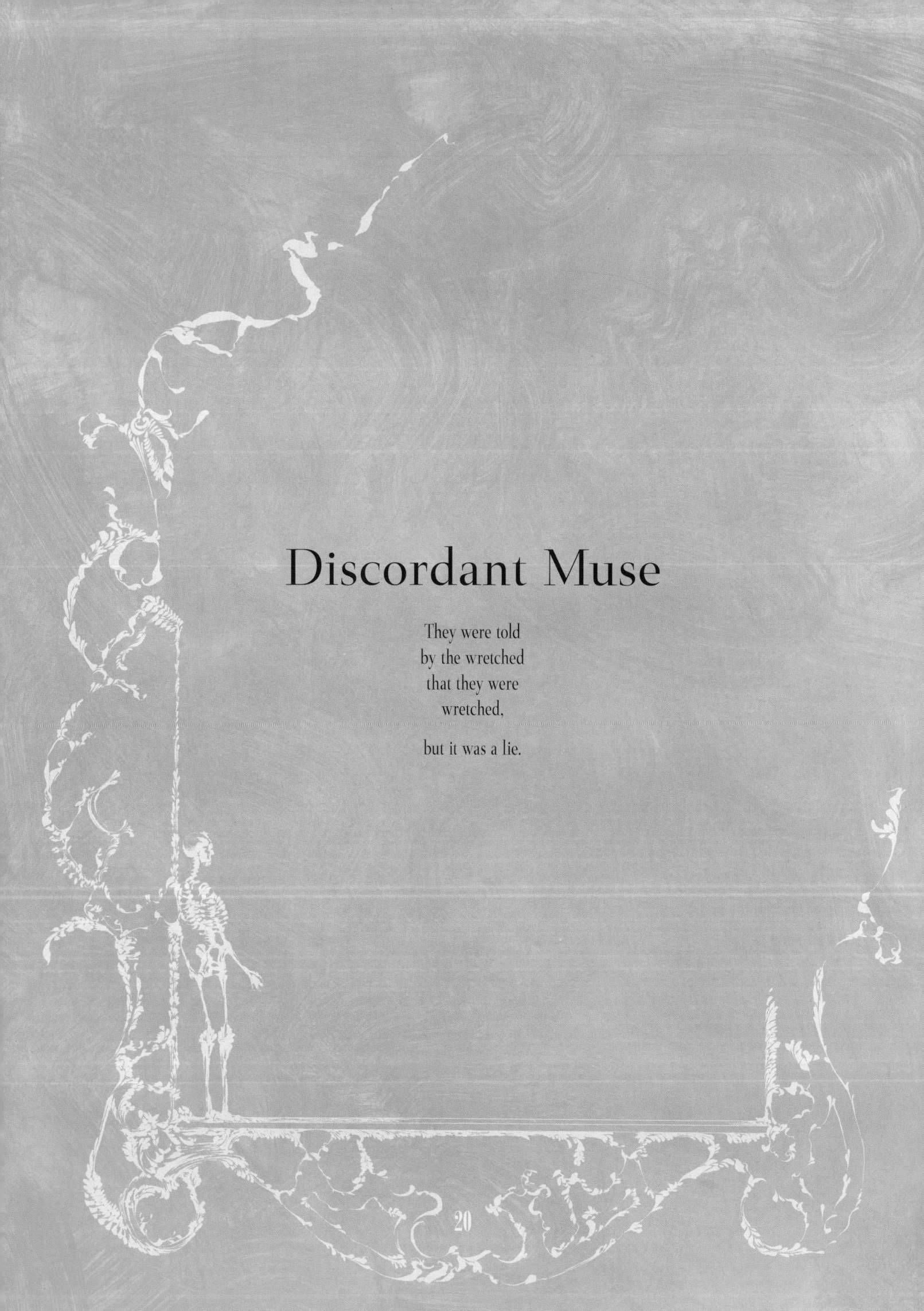

Discordant Muse

They were told
by the wretched
that they were
wretched,

but it was a lie.

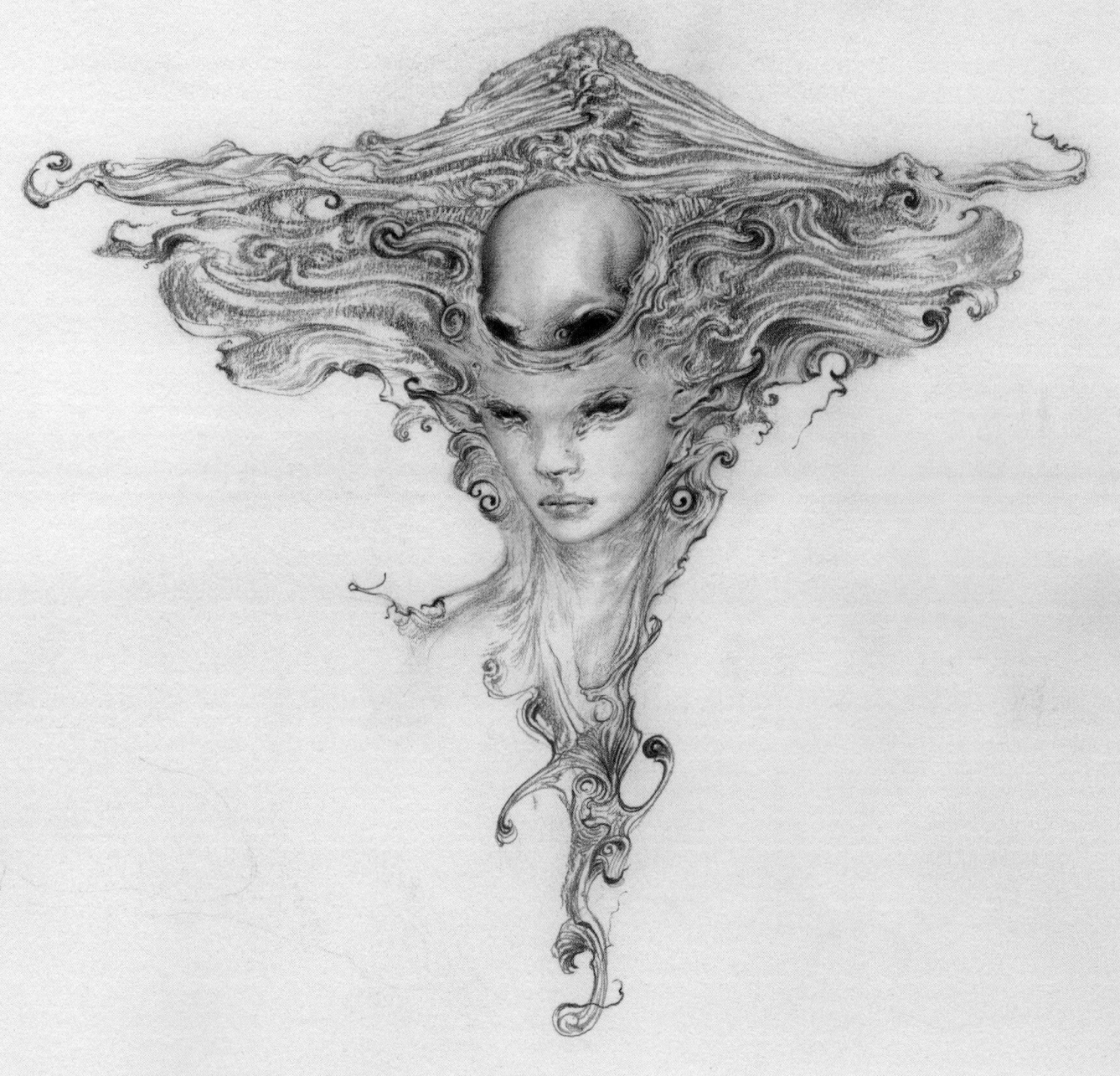

The Discordant Muse.

They were told by the wretched, that they where wretched.
but it was a lie.

Blackshear

Kae: What are you doing?

Blackshear: Fishing.

Kae: No fish in this pool, never have been.

Blackshear: Not fishing for fish.

Kae: Then what?

Blackshear: Stars.

Kae: Stars not in pool... stars up above.

Blackshear: Not the actual bright and shiny ones...
the pale ones, on the water.

Kae: Oh... why?

Blackshear: We Djinn, each and every, are forbidden
by Solomon to look upon the stars. So our lands are veiled
in a darkness through which their light does not wander...
except here. We are given this reflecting pool so that
we may see their beauty...
but to do so we must ever bow our heads.

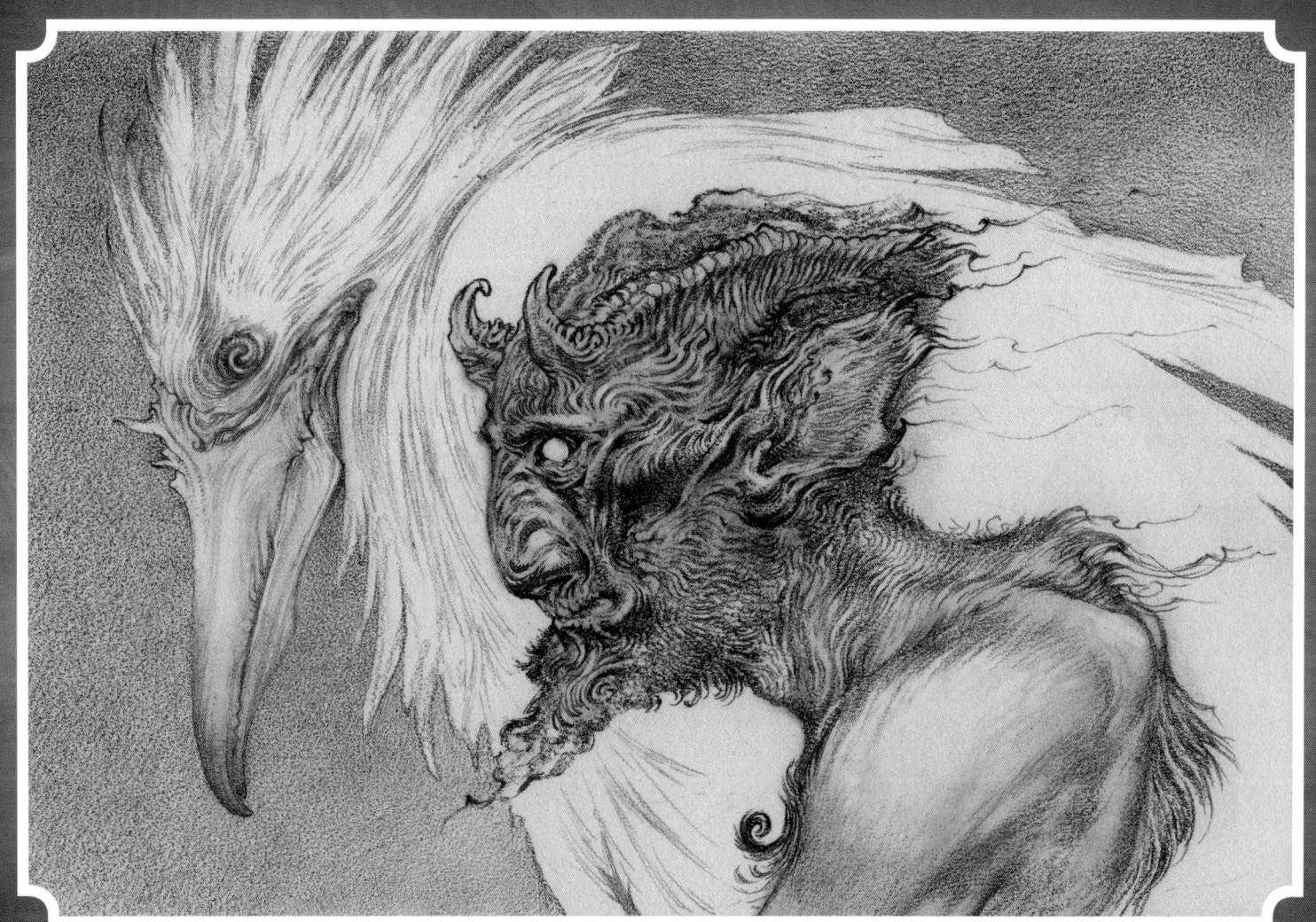

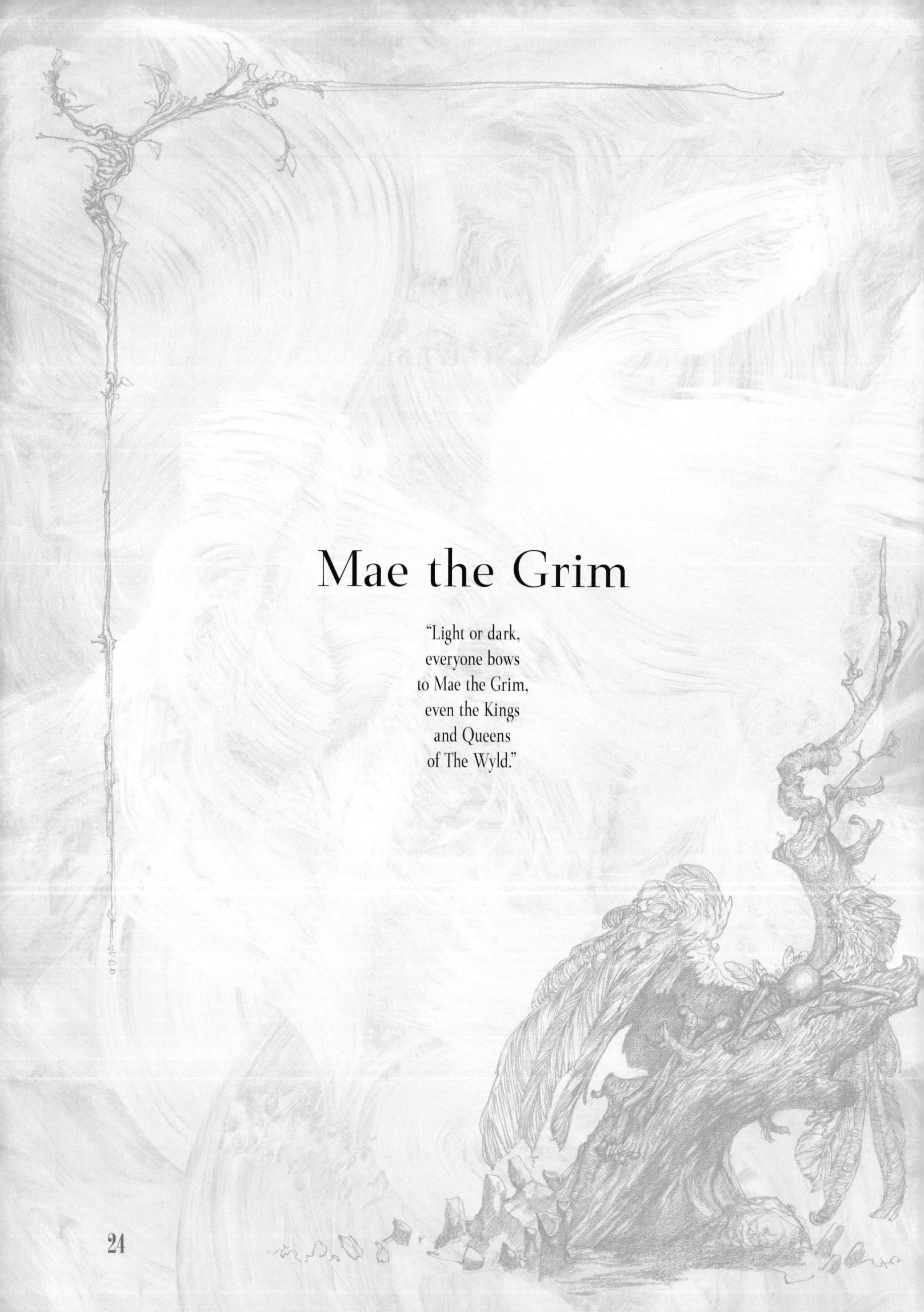

Mae the Grim

"Light or dark,
everyone bows
to Mae the Grim,
even the Kings
and Queens
of The Wyld."

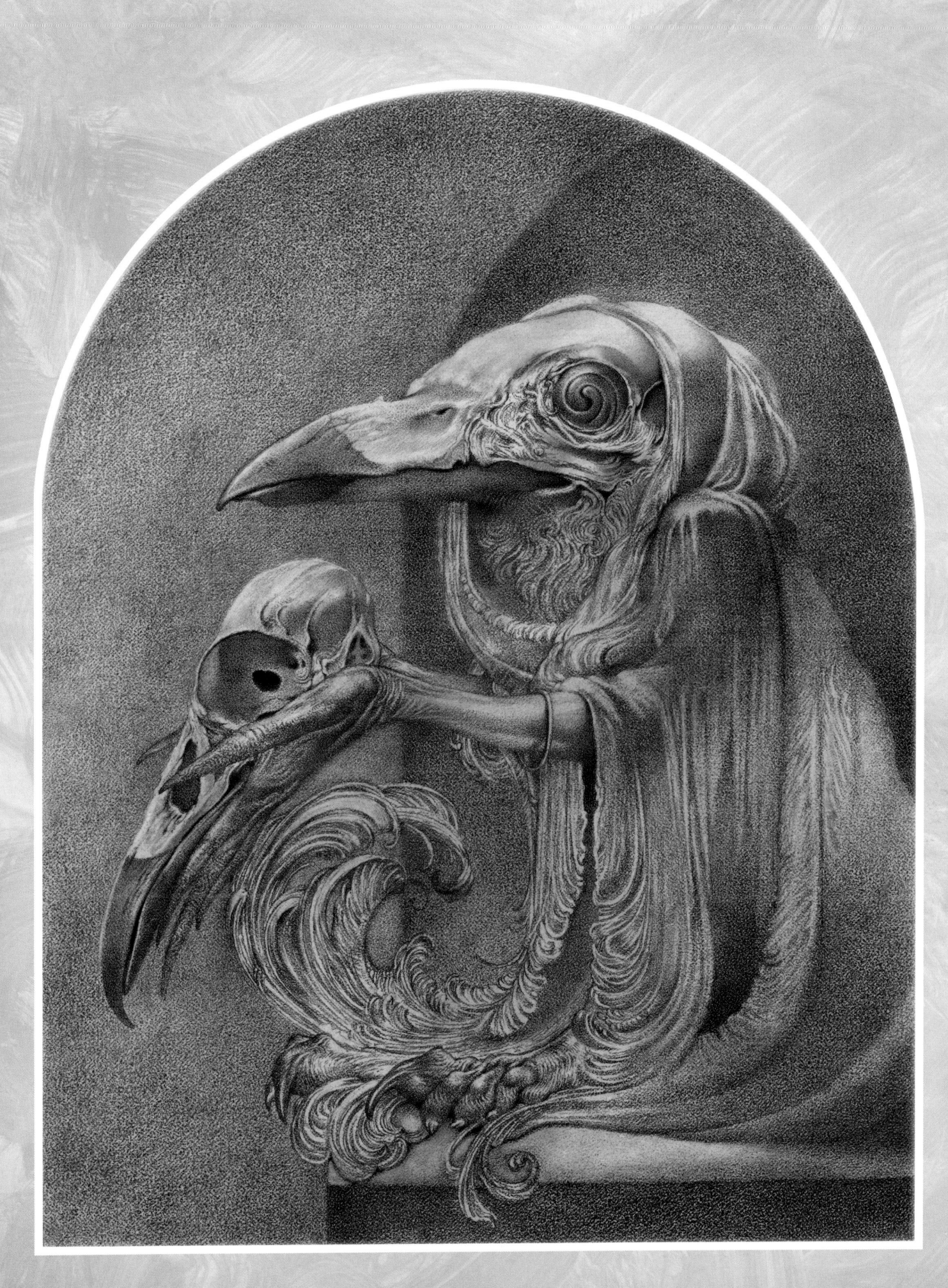

Gaunt Blight

"They're from the Dreaming
Lands. They're the only things
that will give chase to a Night
Gaunt and the only things from
which a Night Gaunt will run.
I've seen two Night Gaunts stand
against a pack of Tindalosian
Hounds; beat them back in a
way that I don't rightly have the
words to describe, yet scramble
in frantic terror at the approach
of a single Gaunt Blight.
It's a mystery."

Excerpt from Earl Ratlitch's
The Gaunt Lands: Kith and Kin

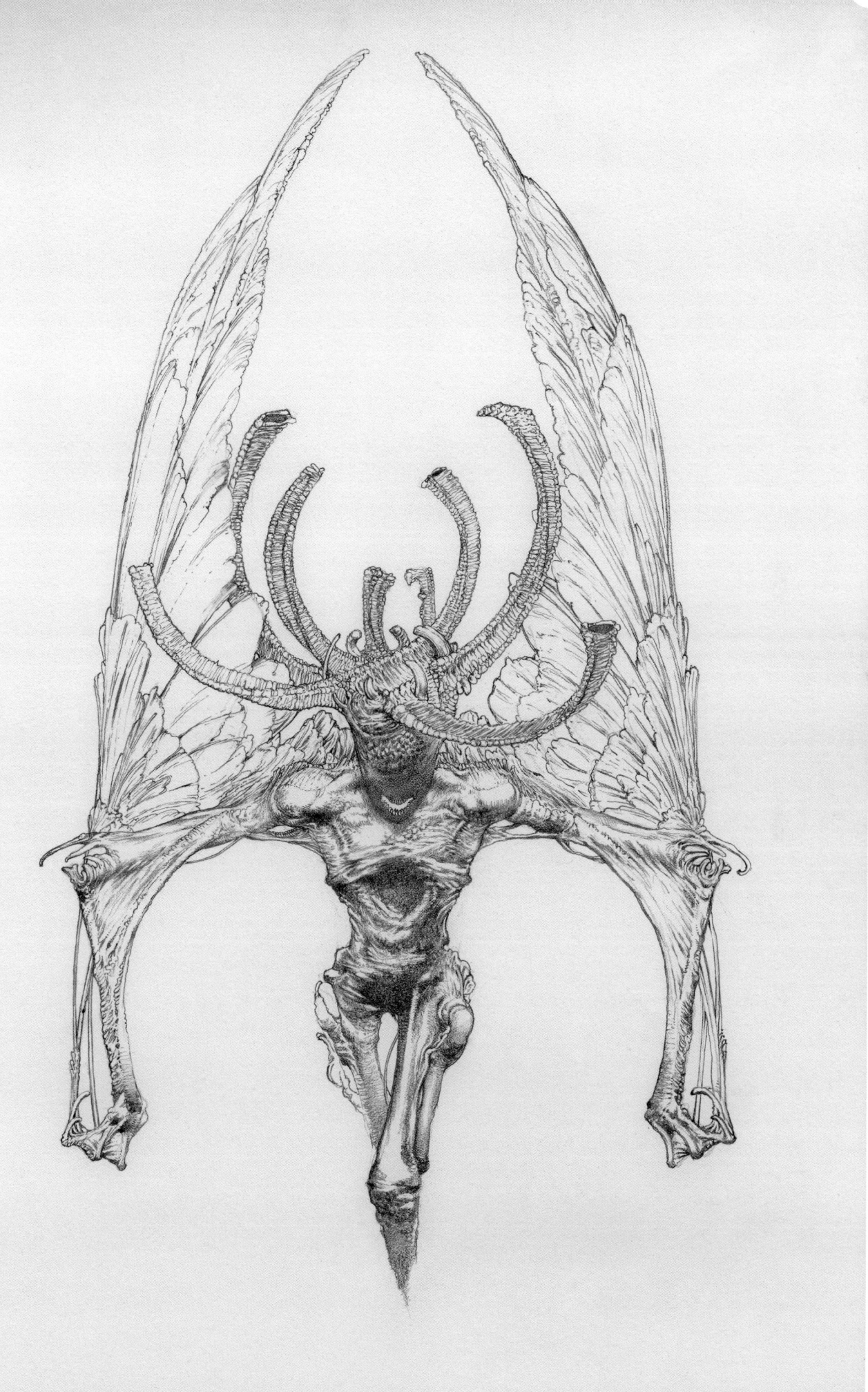

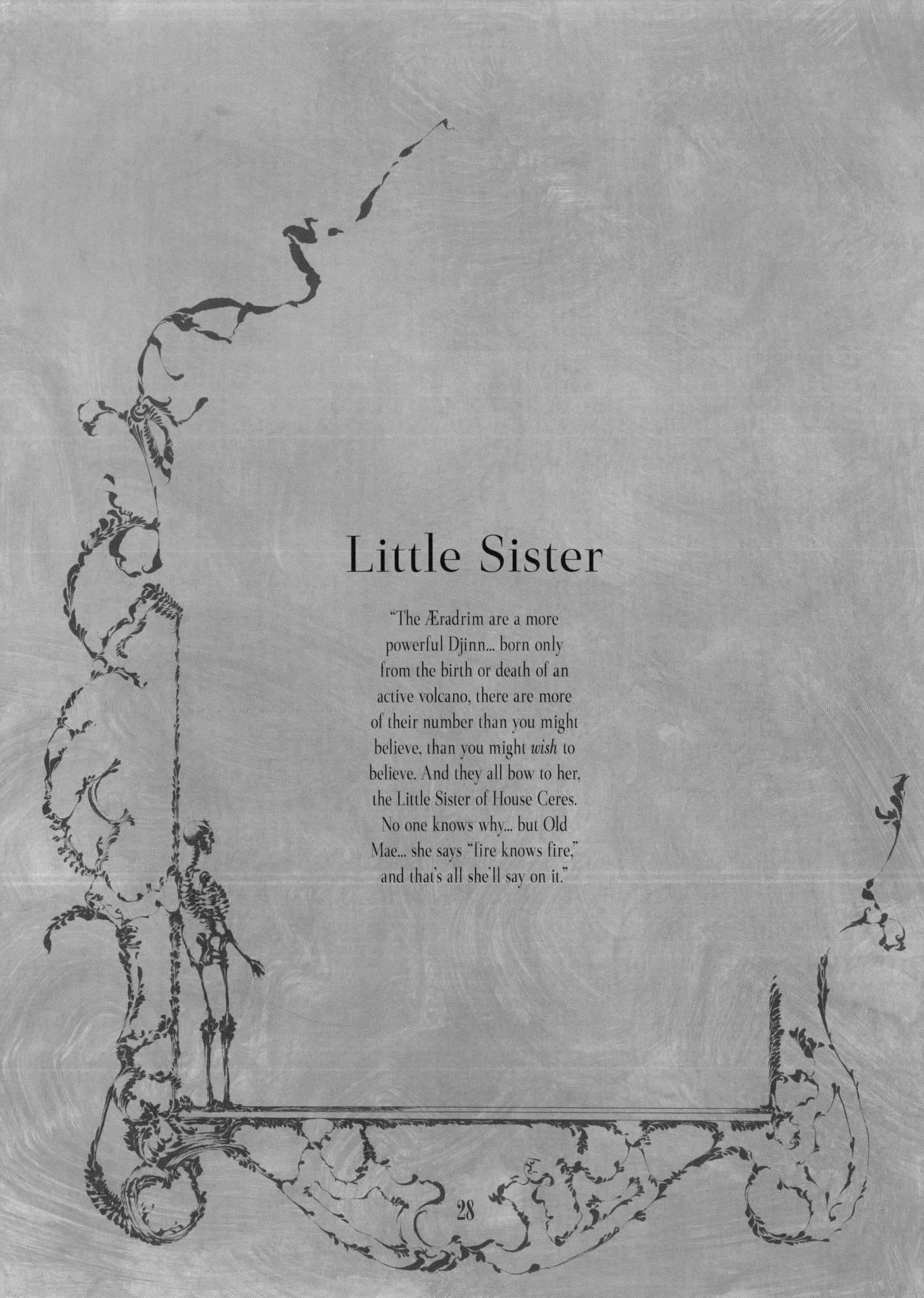

Little Sister

"The Æradrim are a more
powerful Djinn... born only
from the birth or death of an
active volcano, there are more
of their number than you might
believe, than you might *wish* to
believe. And they all bow to her,
the Little Sister of House Ceres.
No one knows why... but Old
Mae... she says "fire knows fire,"
and that's all she'll say on it."

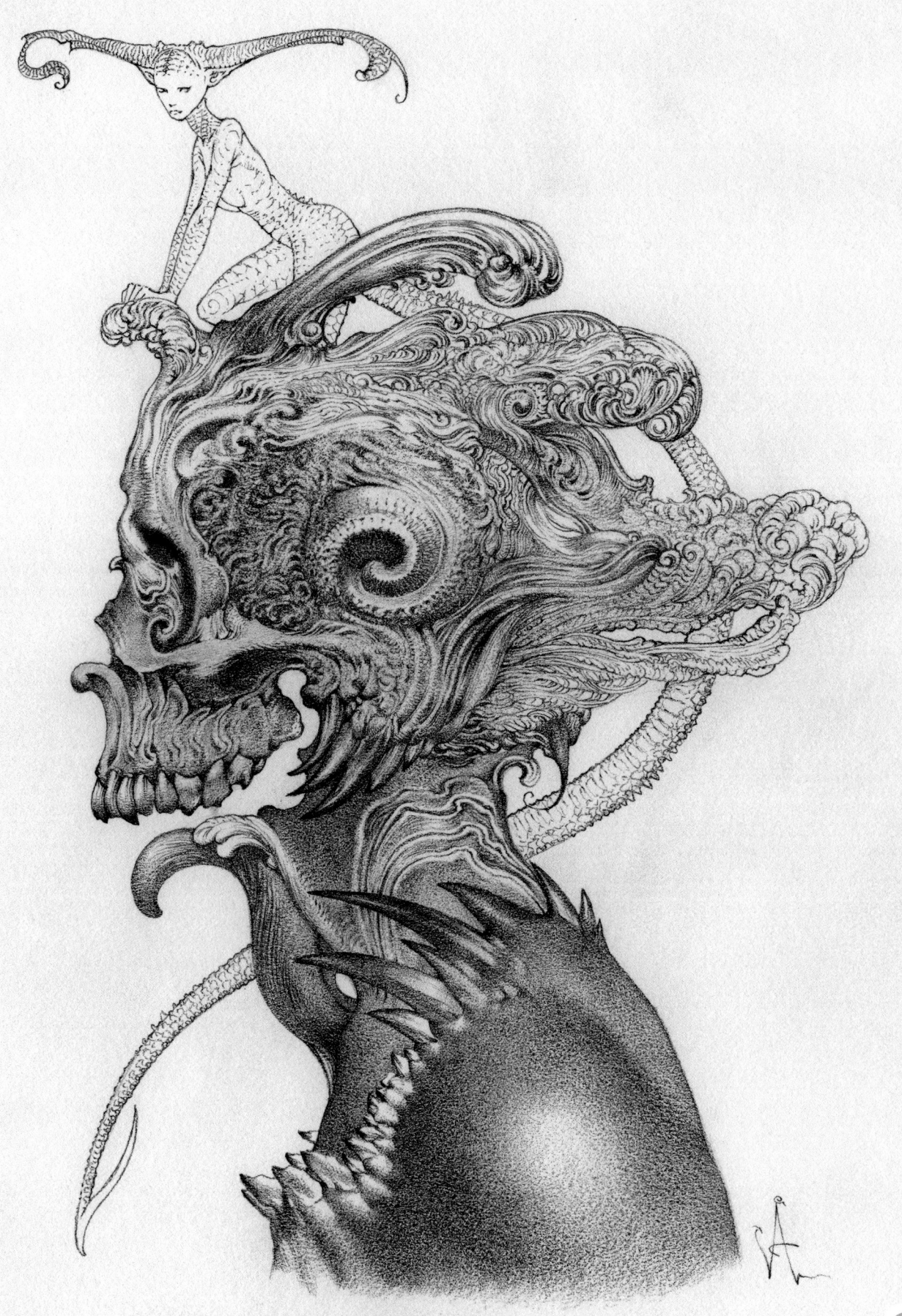

The Clearing

The marksman
sets upon
The Clearing,
not knowing it is hers...
And they
who never miss
their shot
do not find their mark.
They do not return,
the hunters who go there.
But they *are* seen again,
Naked,
sleeping amongst
their kin.

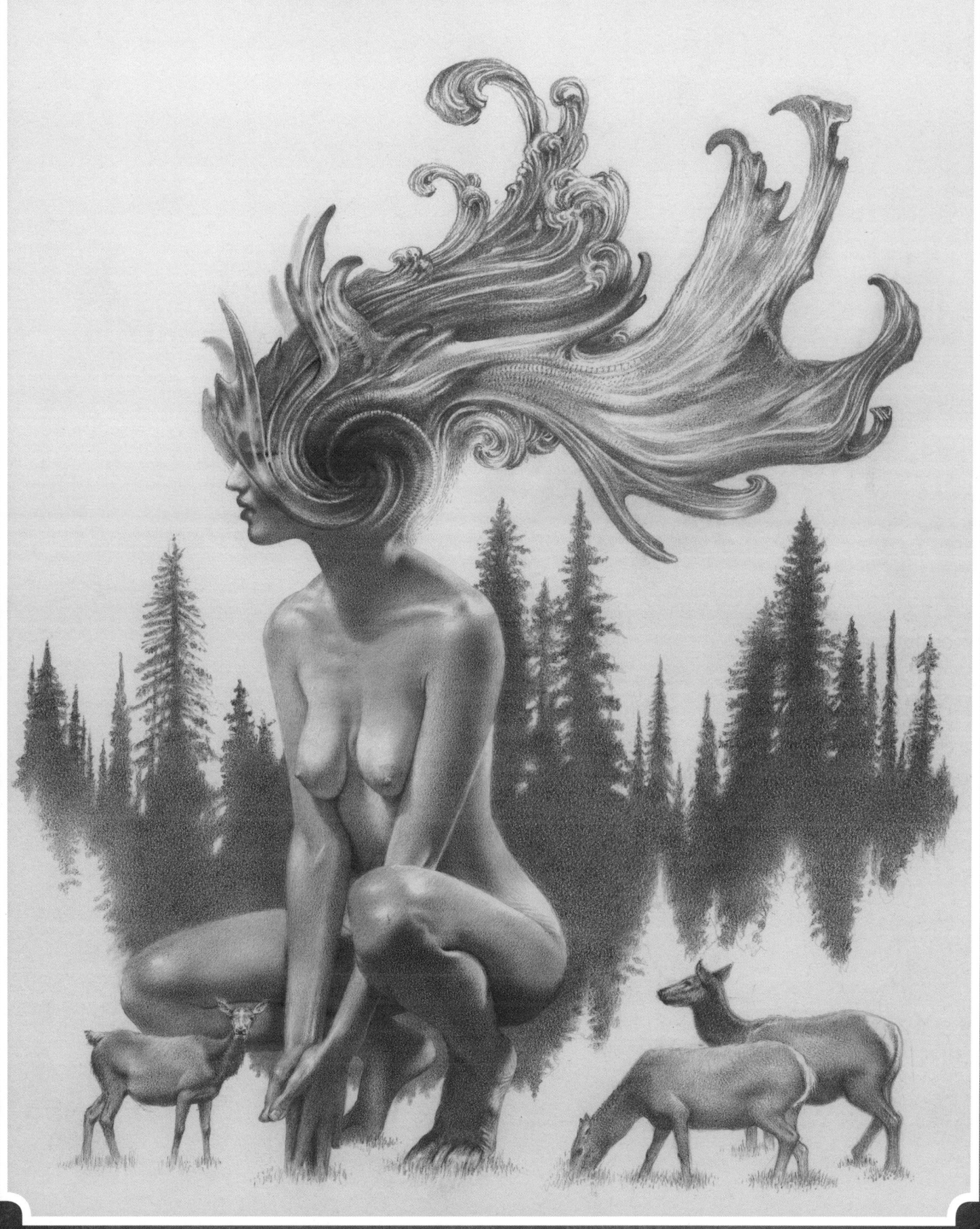

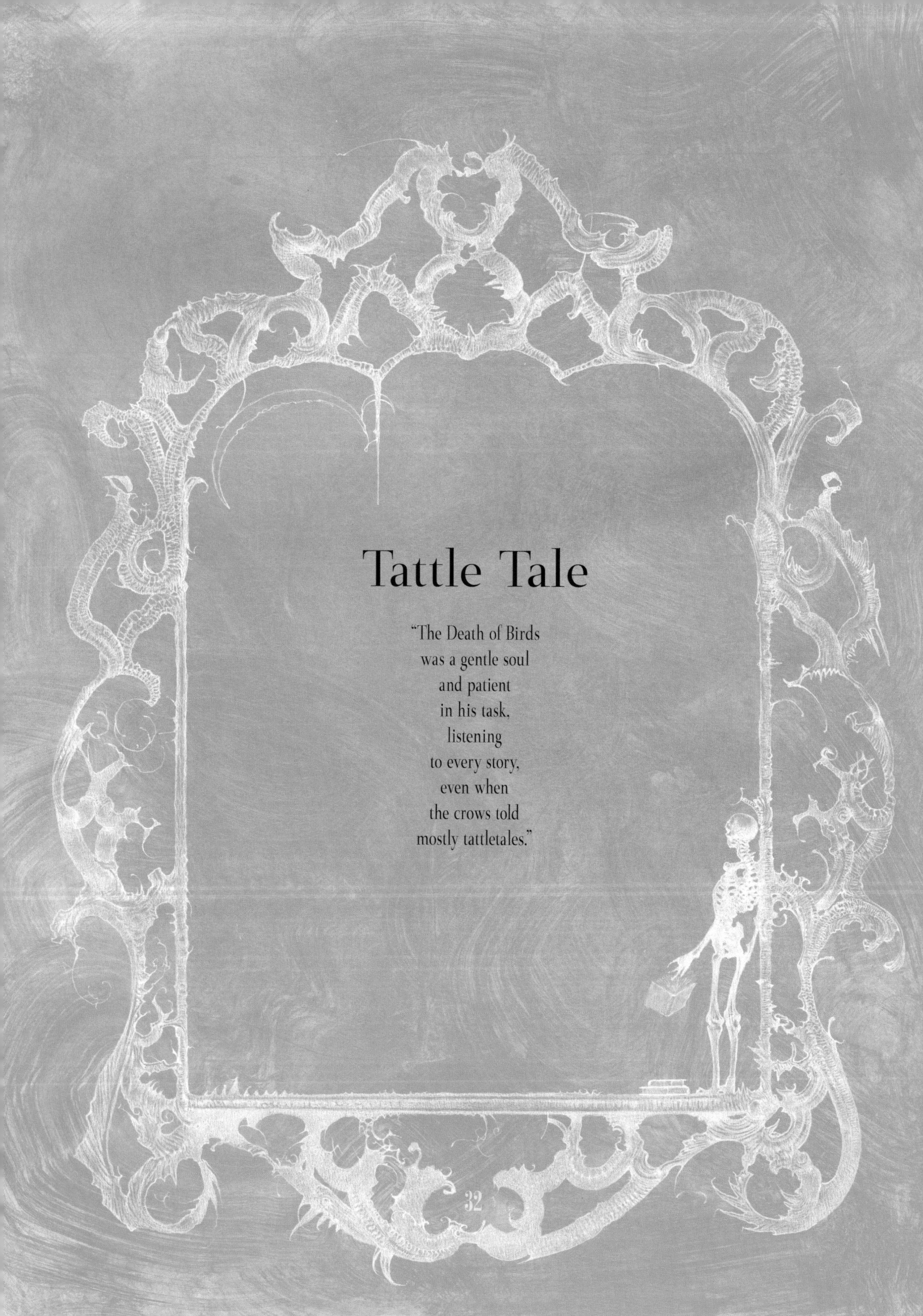

Tattle Tale

"The Death of Birds
was a gentle soul
and patient
in his task,
listening
to every story,
even when
the crows told
mostly tattletales."

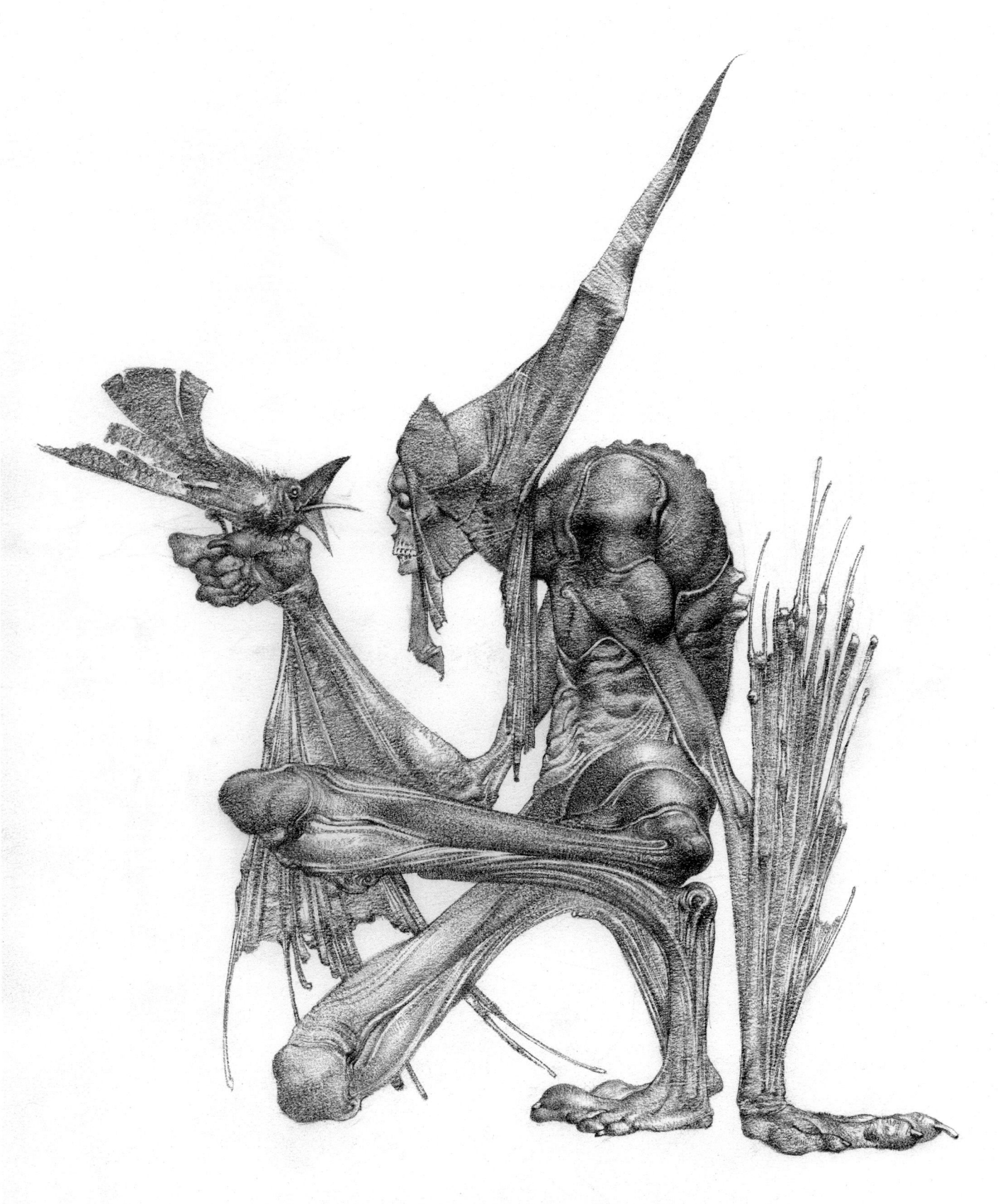

Wayward

It was obvious
that he was
born under
a bright star.
The question was...

how long would it
follow him?

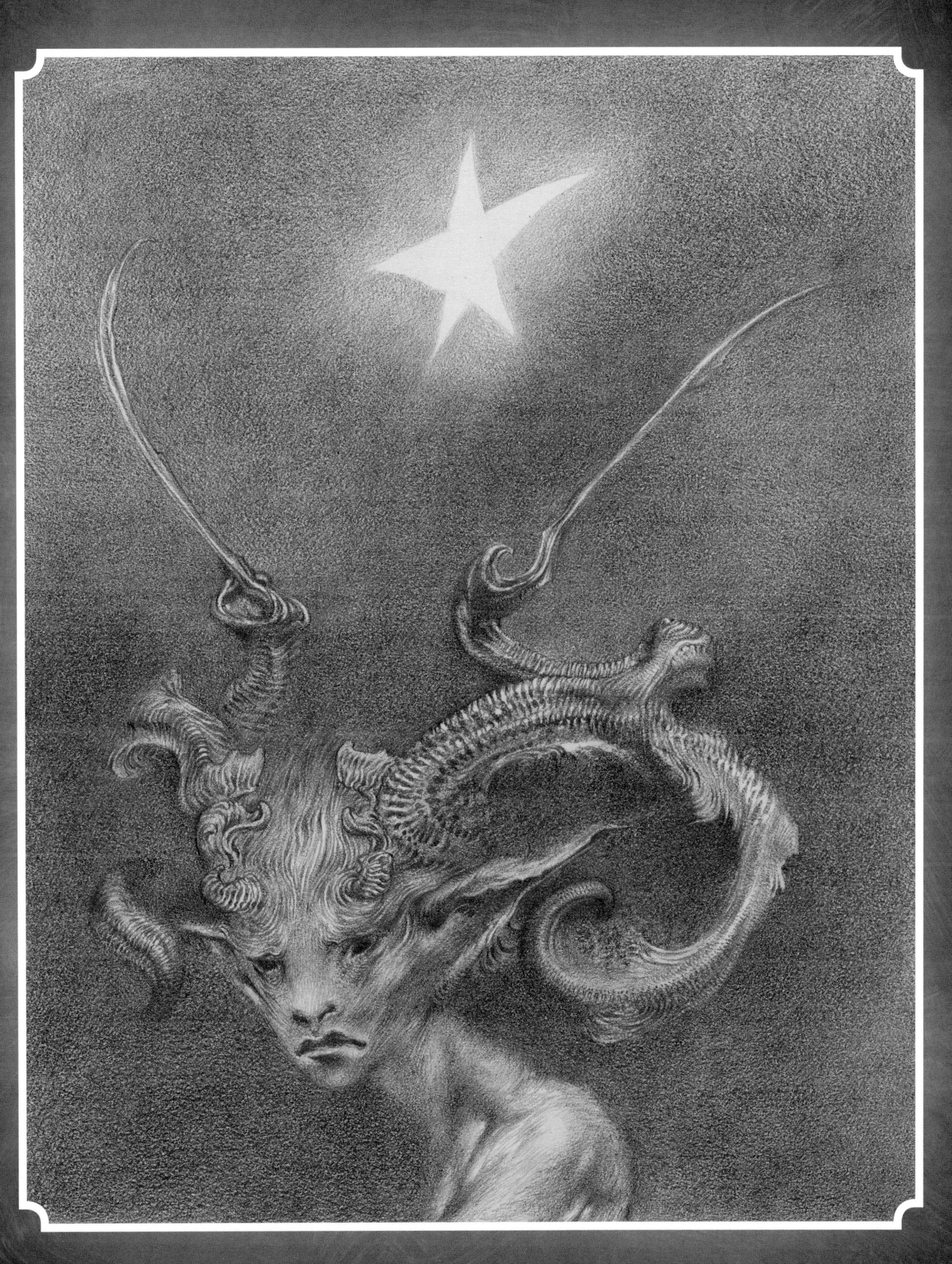

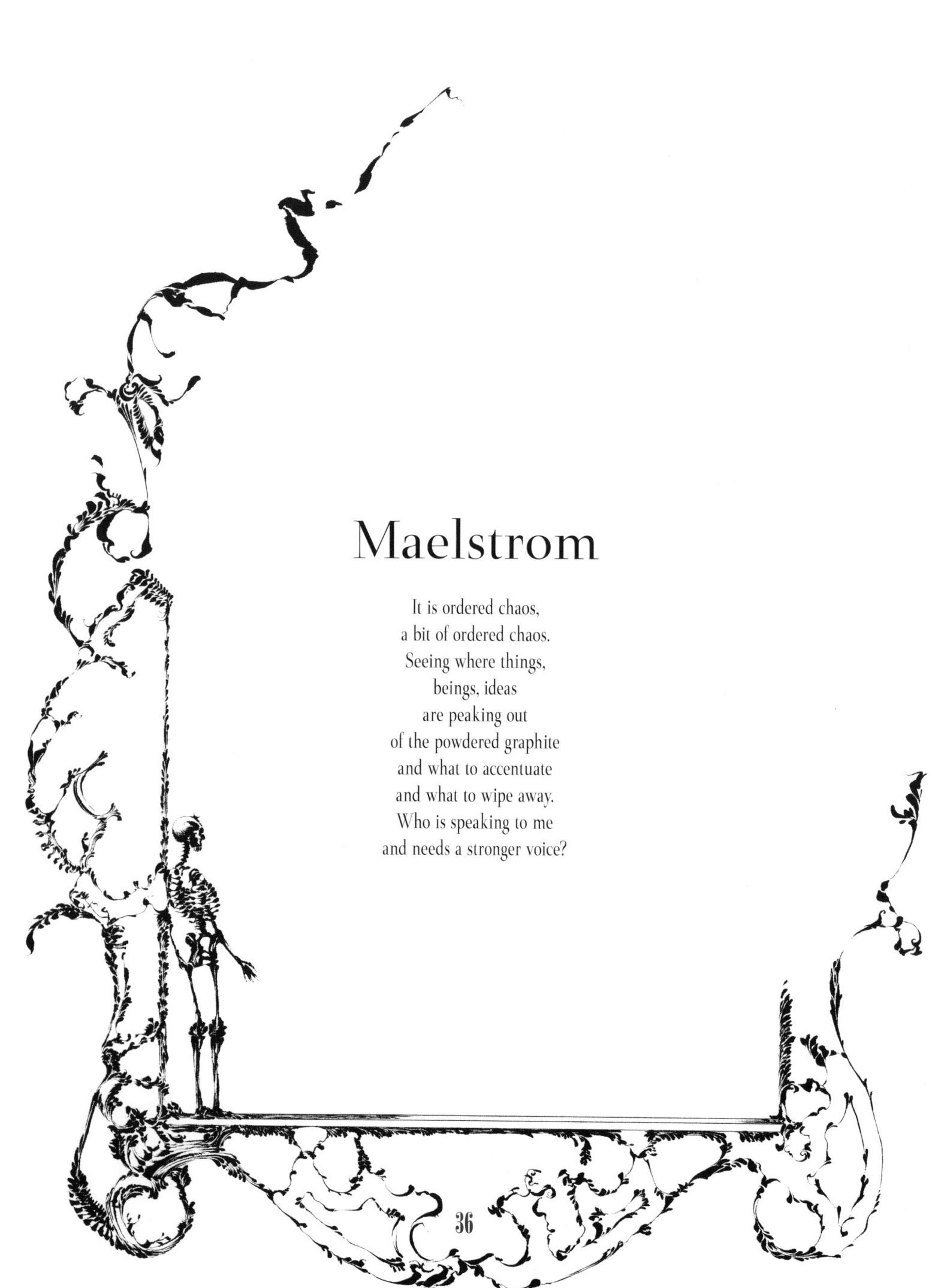

Maelstrom

It is ordered chaos,
a bit of ordered chaos.
Seeing where things,
beings, ideas
are peaking out
of the powdered graphite
and what to accentuate
and what to wipe away.
Who is speaking to me
and needs a stronger voice?

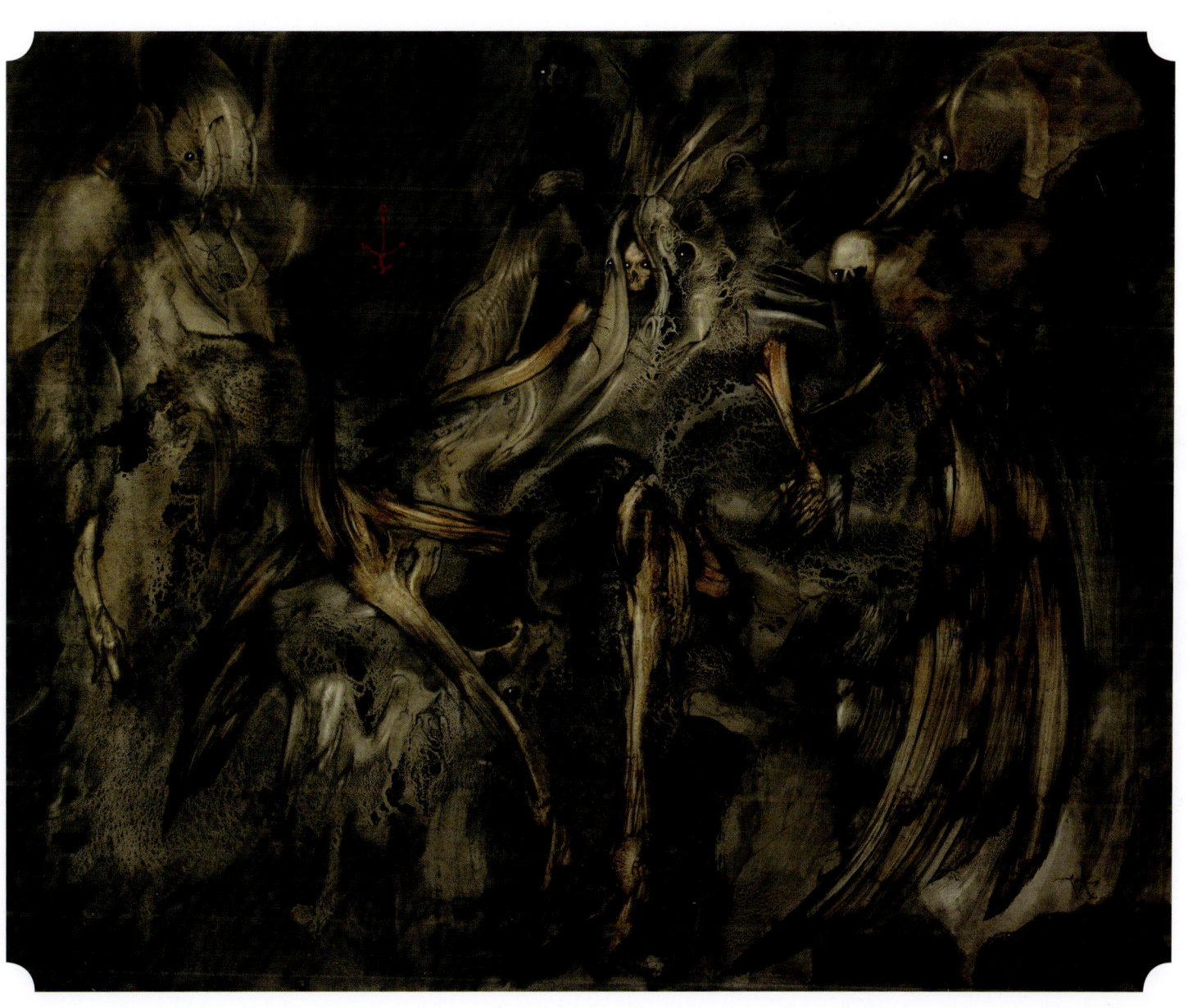

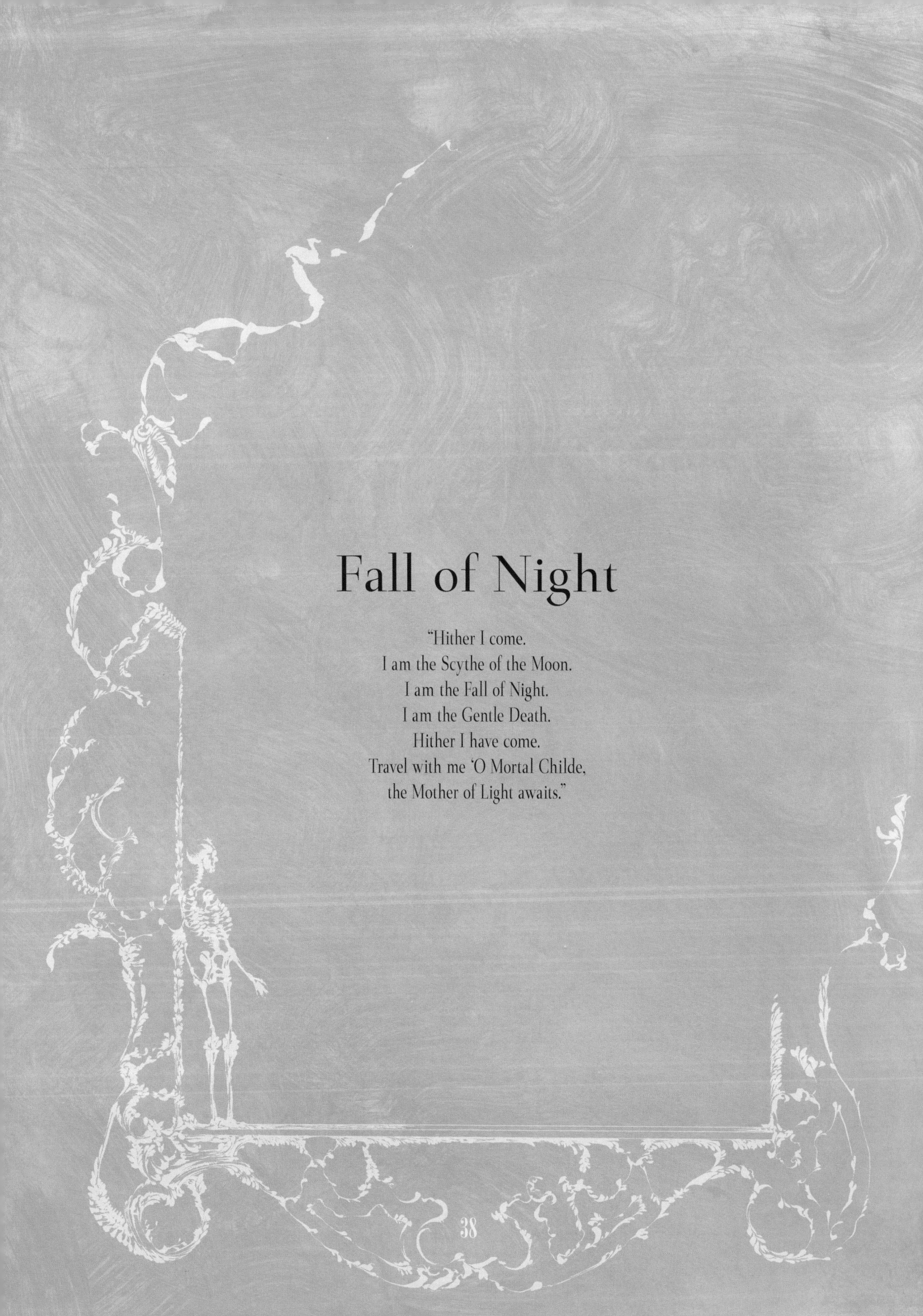

Fall of Night

"Hither I come.
I am the Scythe of the Moon.
I am the Fall of Night.
I am the Gentle Death.
Hither I have come.
Travel with me 'O Mortal Childe,
the Mother of Light awaits."

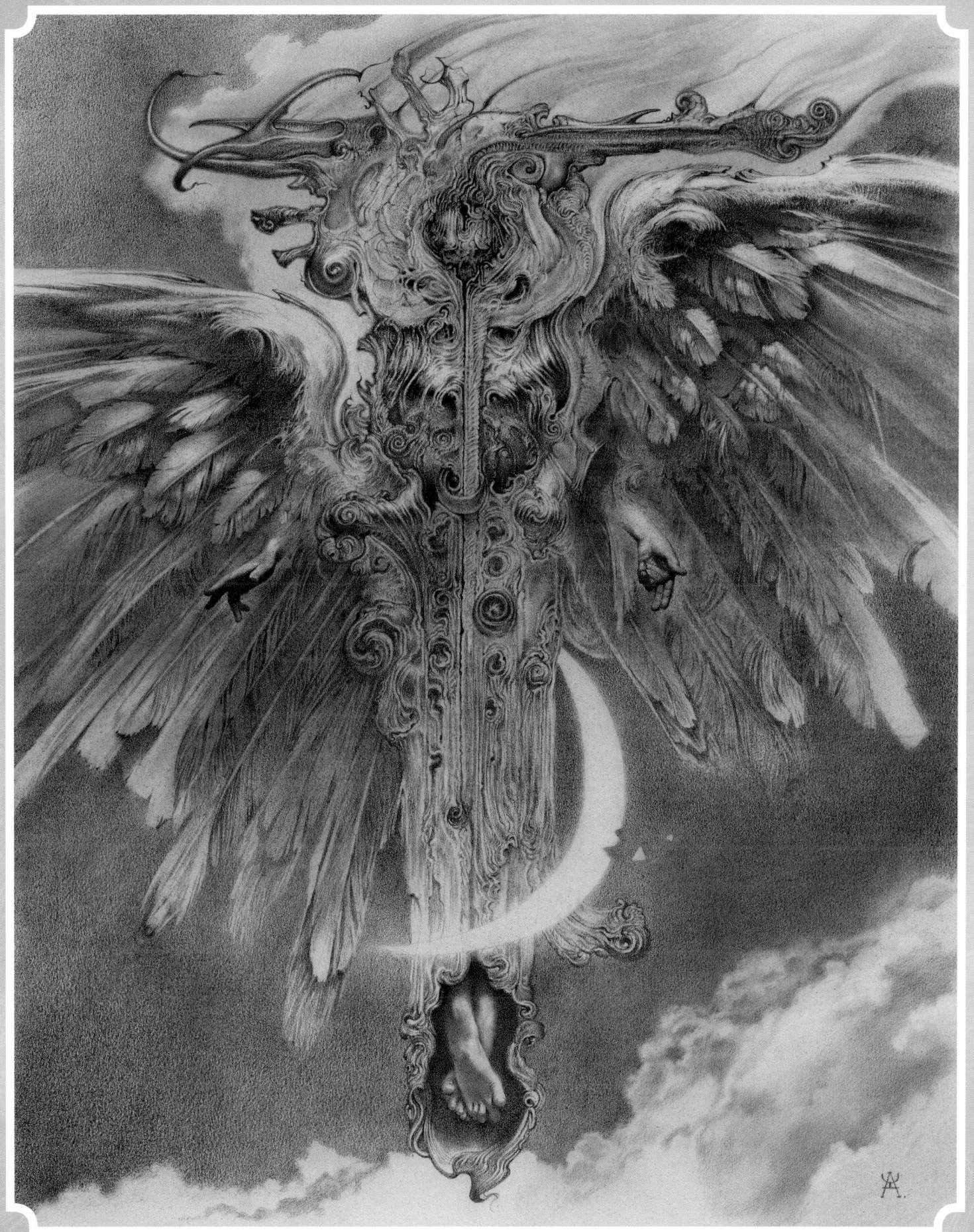

Child of the Broken Star

"I love you too much,"
he said.
"What do you mean?"
asked the child.
"It is good that I am
no longer divine...
I would Unmake creation
to keep you safe...
I love you too much."

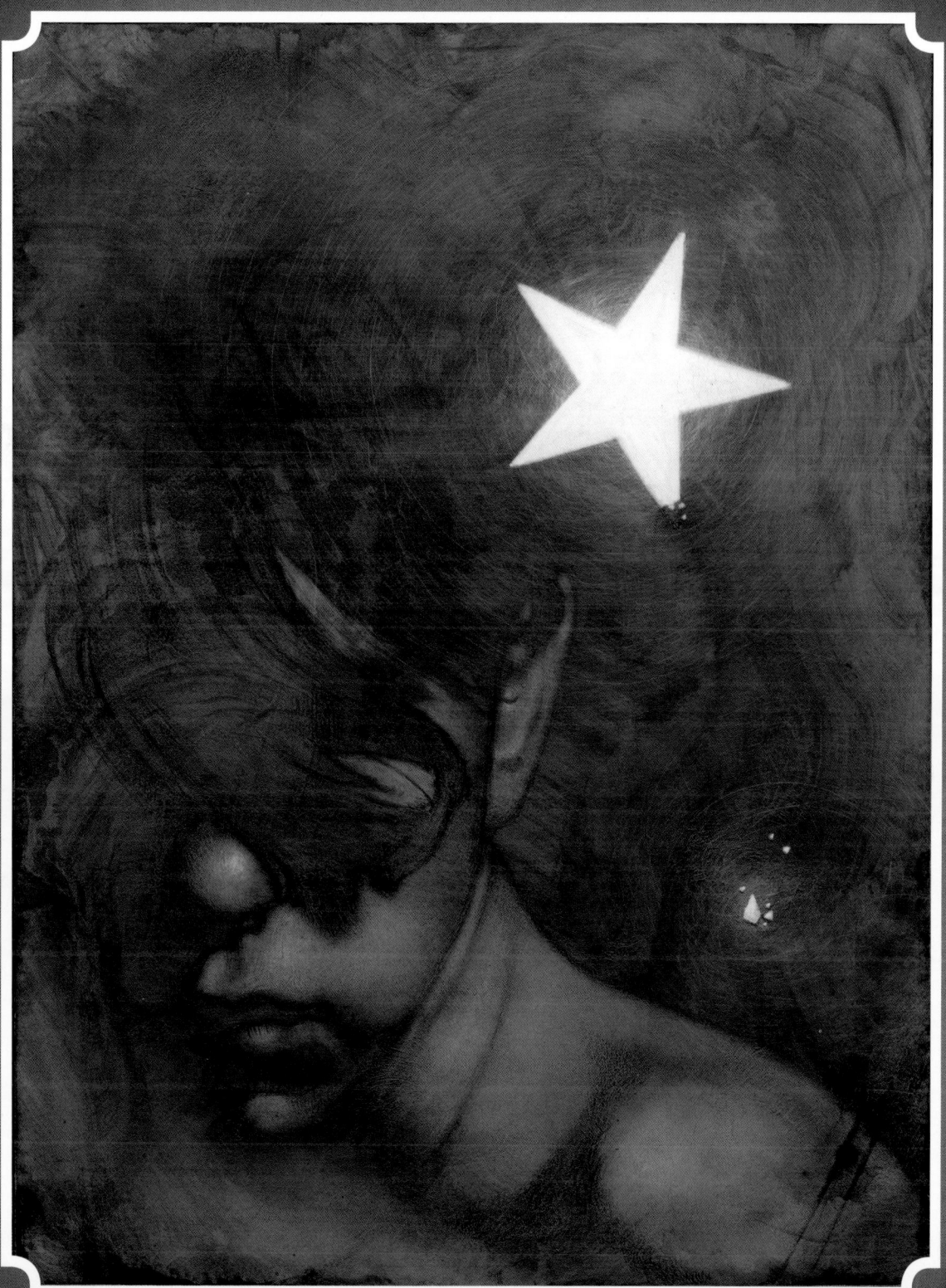

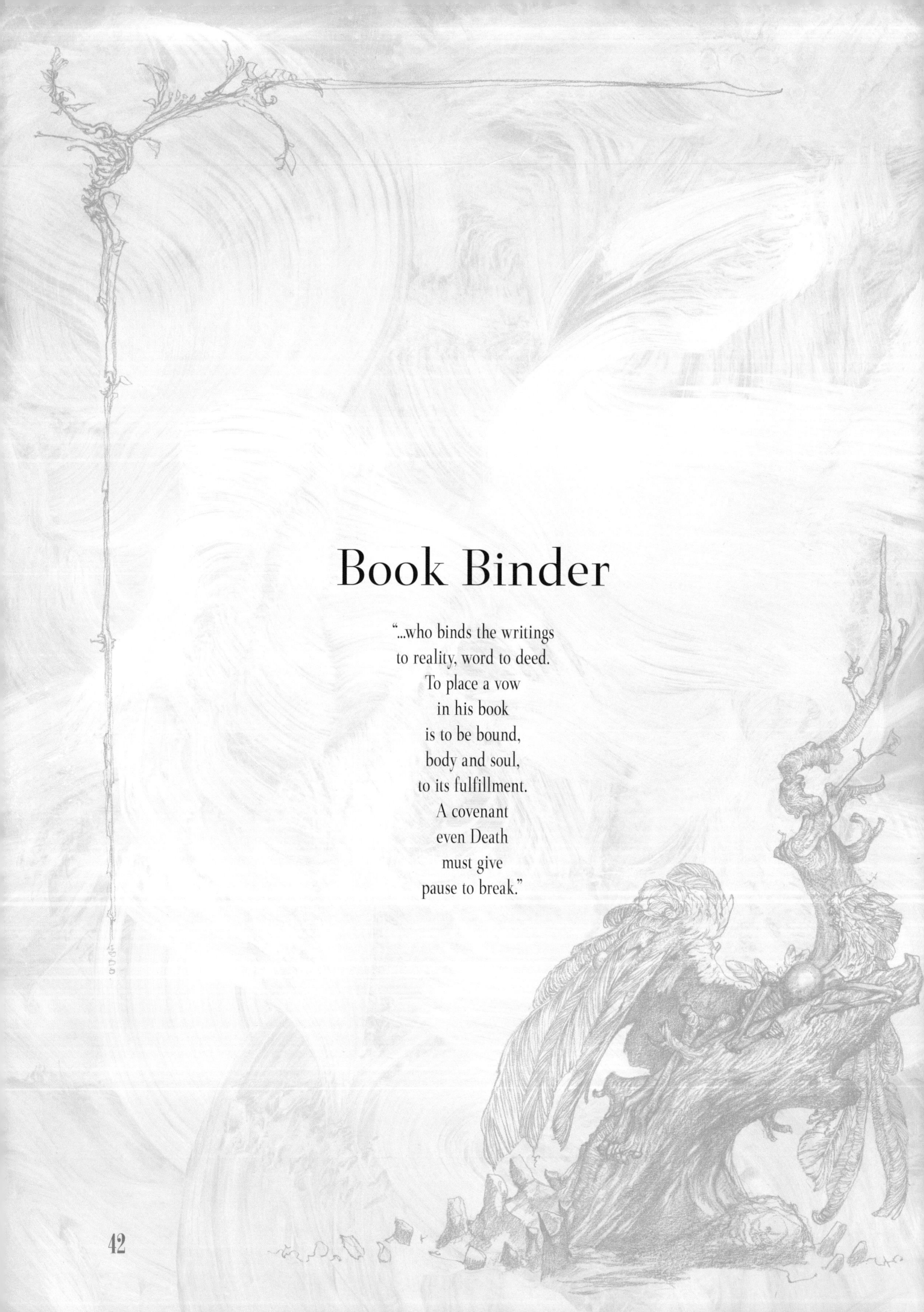

Book Binder

"...who binds the writings
to reality, word to deed.
To place a vow
in his book
is to be bound,
body and soul,
to its fulfillment.
A covenant
even Death
must give
pause to break."

The Reader

The Speaker of Names
The Warrant
The Uncrowned King
He shall measure their number,
the wretched, and he will set
their names apart.
His is the hand that writes, his
is the hand that marks.
He shall call them like thunder
in the stillness of night

...and they shall be fearful
that their names be unsown.

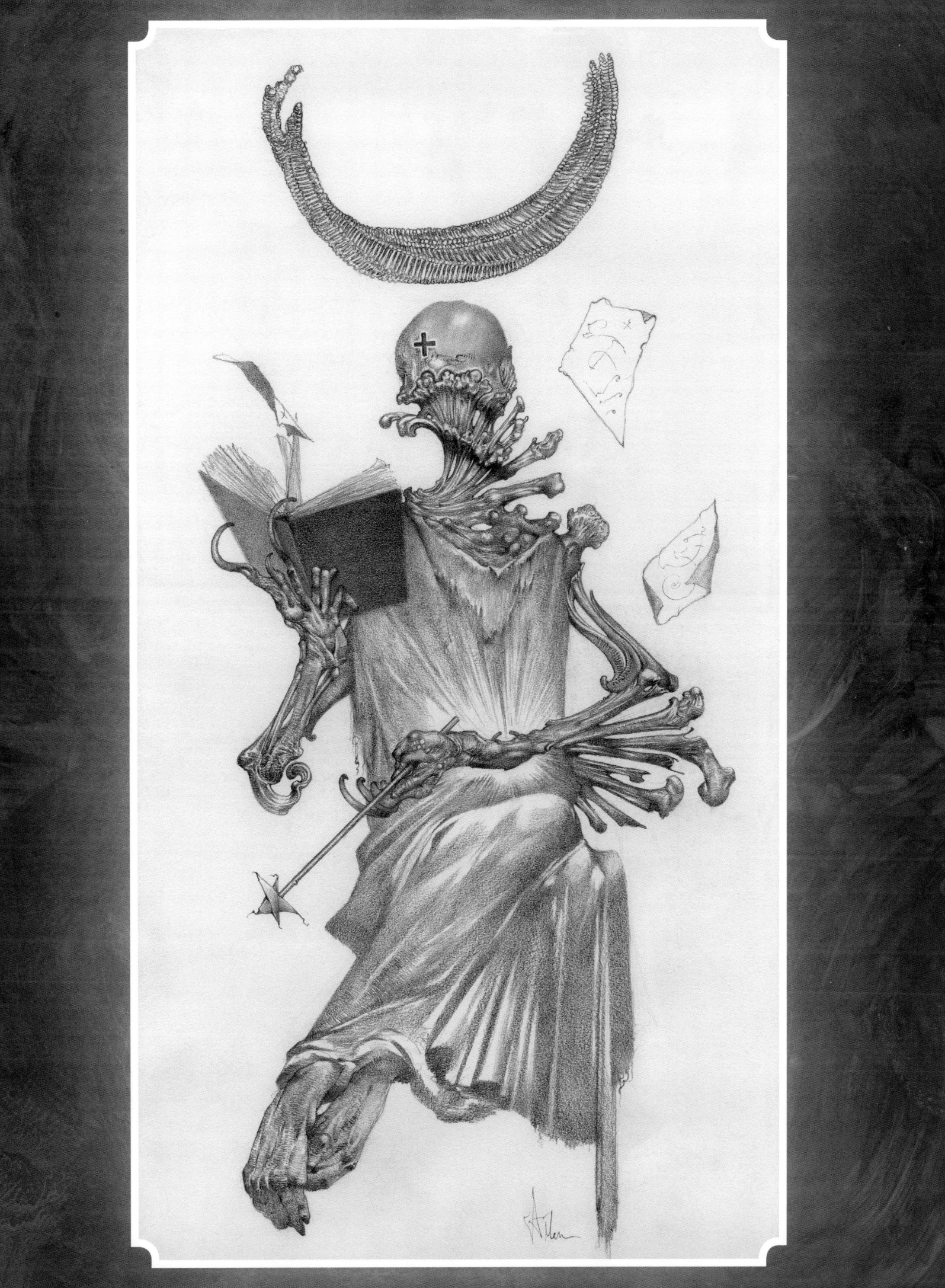

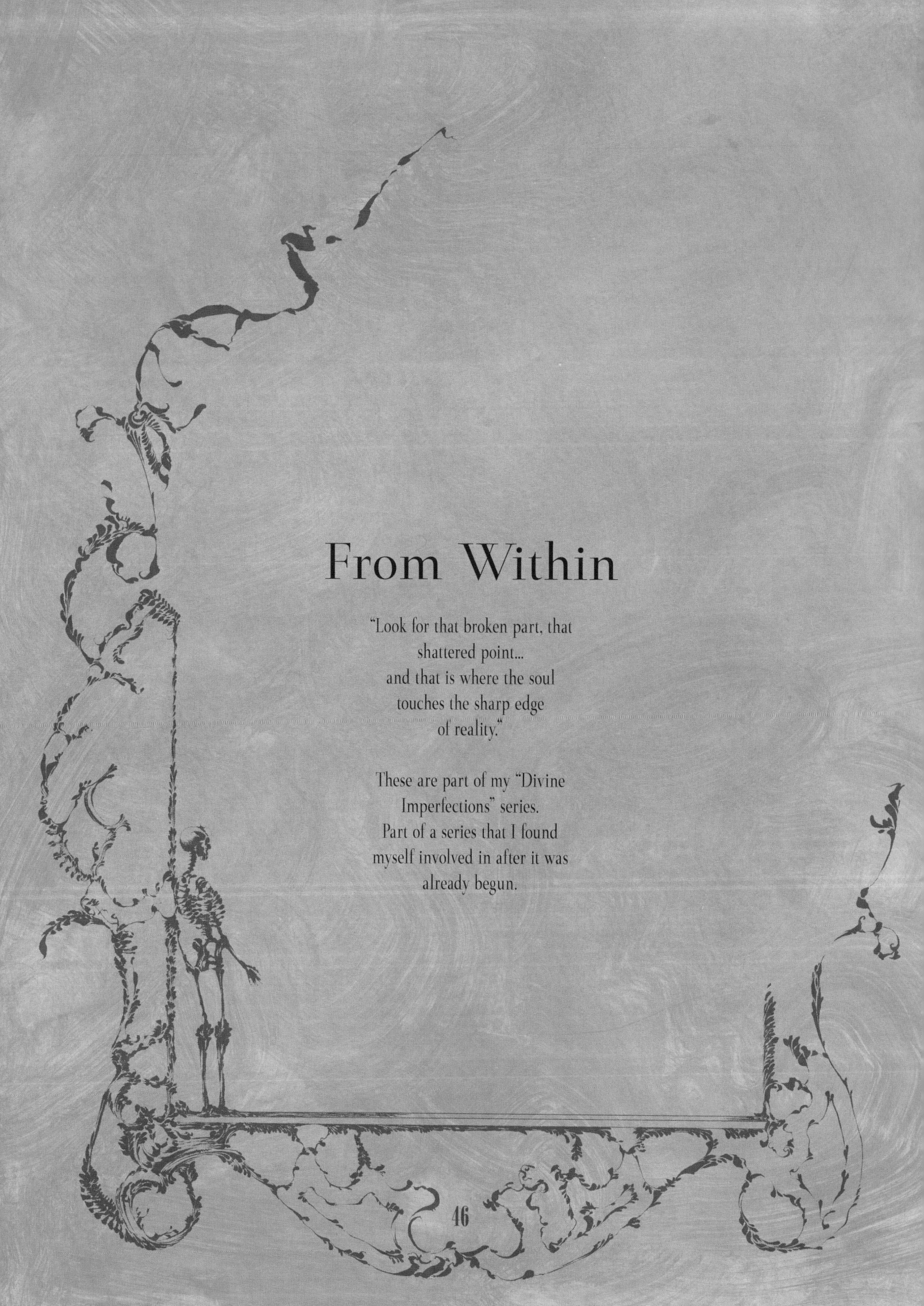

From Within

"Look for that broken part, that
shattered point...
and that is where the soul
touches the sharp edge
of reality."

These are part of my "Divine
Imperfections" series.
Part of a series that I found
myself involved in after it was
already begun.

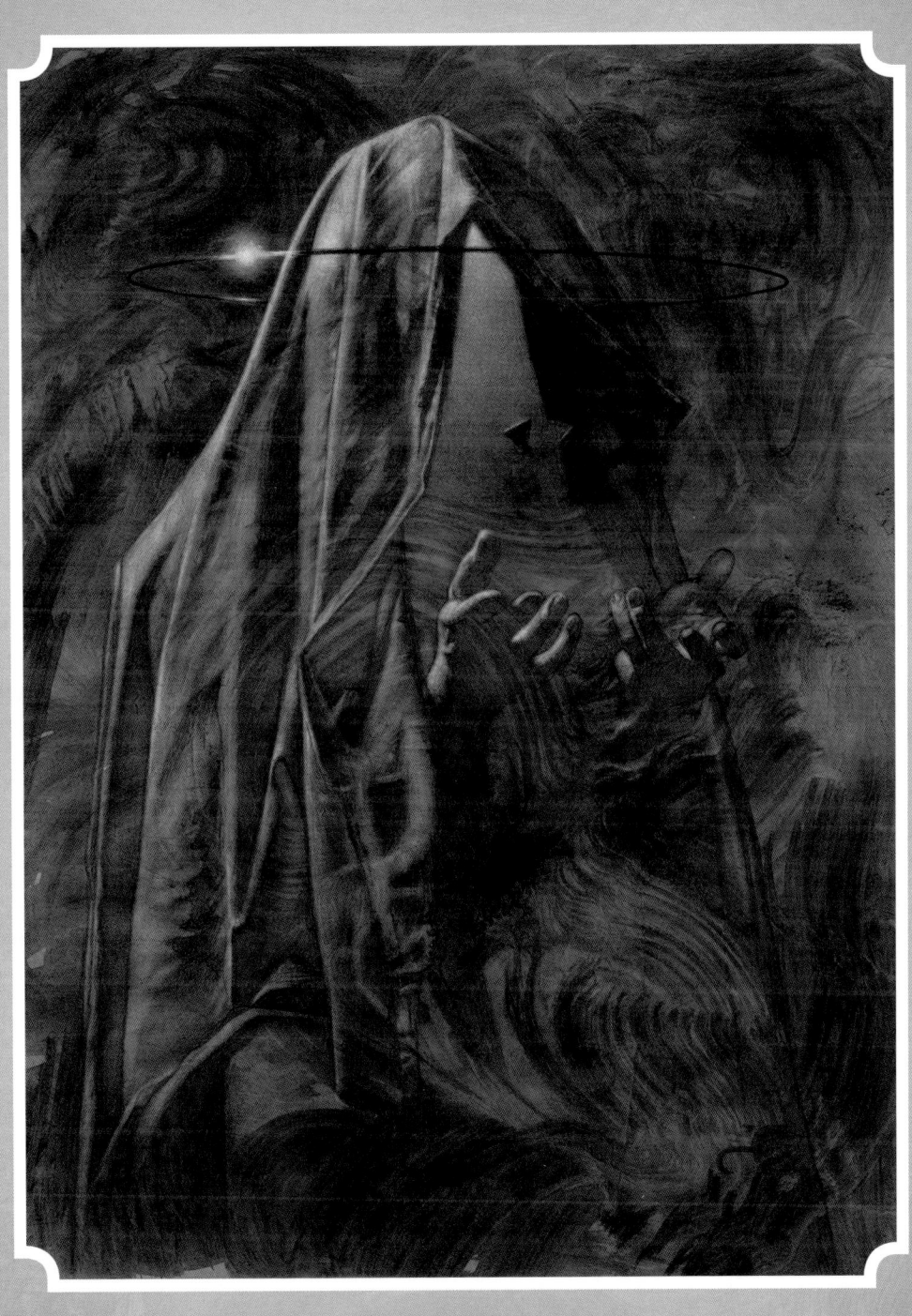

Reborn

Her light is small
yet powerful... and growing...
But make no mistake,
she is accustomed
and fearless
and loving
of the night.

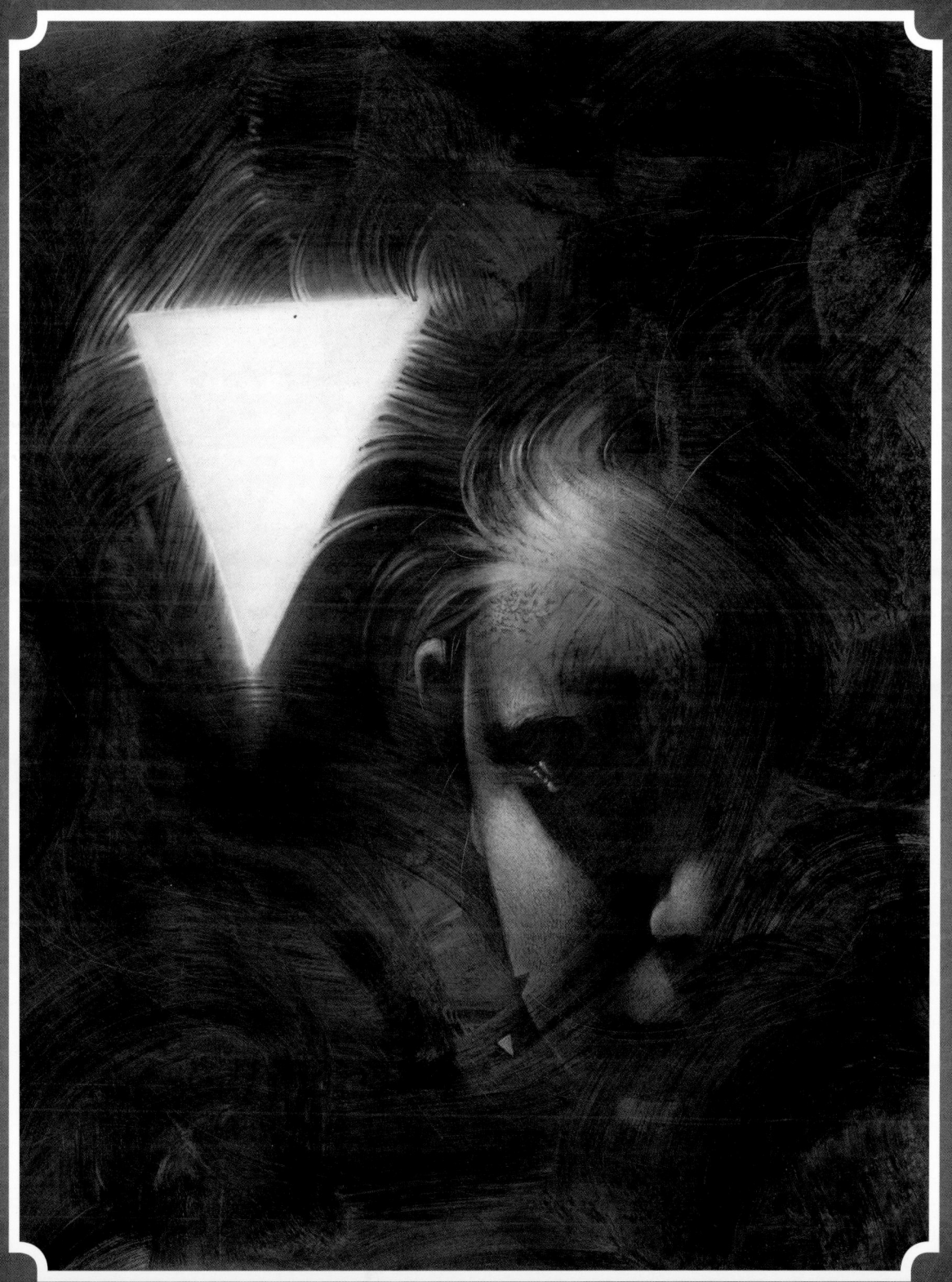

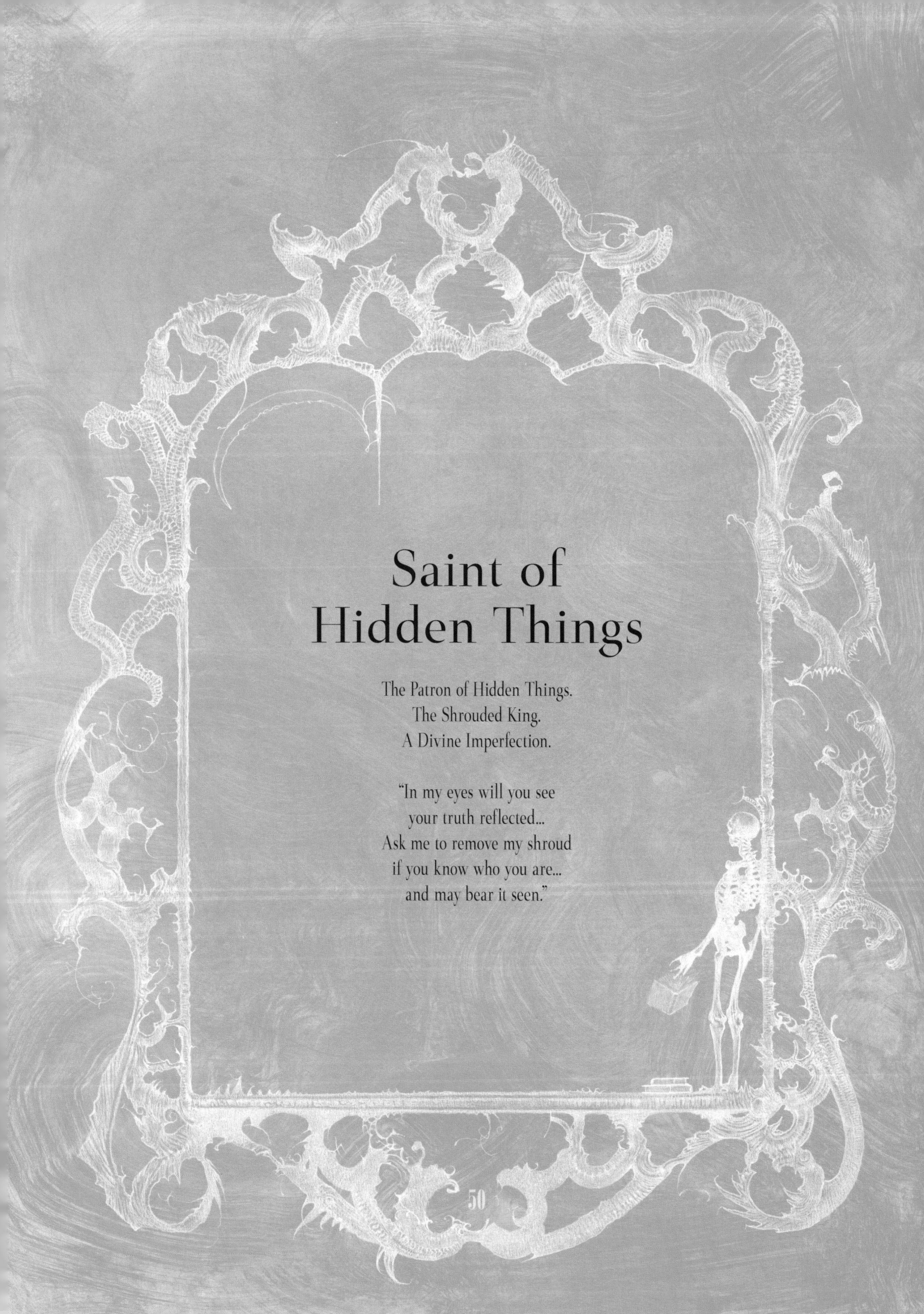

Saint of Hidden Things

The Patron of Hidden Things.
The Shrouded King.
A Divine Imperfection.

"In my eyes will you see
your truth reflected...
Ask me to remove my shroud
if you know who you are...
and may bear it seen."

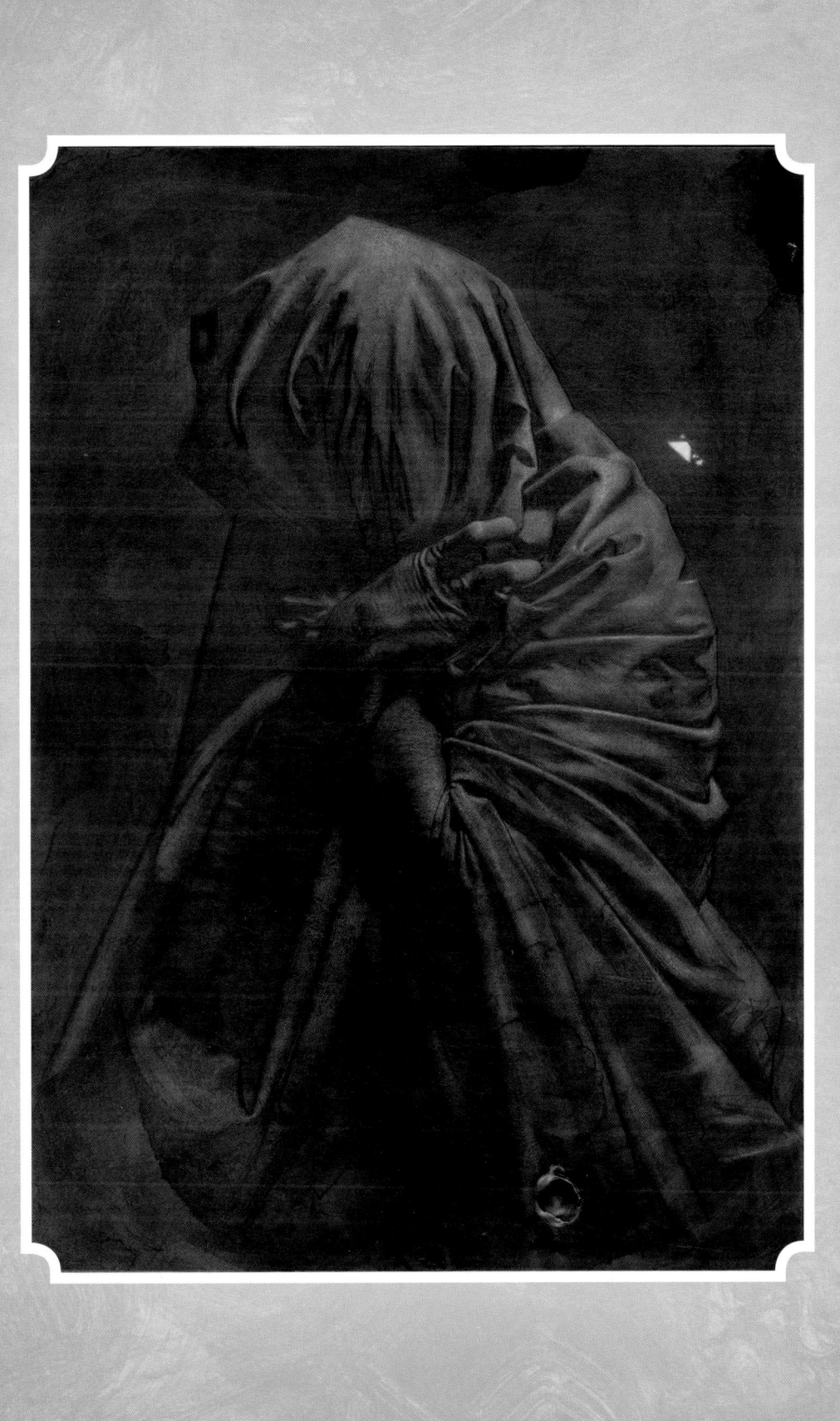

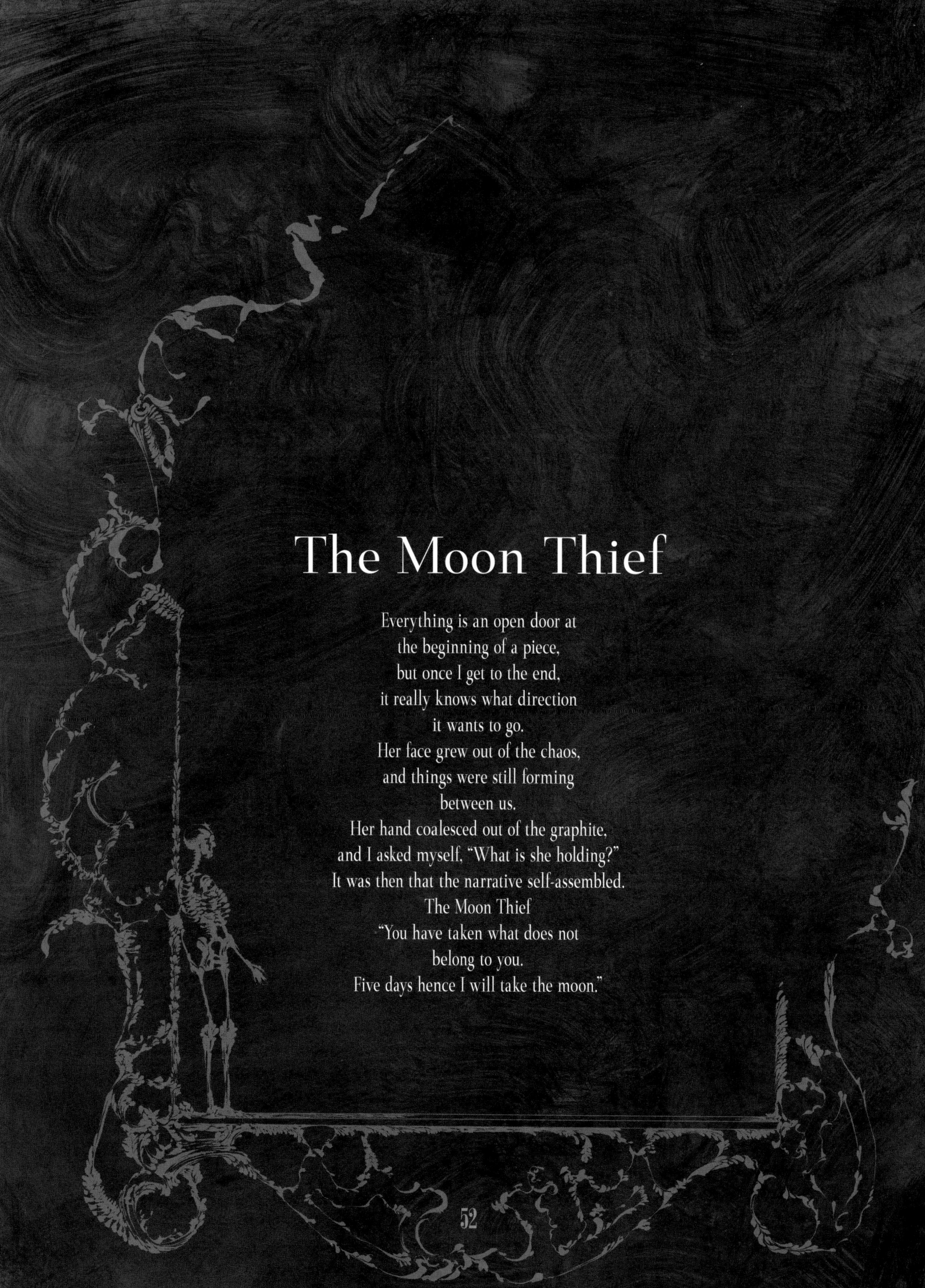

The Moon Thief

Everything is an open door at
the beginning of a piece,
but once I get to the end,
it really knows what direction
it wants to go.
Her face grew out of the chaos,
and things were still forming
between us.
Her hand coalesced out of the graphite,
and I asked myself, "What is she holding?"
It was then that the narrative self-assembled.
The Moon Thief
"You have taken what does not
belong to you.
Five days hence I will take the moon."

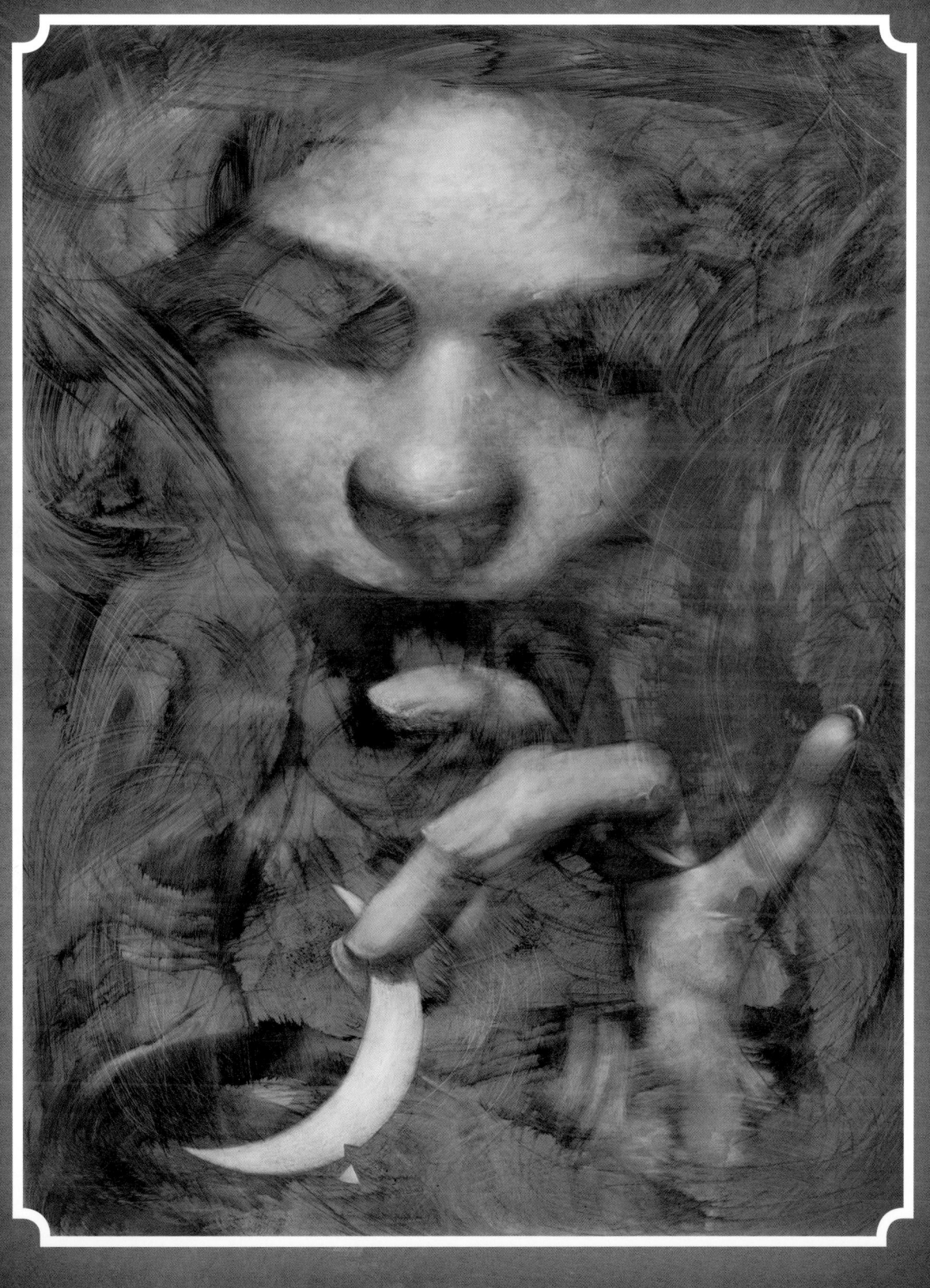

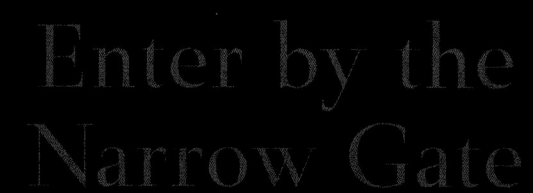

Enter by the
Narrow Gate

Enter by the
Narrow Gate
It is hidden
and its toll keepers
fearsome, and yet
it is the only way...

the width of
one soul.

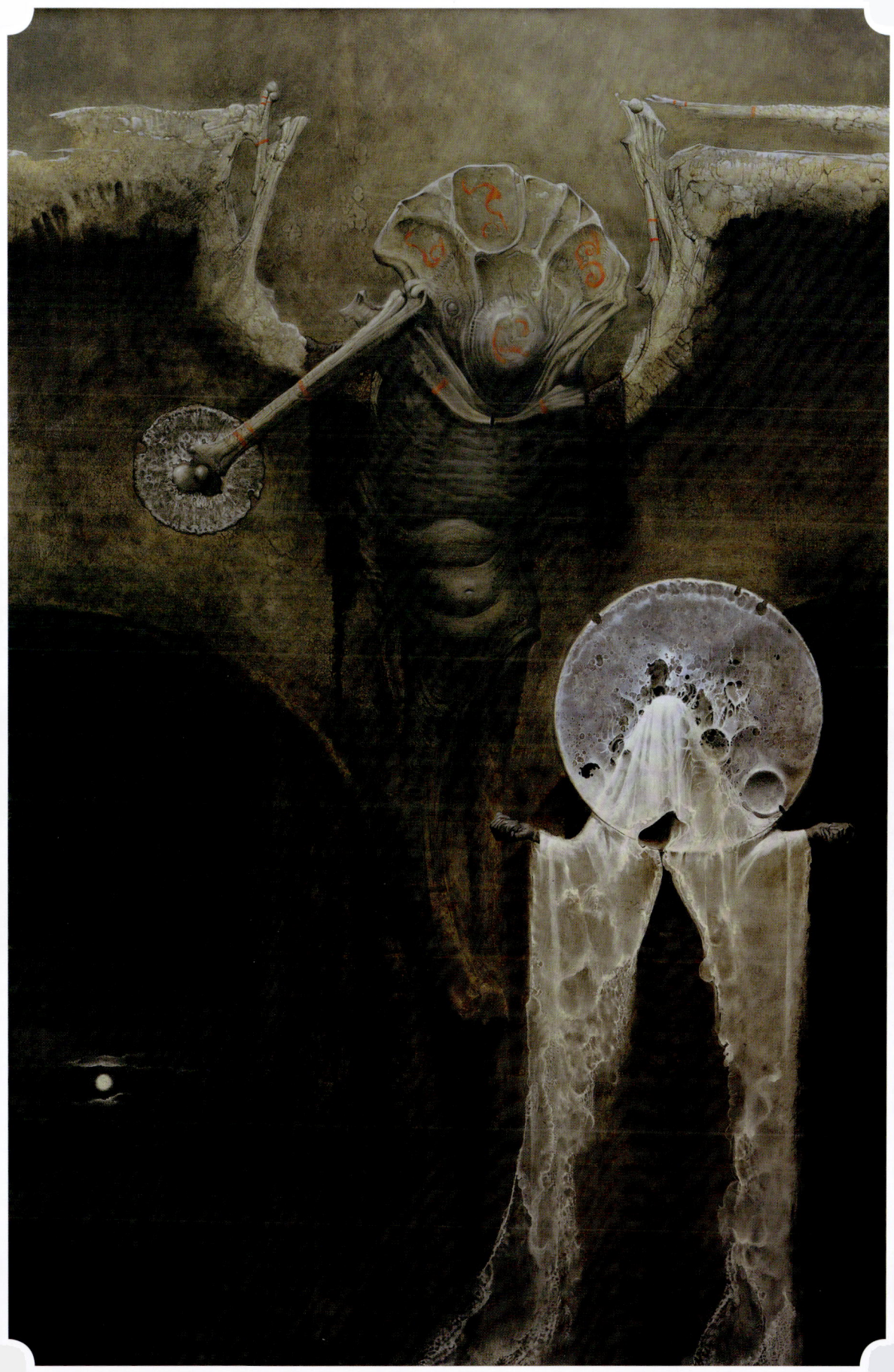

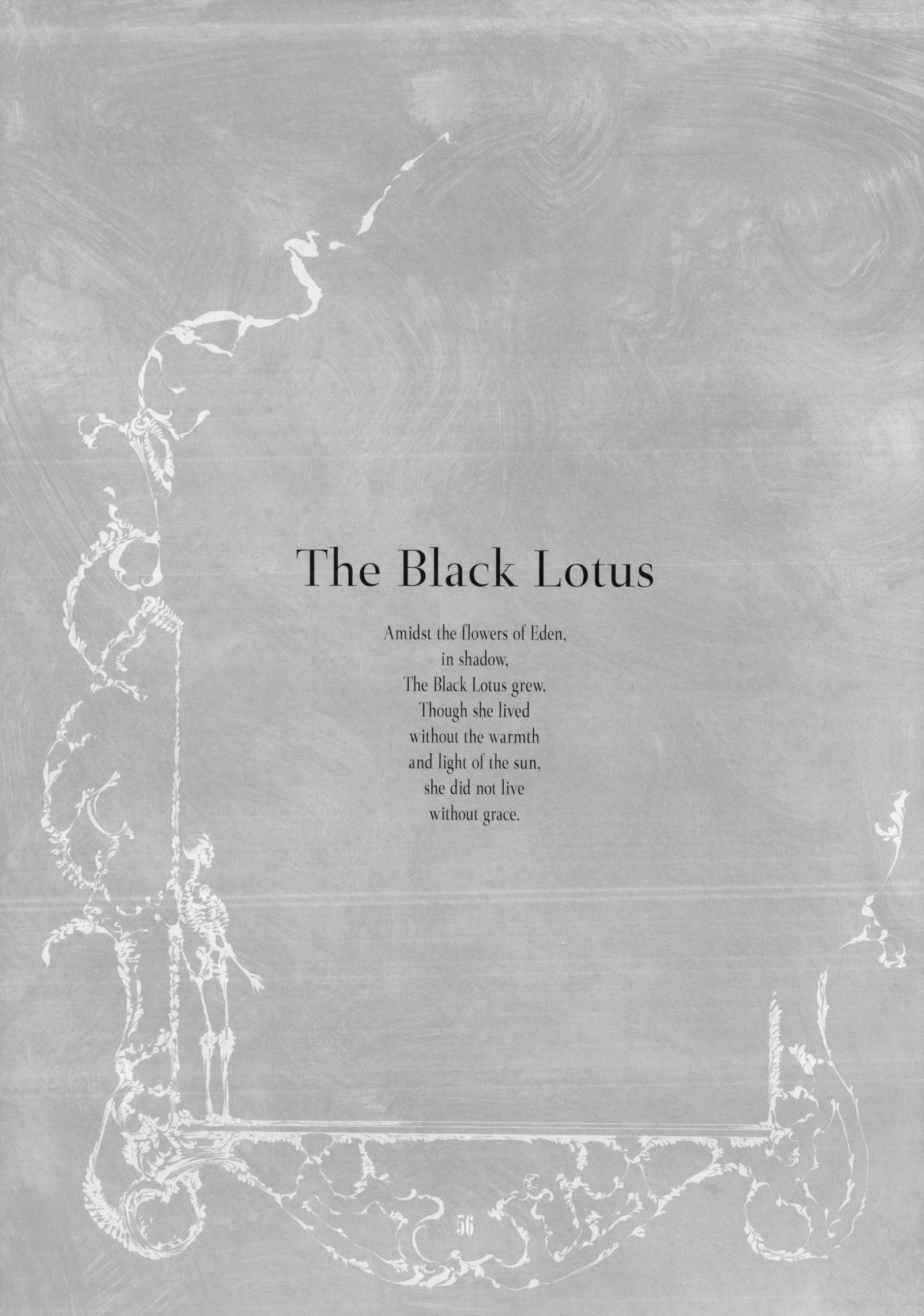

The Black Lotus

Amidst the flowers of Eden,
in shadow,
The Black Lotus grew.
Though she lived
without the warmth
and light of the sun,
she did not live
without grace.

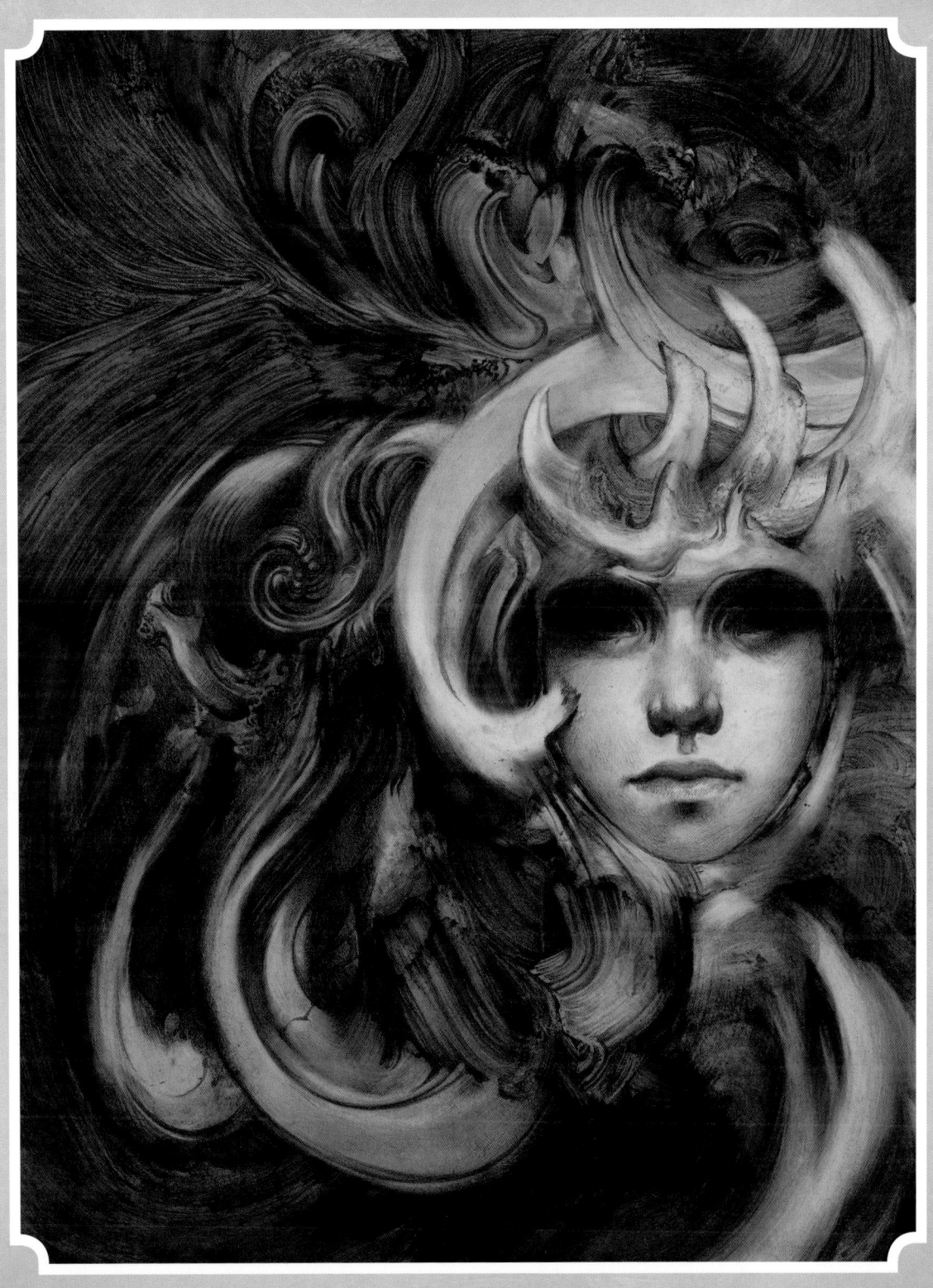

Within Reach

I am the Moon,
so dark
yet not unknown
to the Light...
and always
within reach.

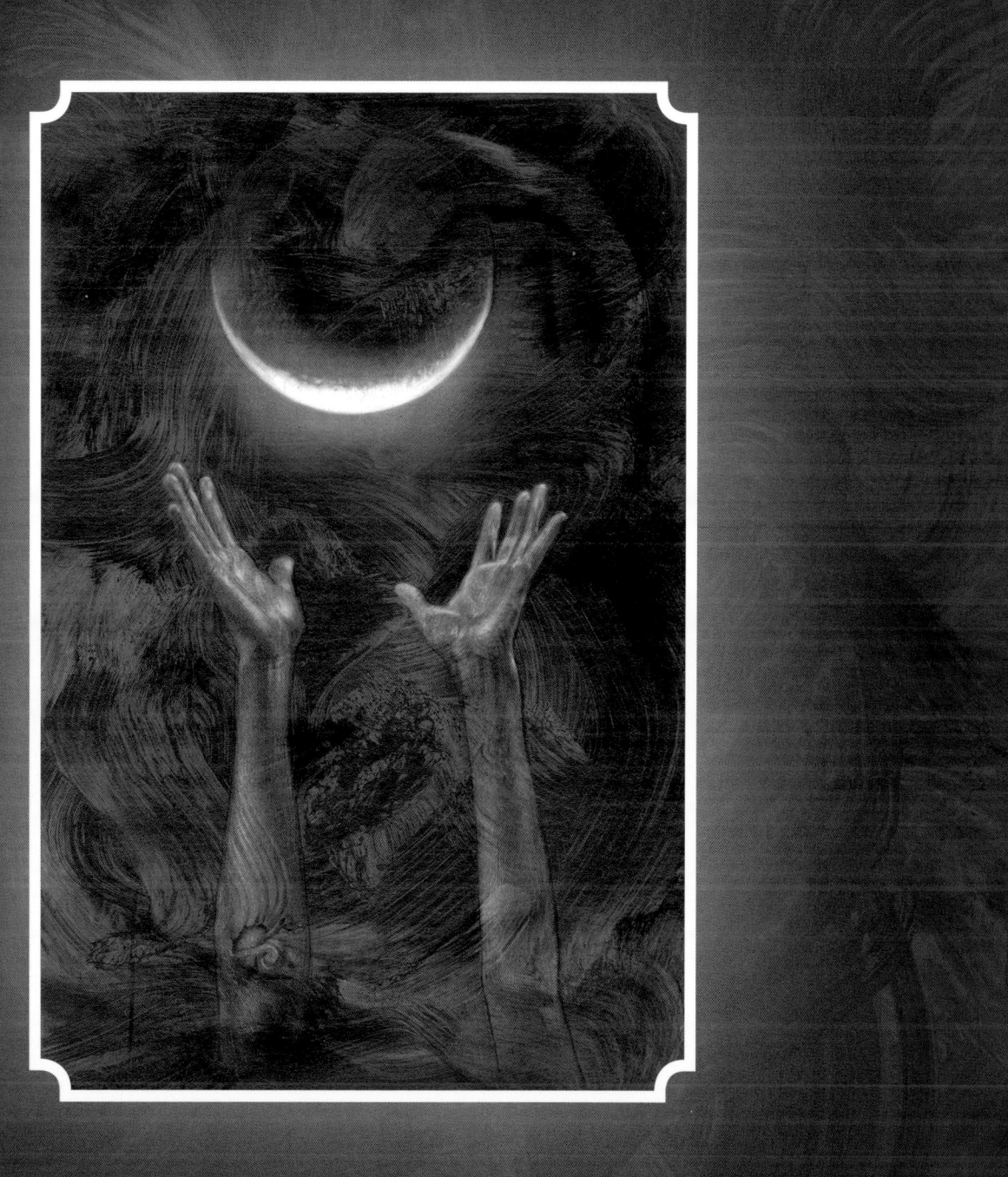

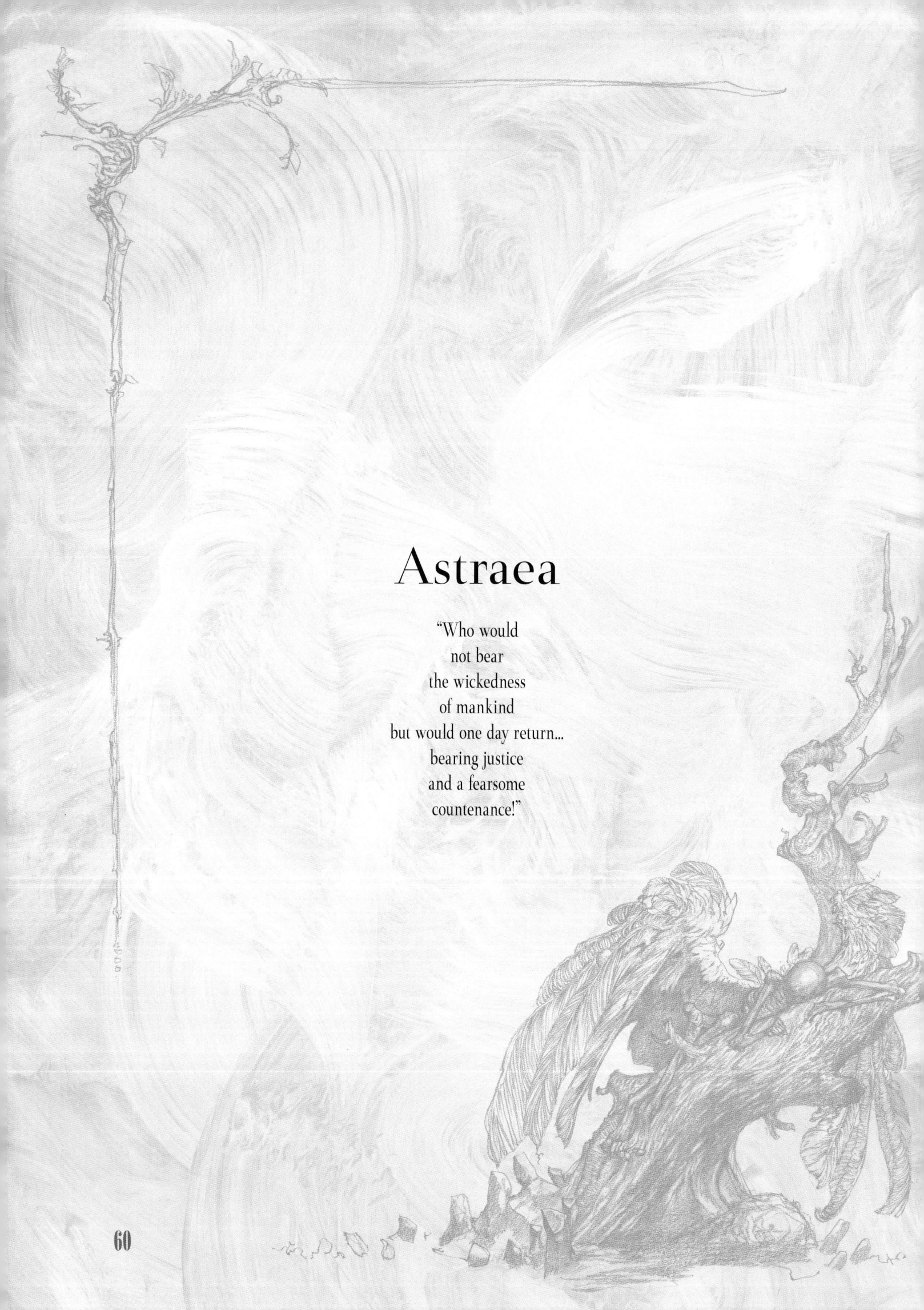

Astraea

"Who would
not bear
the wickedness
of mankind
but would one day return...
bearing justice
and a fearsome
countenance!"

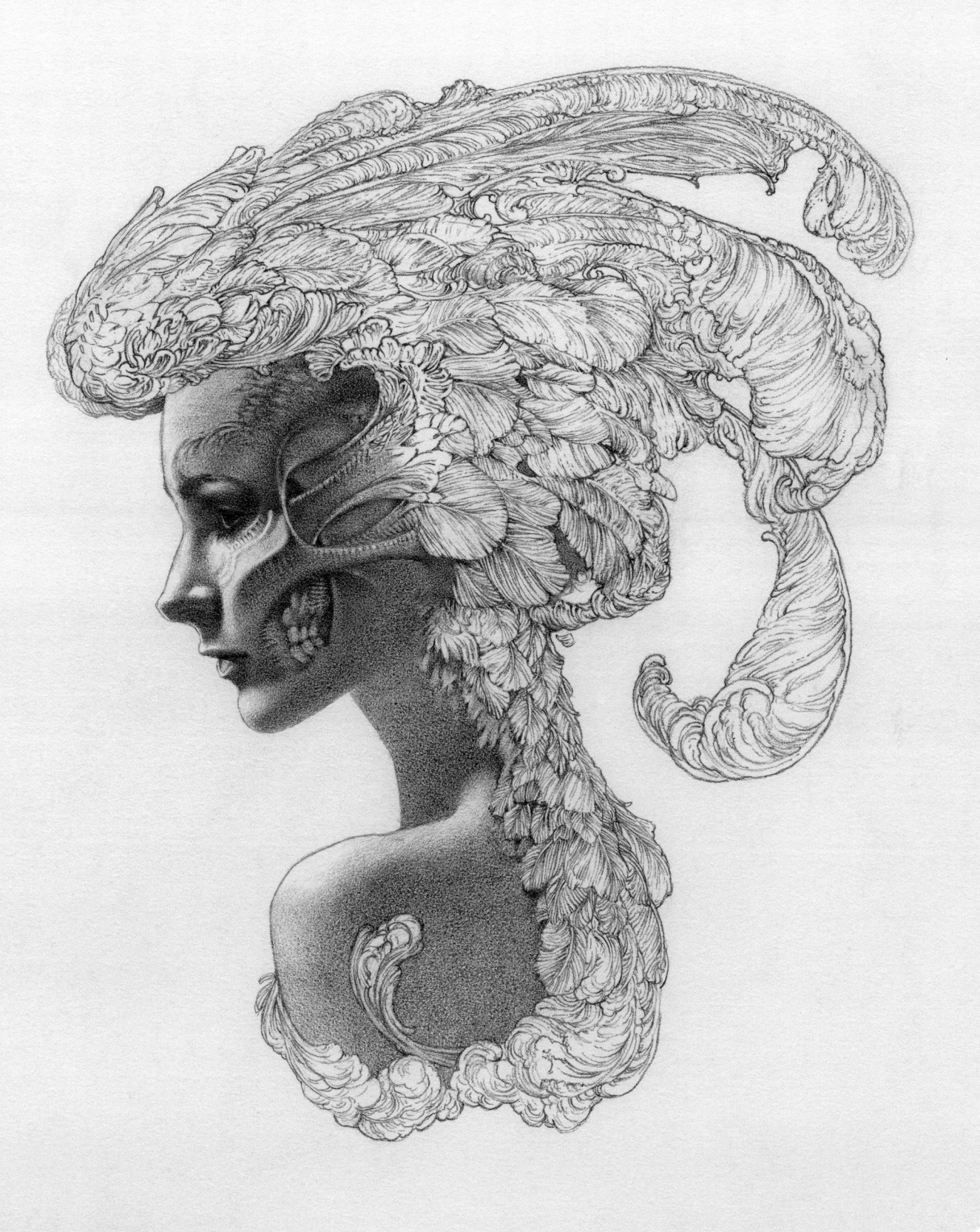

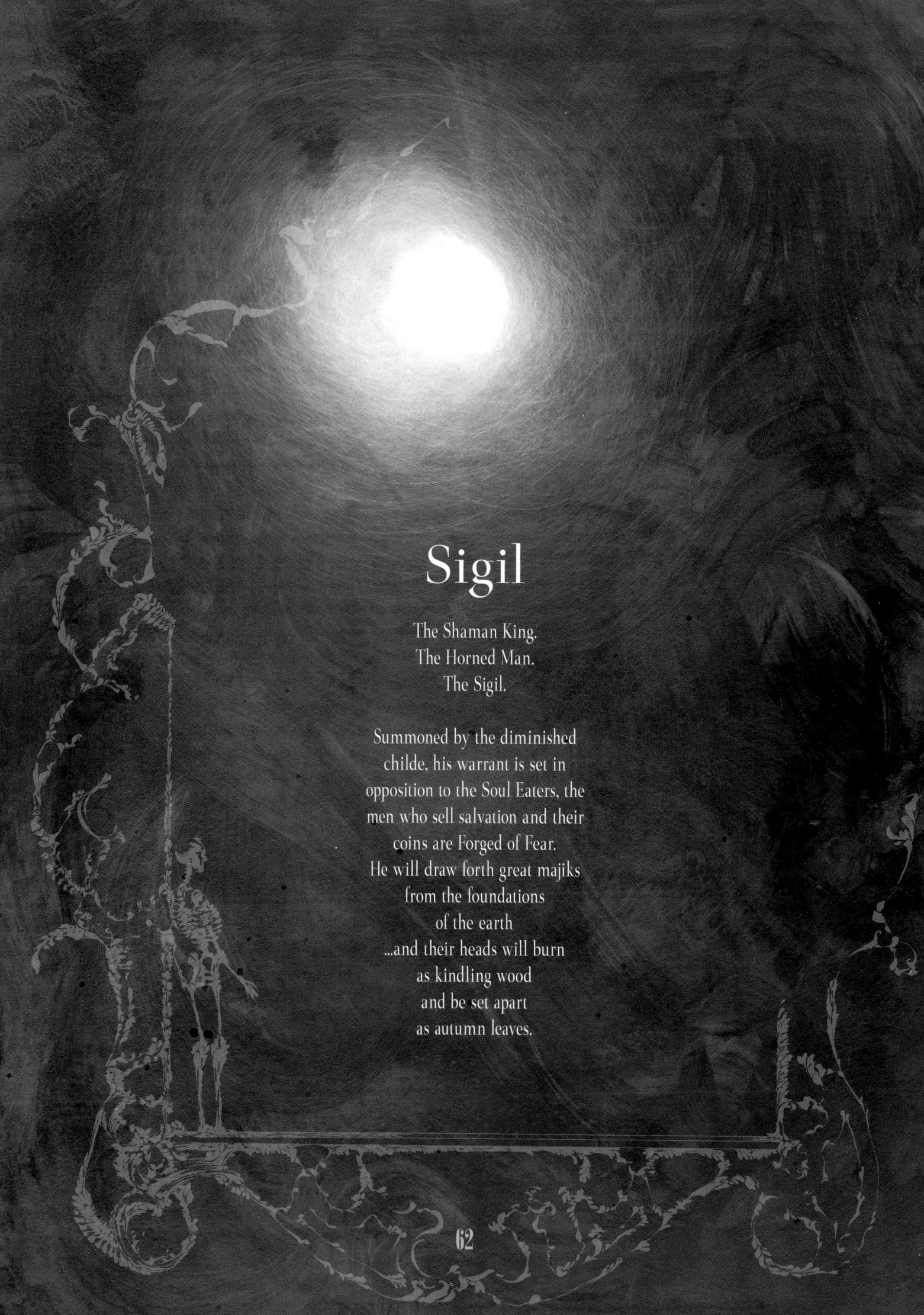

Sigil

The Shaman King.
The Horned Man.
The Sigil.

Summoned by the diminished
childe, his warrant is set in
opposition to the Soul Eaters, the
men who sell salvation and their
coins are Forged of Fear.
He will draw forth great majiks
from the foundations
of the earth
...and their heads will burn
as kindling wood
and be set apart
as autumn leaves.

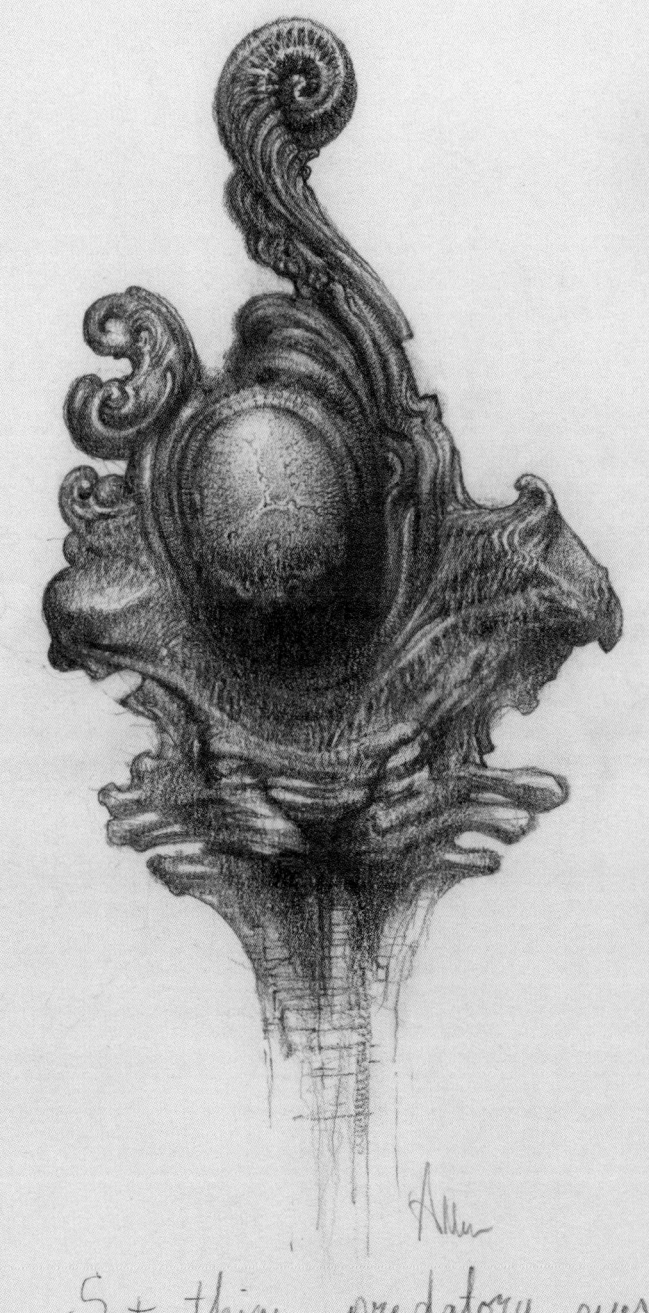

Set thine predatory eyes
Upon the innocent
and mine eyes
Will set upon thee.

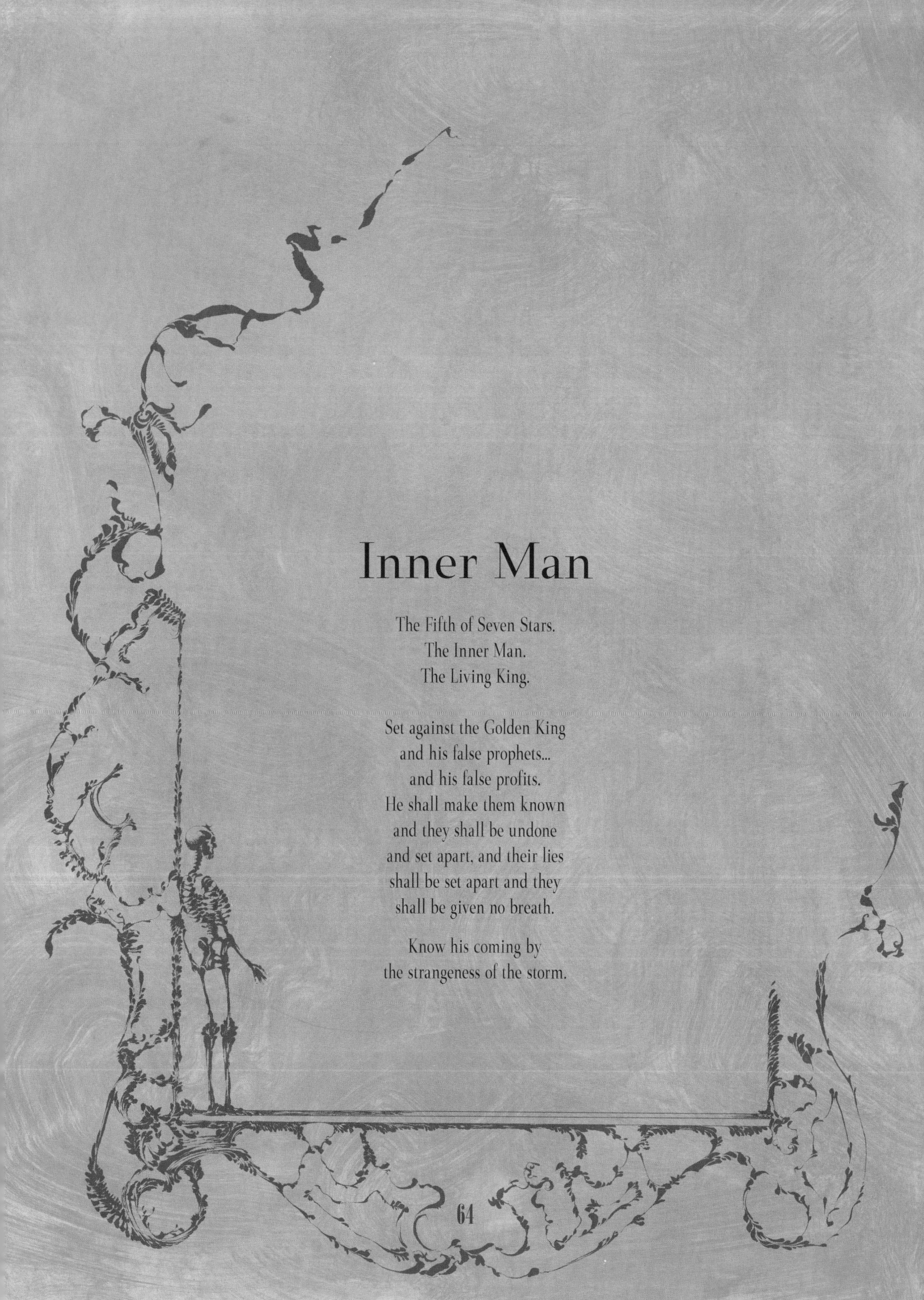

Inner Man

The Fifth of Seven Stars.
The Inner Man.
The Living King.

Set against the Golden King
and his false prophets...
and his false profits.
He shall make them known
and they shall be undone
and set apart, and their lies
shall be set apart and they
shall be given no breath.

Know his coming by
the strangeness of the storm.

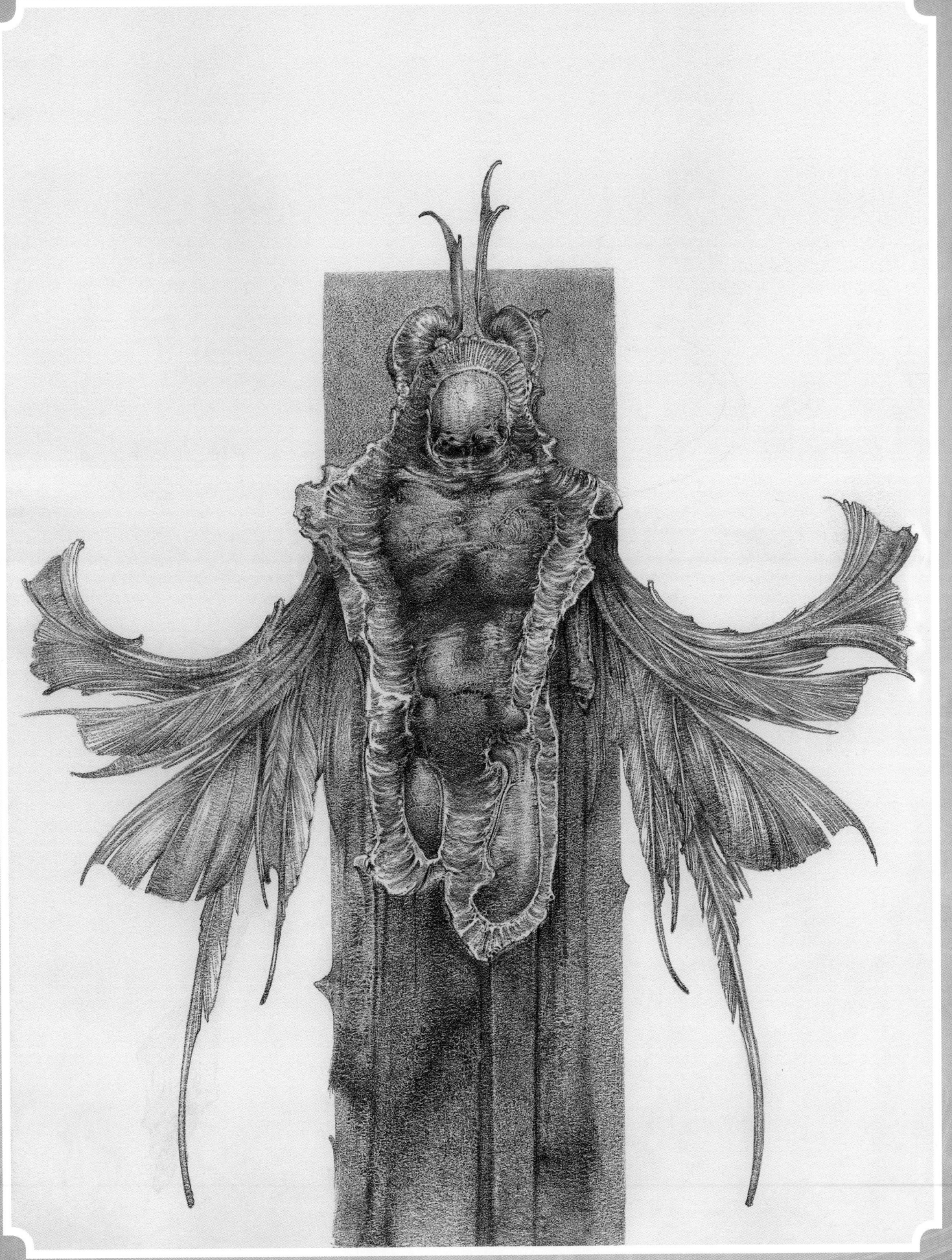

Sarcophagus III

I hold within me
every evil, every
wretched thing that
has come before me.
Everything with dark
desire that has tried
to cross my path
is herein.
Their presence has
corrupted, tortured
my manifest form,
but I will never
release them...

I am their Hell.

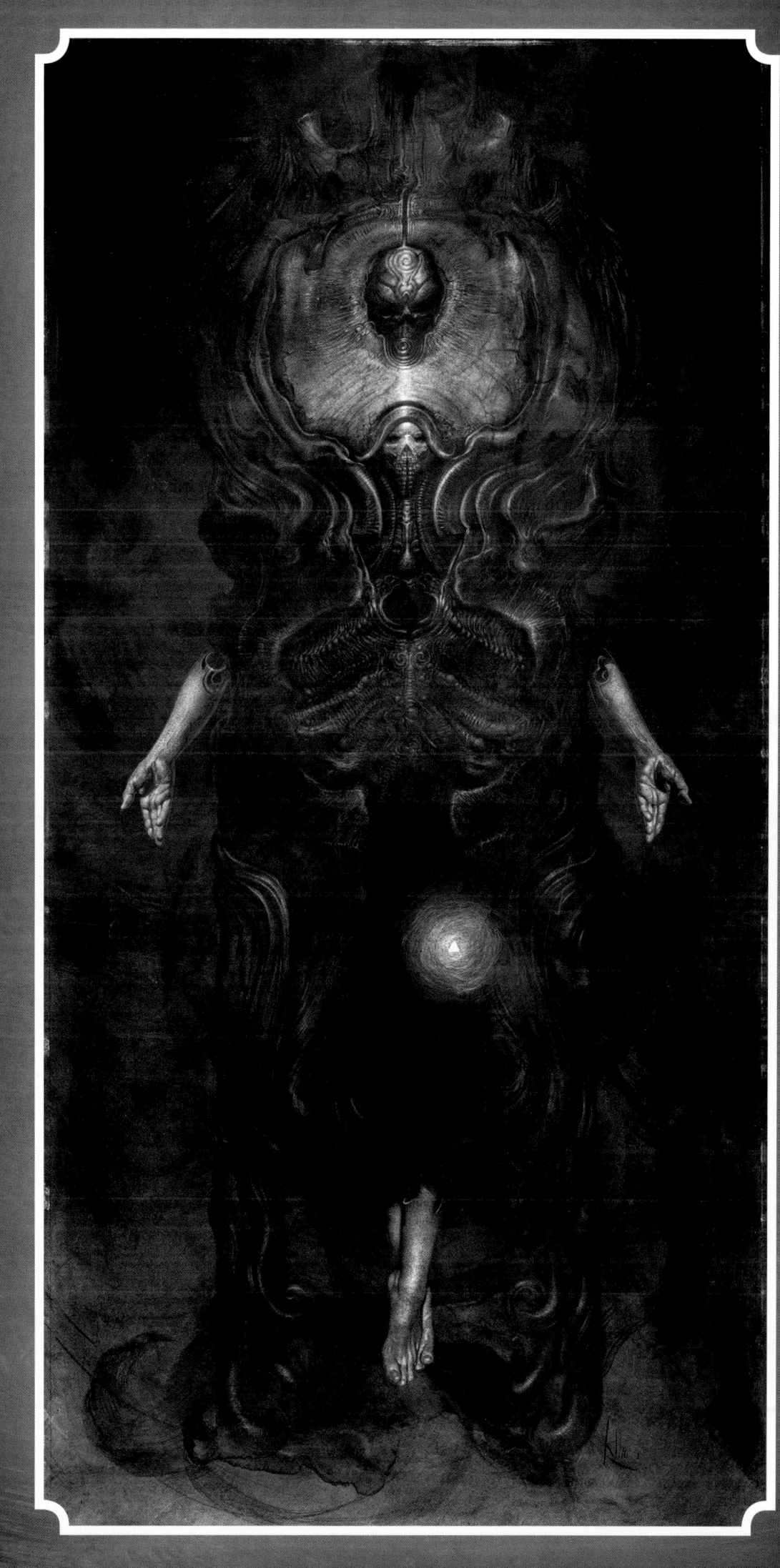

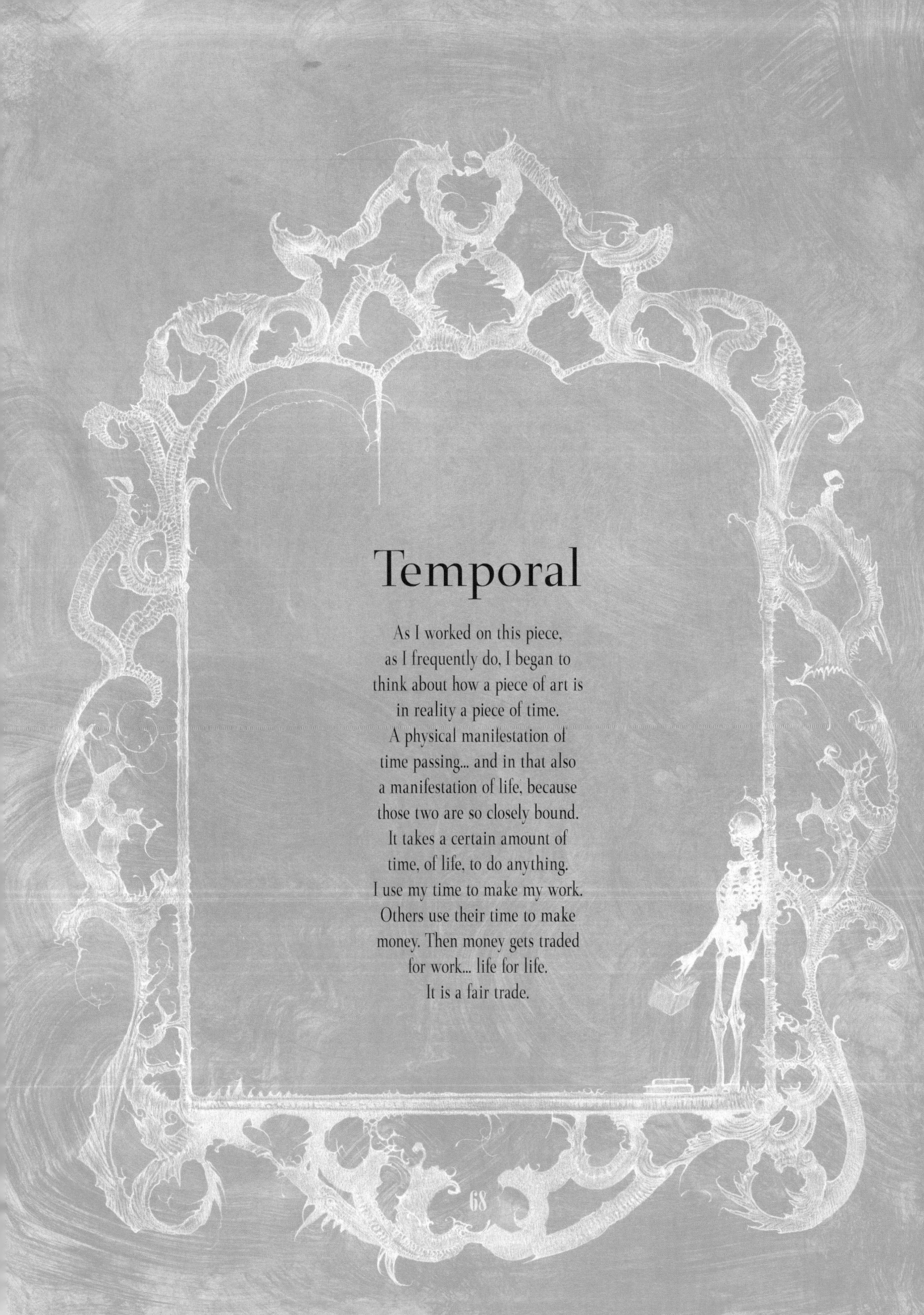

Temporal

As I worked on this piece,
as I frequently do, I began to
think about how a piece of art is
in reality a piece of time.
A physical manifestation of
time passing... and in that also
a manifestation of life, because
those two are so closely bound.
It takes a certain amount of
time, of life, to do anything.
I use my time to make my work.
Others use their time to make
money. Then money gets traded
for work... life for life.
It is a fair trade.

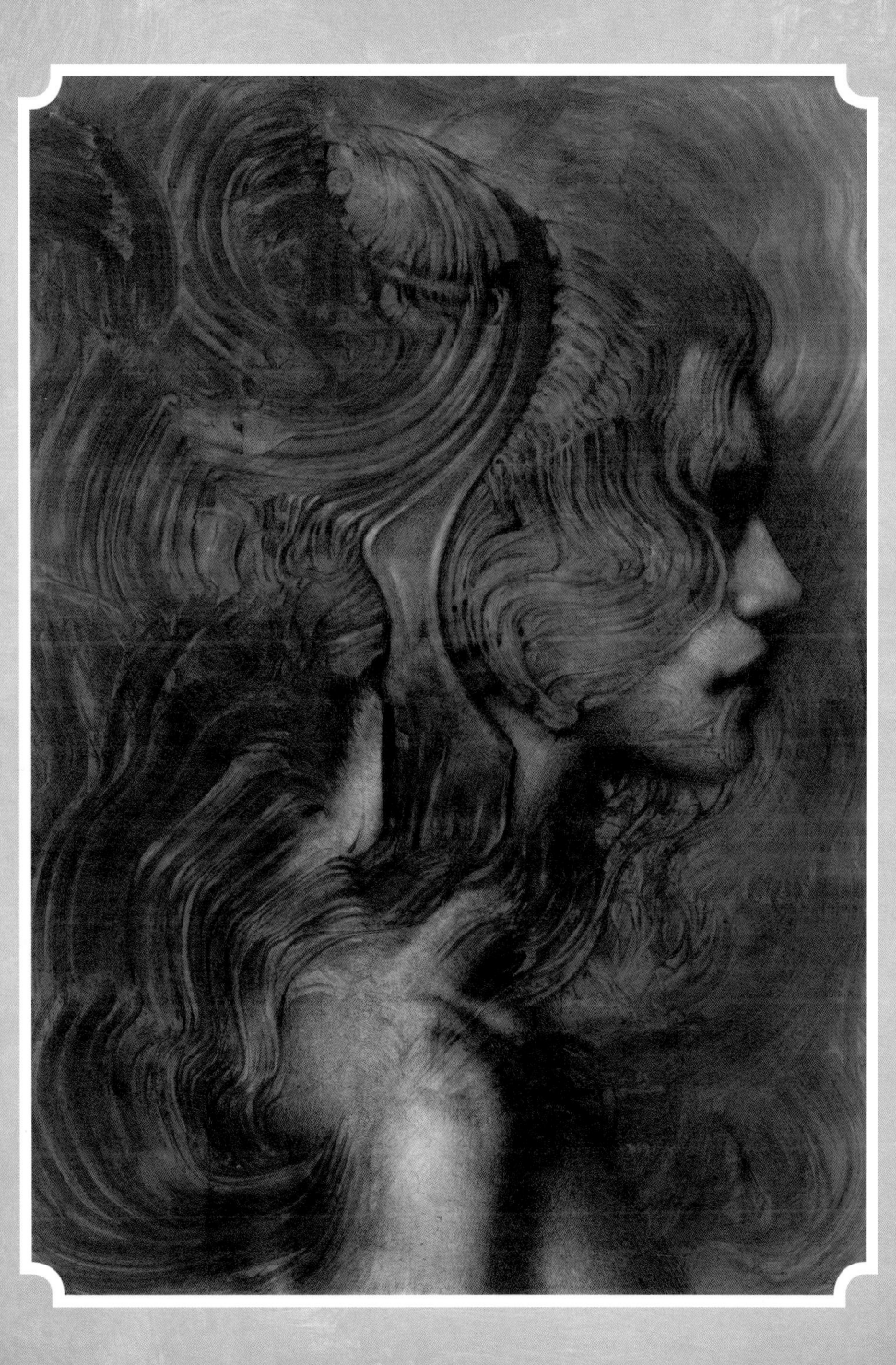

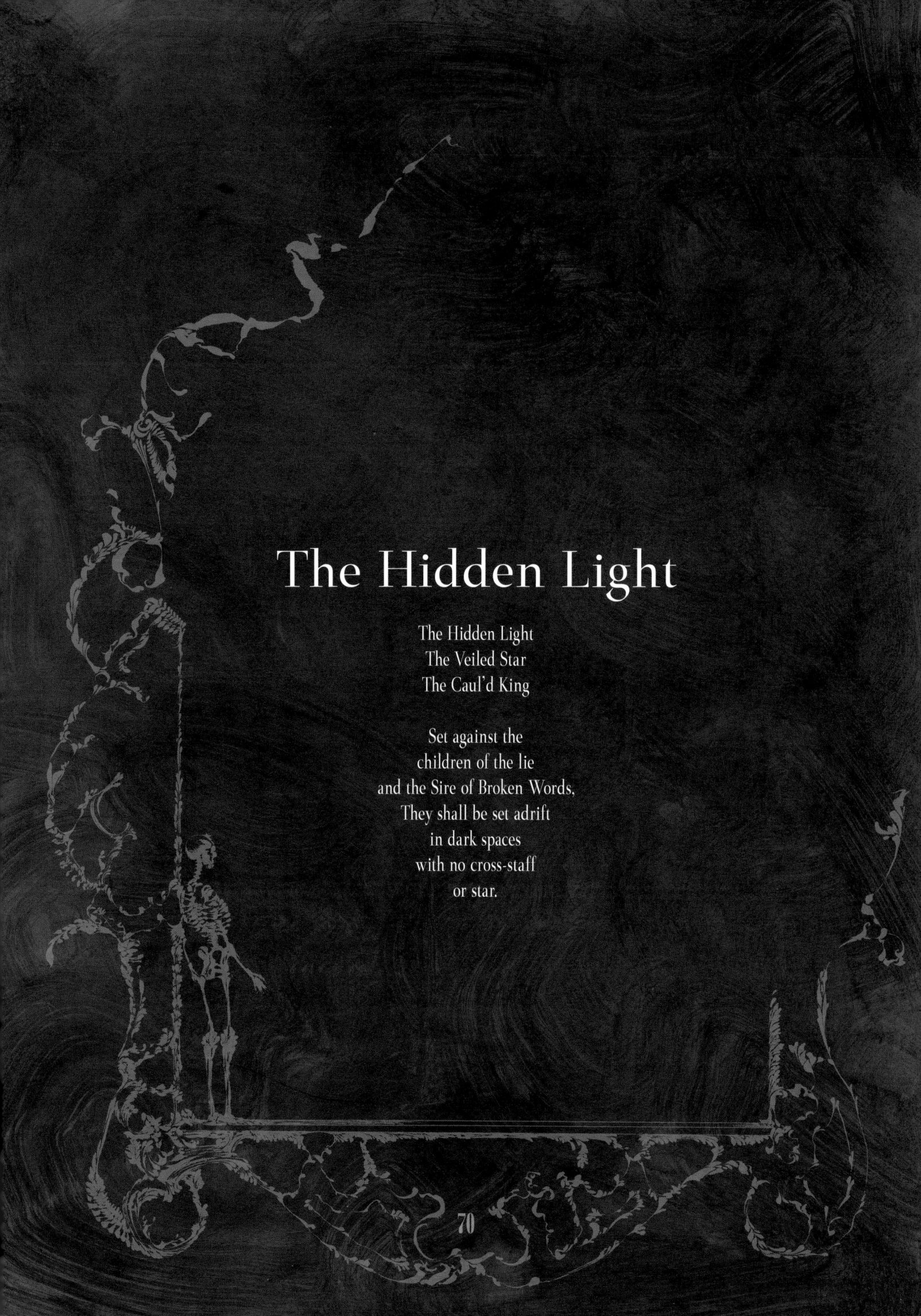

The Hidden Light

The Hidden Light
The Veiled Star
The Caul'd King

Set against the
children of the lie
and the Sire of Broken Words,
They shall be set adrift
in dark spaces
with no cross-staff
or star.

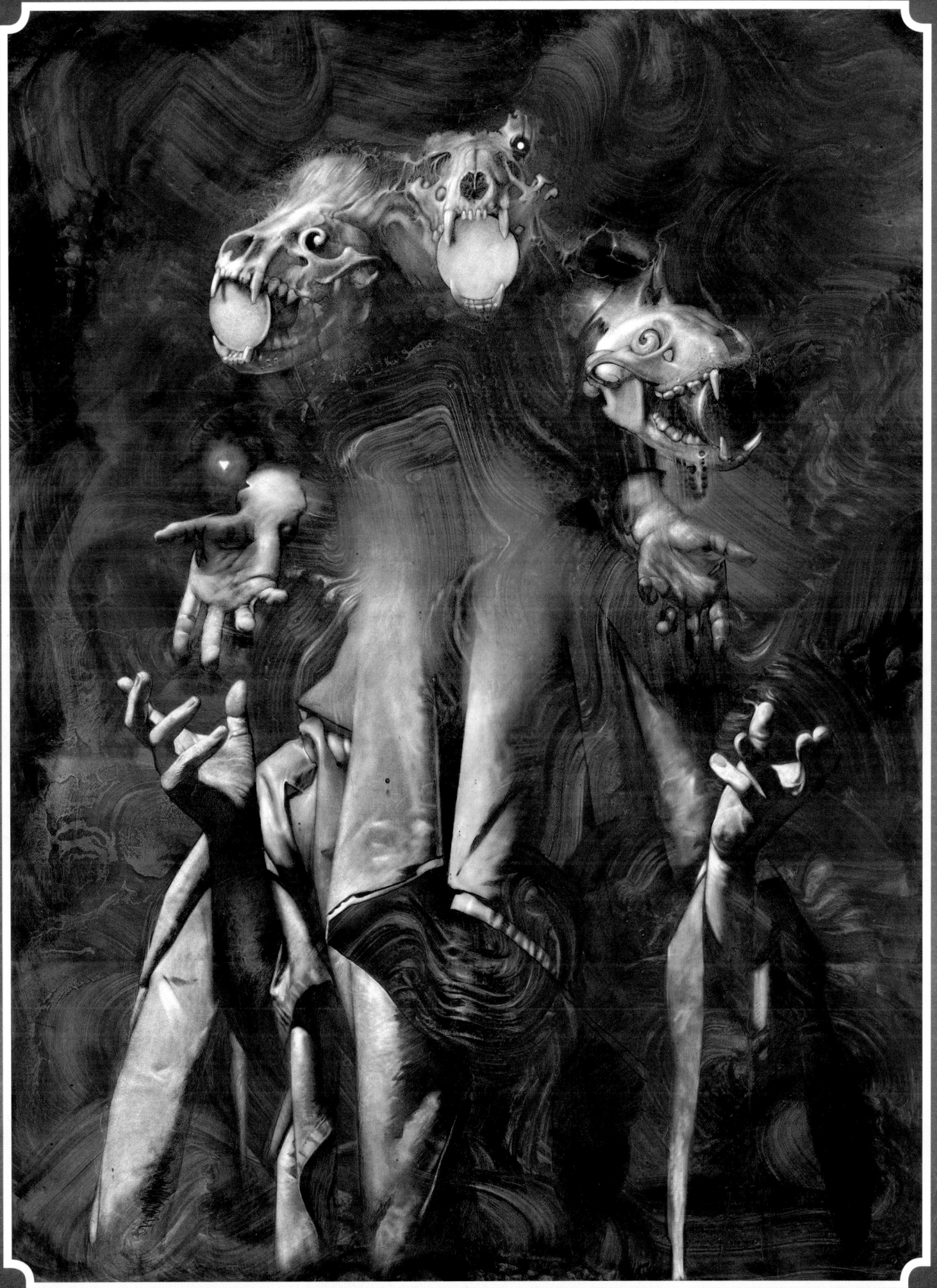

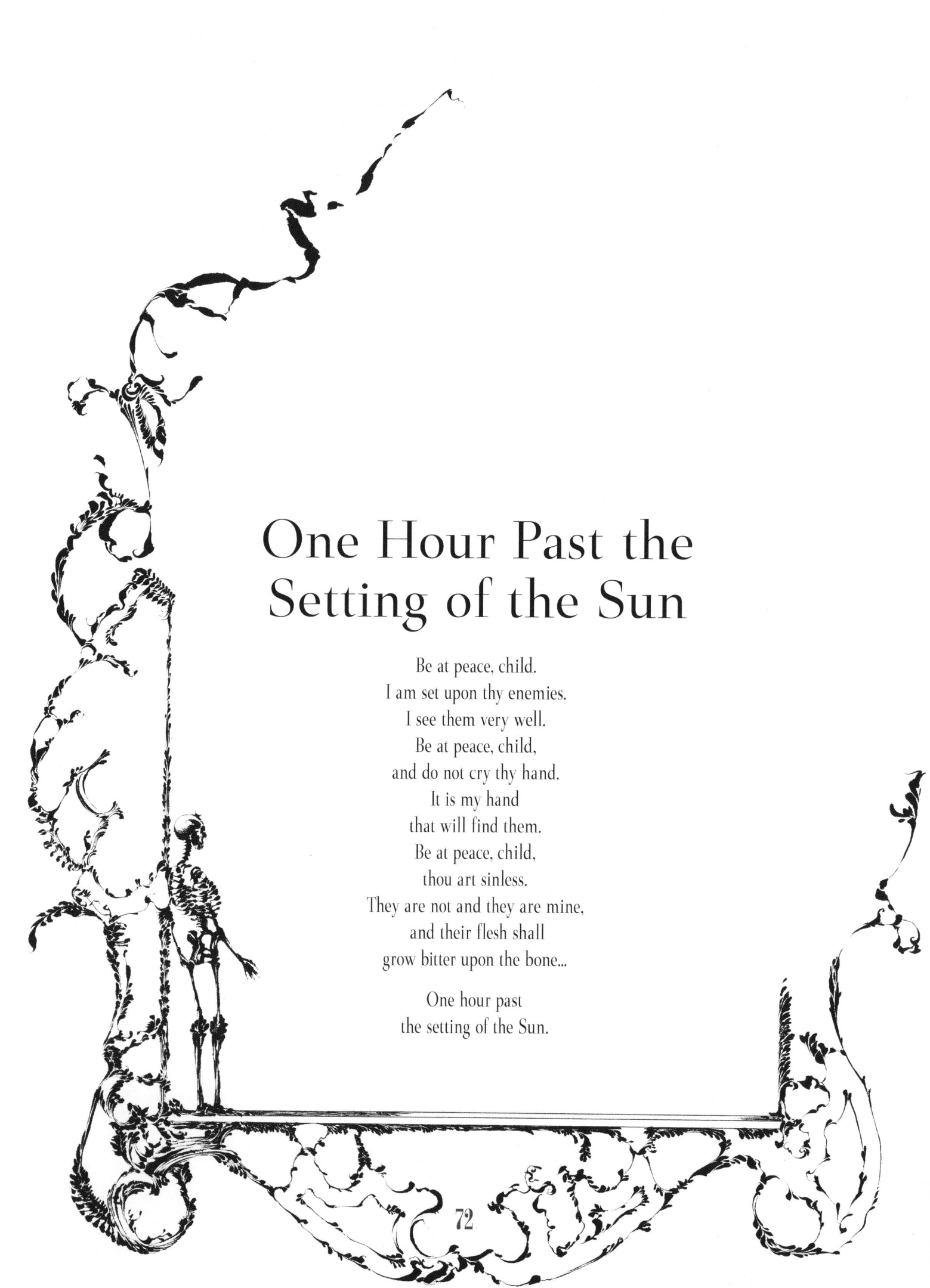

One Hour Past the Setting of the Sun

Be at peace, child.
I am set upon thy enemies.
I see them very well.
Be at peace, child,
and do not cry thy hand.
It is my hand
that will find them.
Be at peace, child,
thou art sinless.
They are not and they are mine,
and their flesh shall
grow bitter upon the bone...

One hour past
the setting of the Sun.

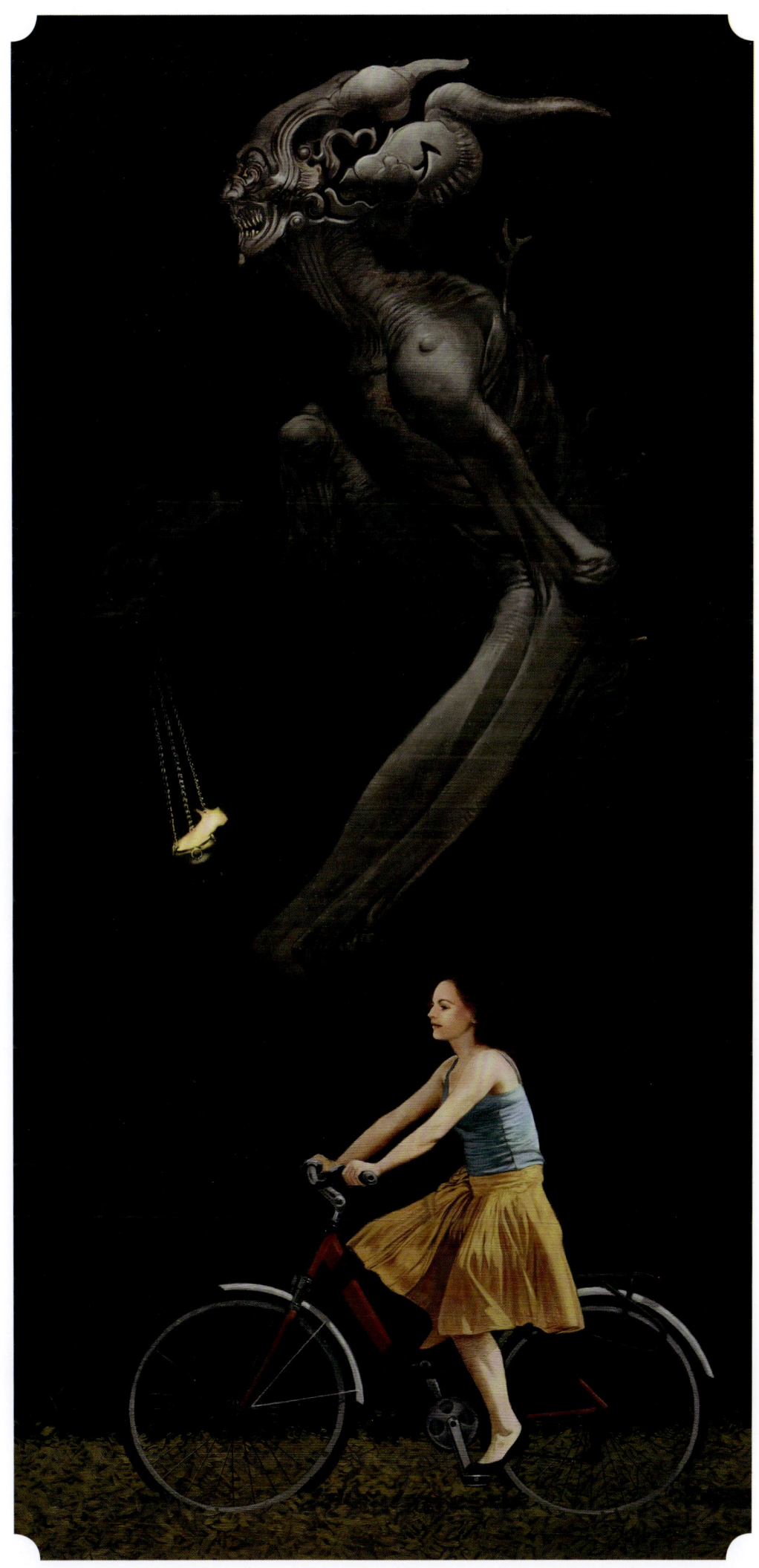

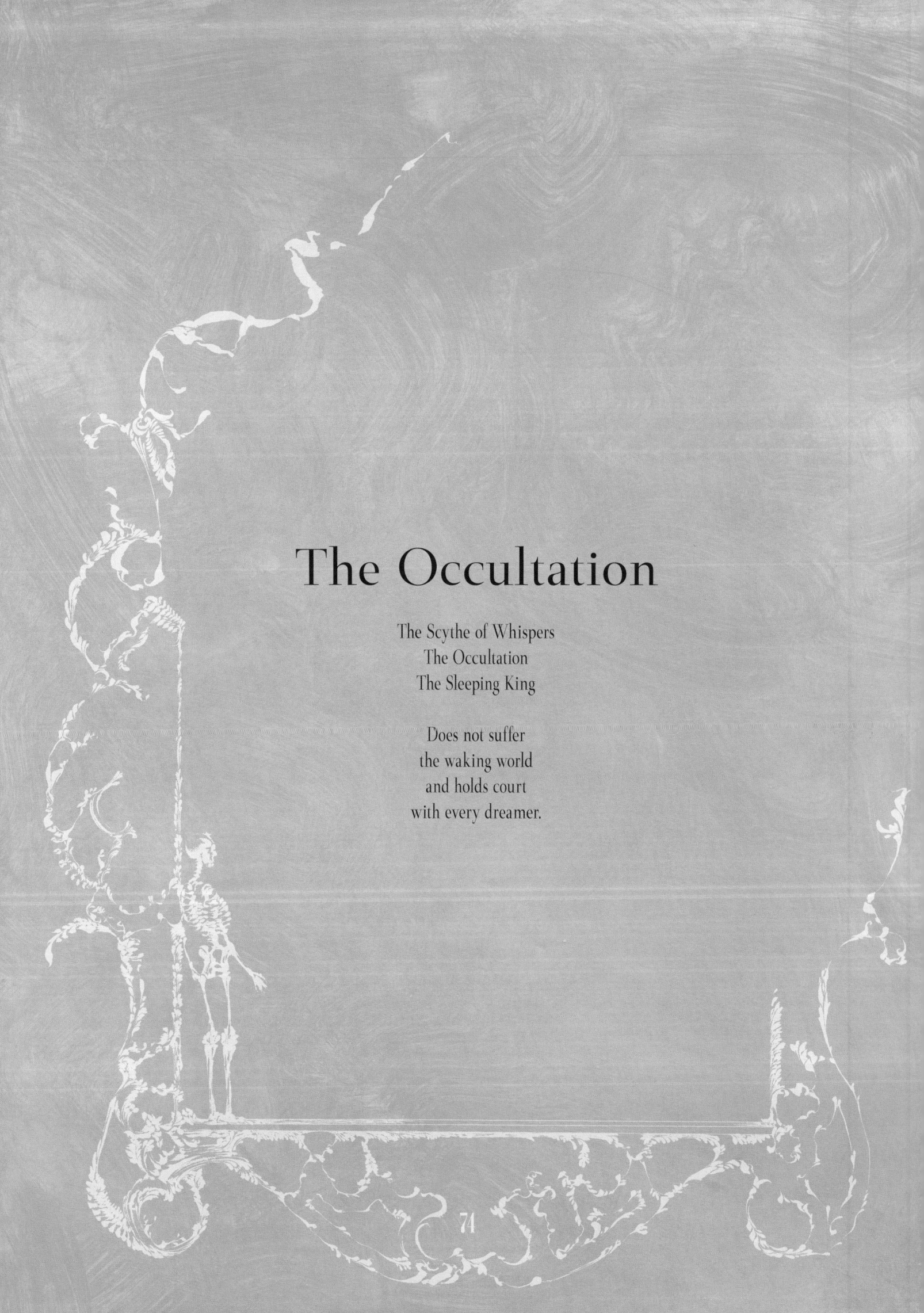

The Occultation

The Scythe of Whispers
The Occultation
The Sleeping King

Does not suffer
the waking world
and holds court
with every dreamer.

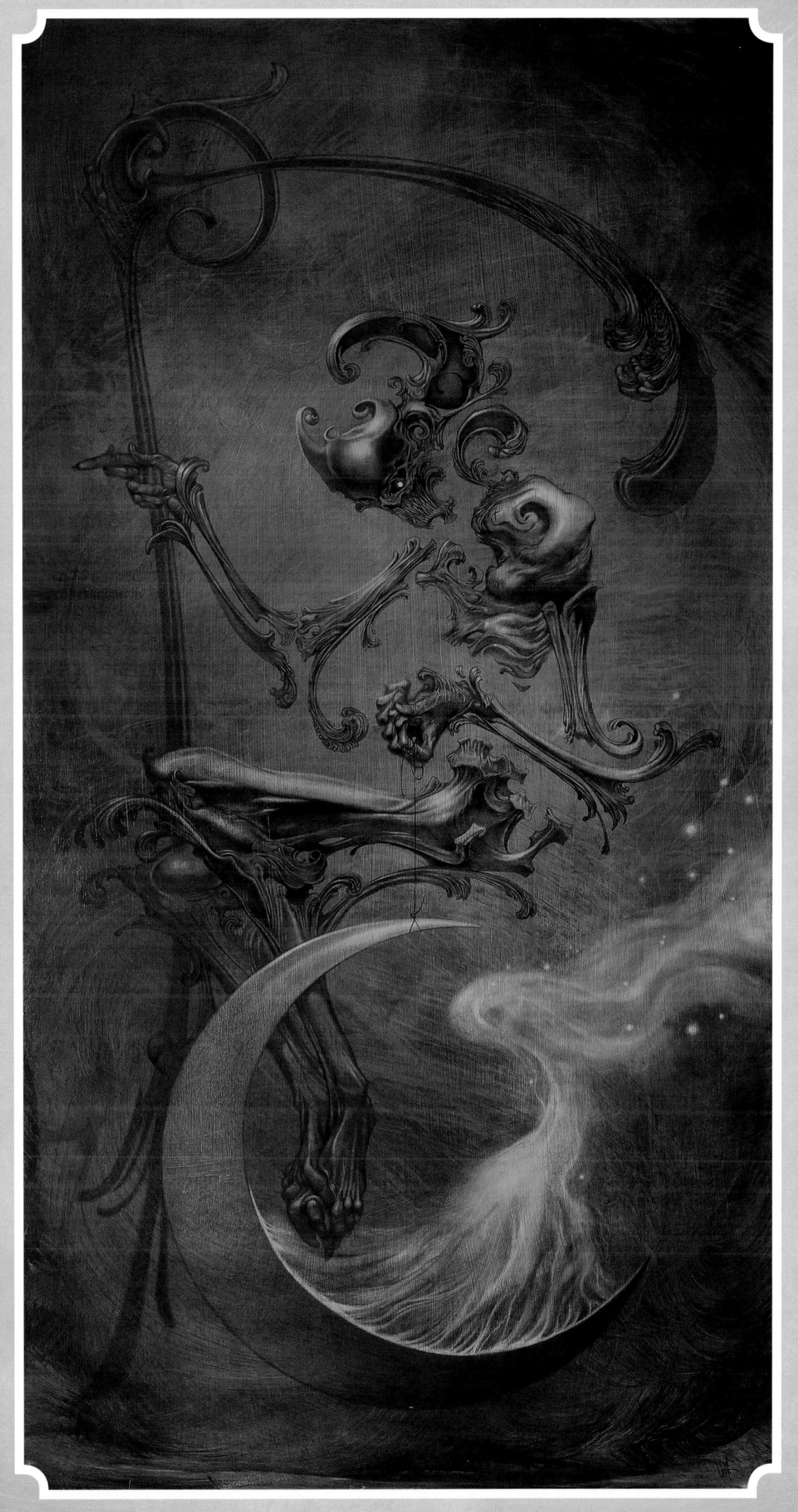

Black Crescent

From an angel
she hath wrested
the meaning
of the Crescent Moon
and brought it
with her
in the service
of humankind.

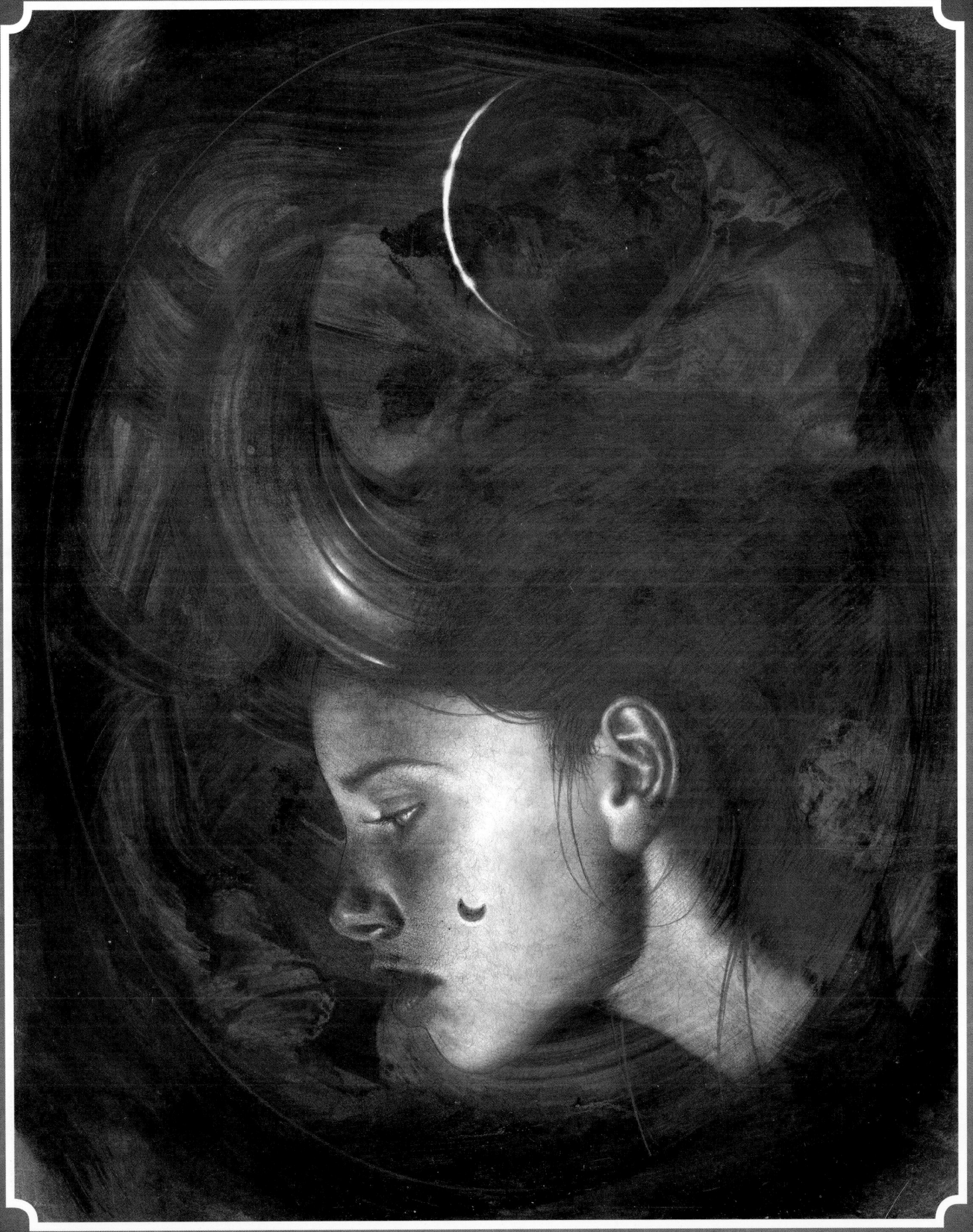

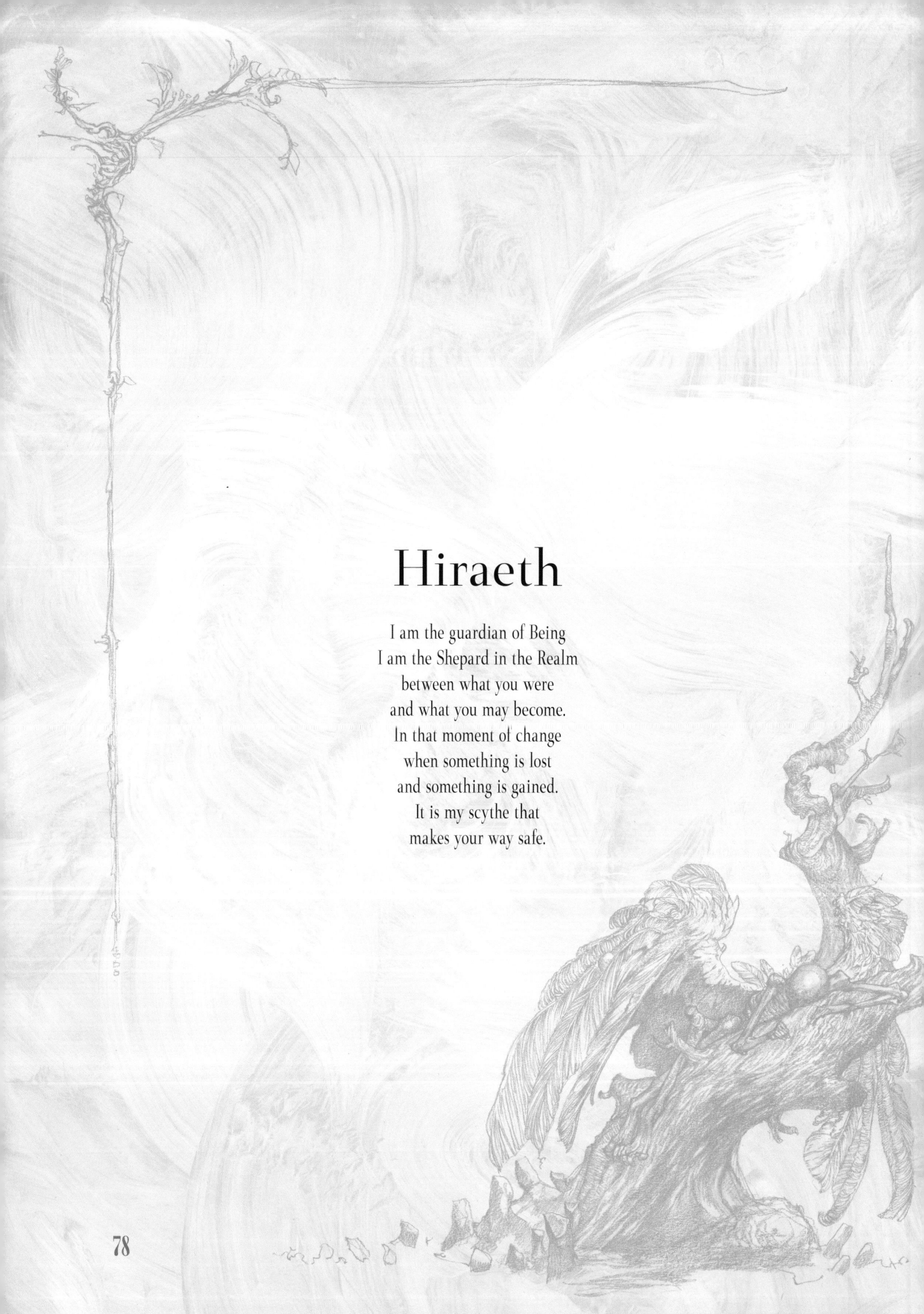

Hiraeth

I am the guardian of Being
I am the Shepard in the Realm
between what you were
and what you may become.
In that moment of change
when something is lost
and something is gained.
It is my scythe that
makes your way safe.

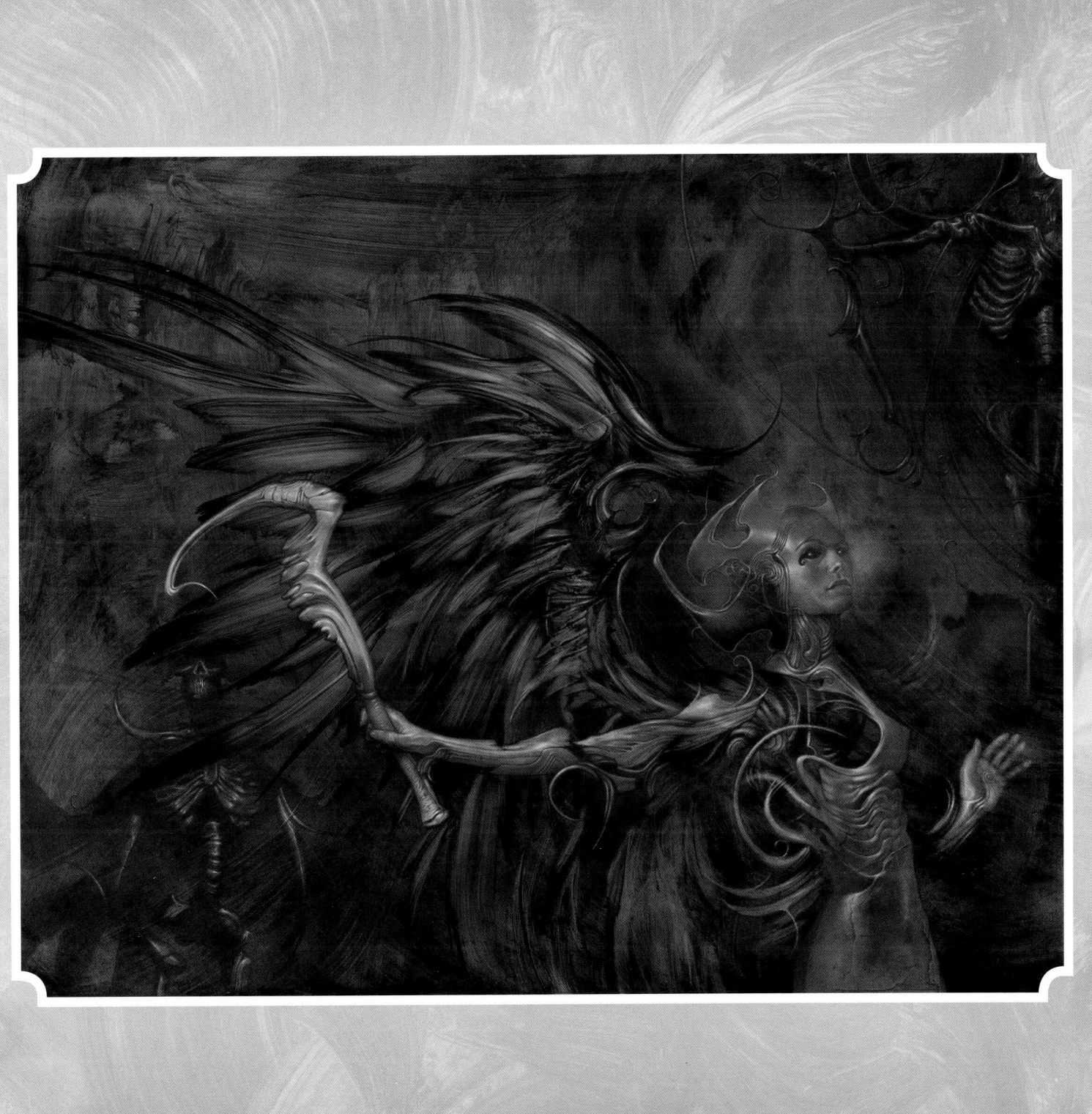

Fallen Star

Since the stars were
first cast like bones
I have been...
and it shall be
my hand
that stays
the last fallen star
from its death,
to begin again.

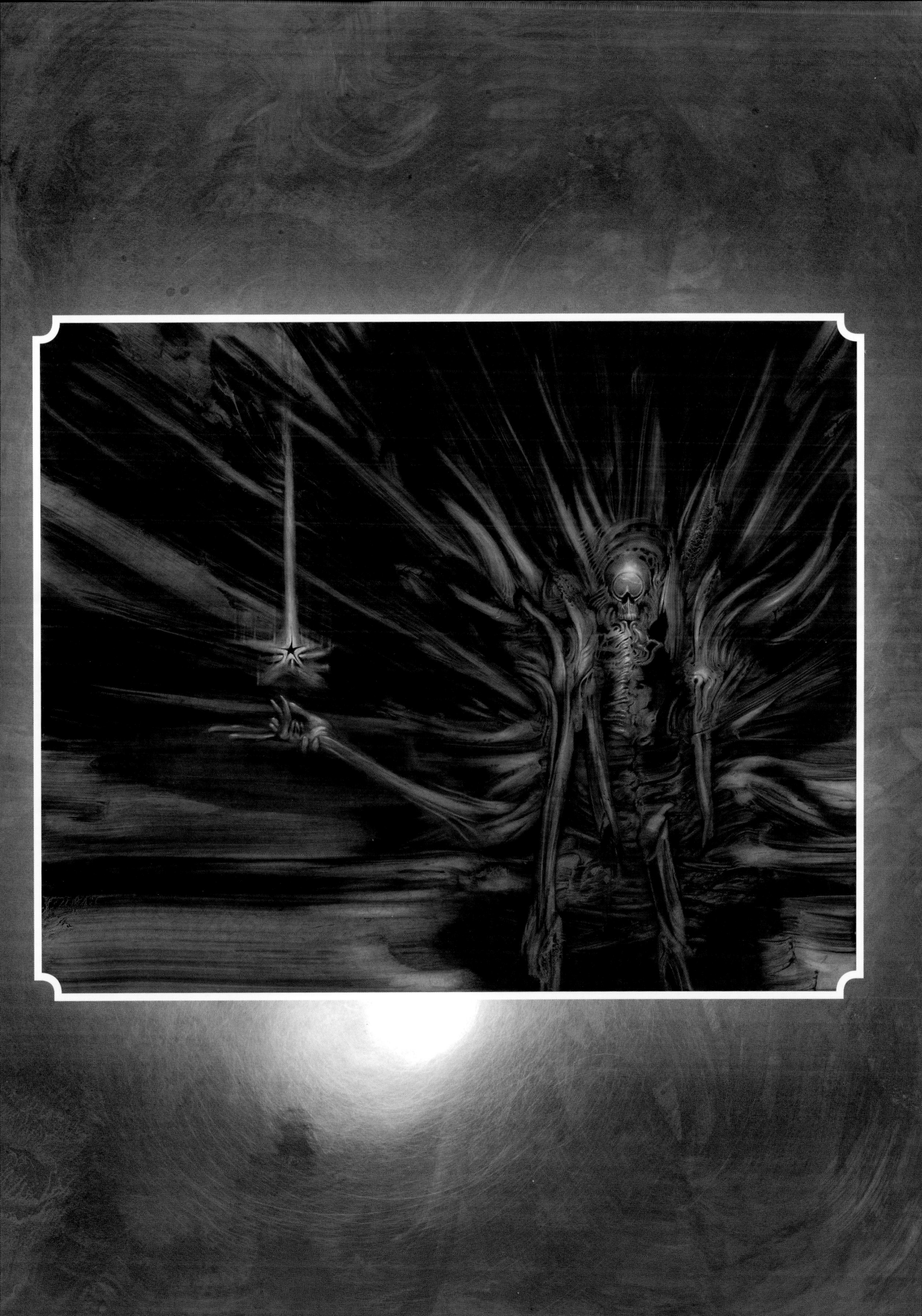

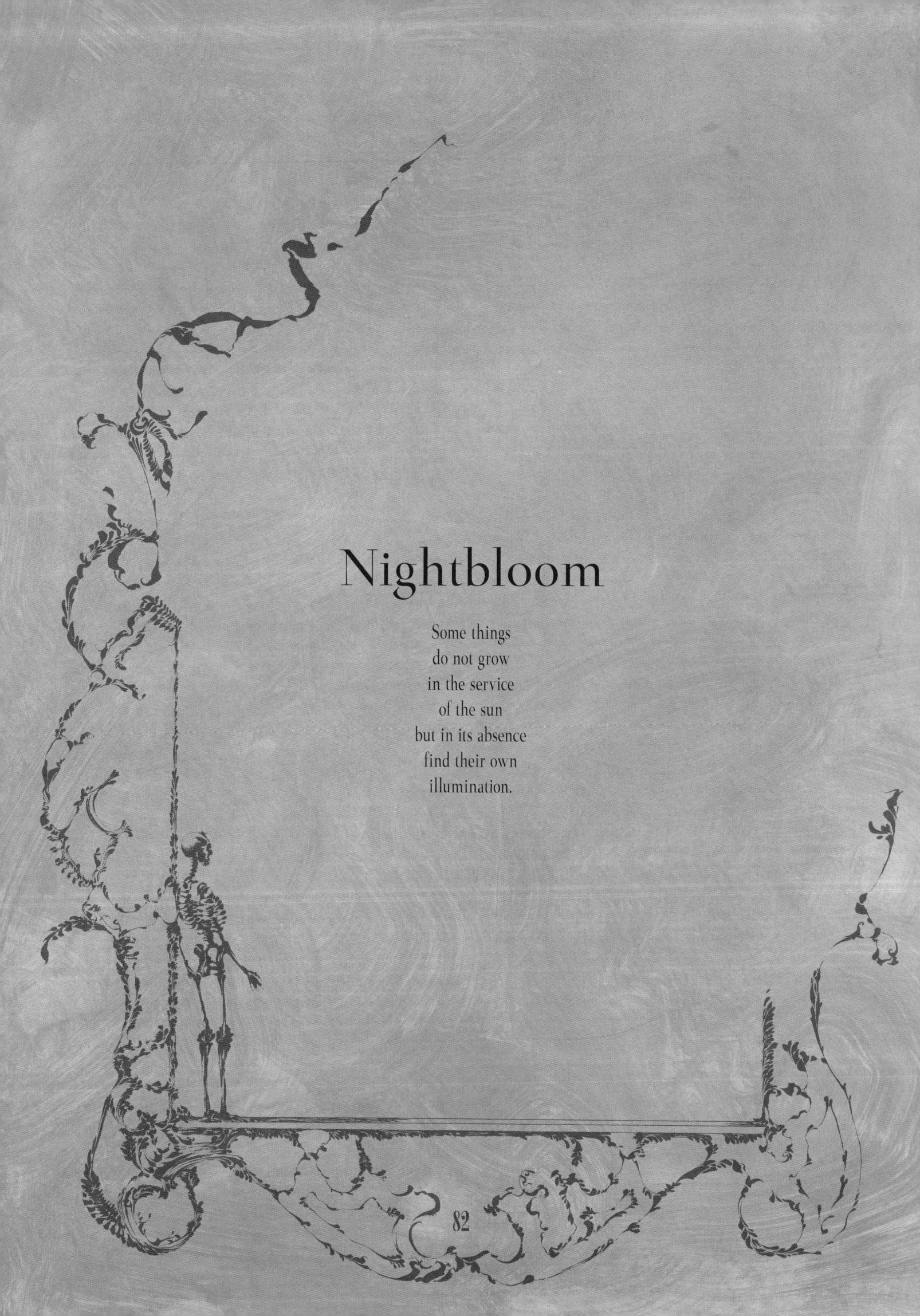

Nightbloom

Some things
do not grow
in the service
of the sun
but in its absence
find their own
illumination.

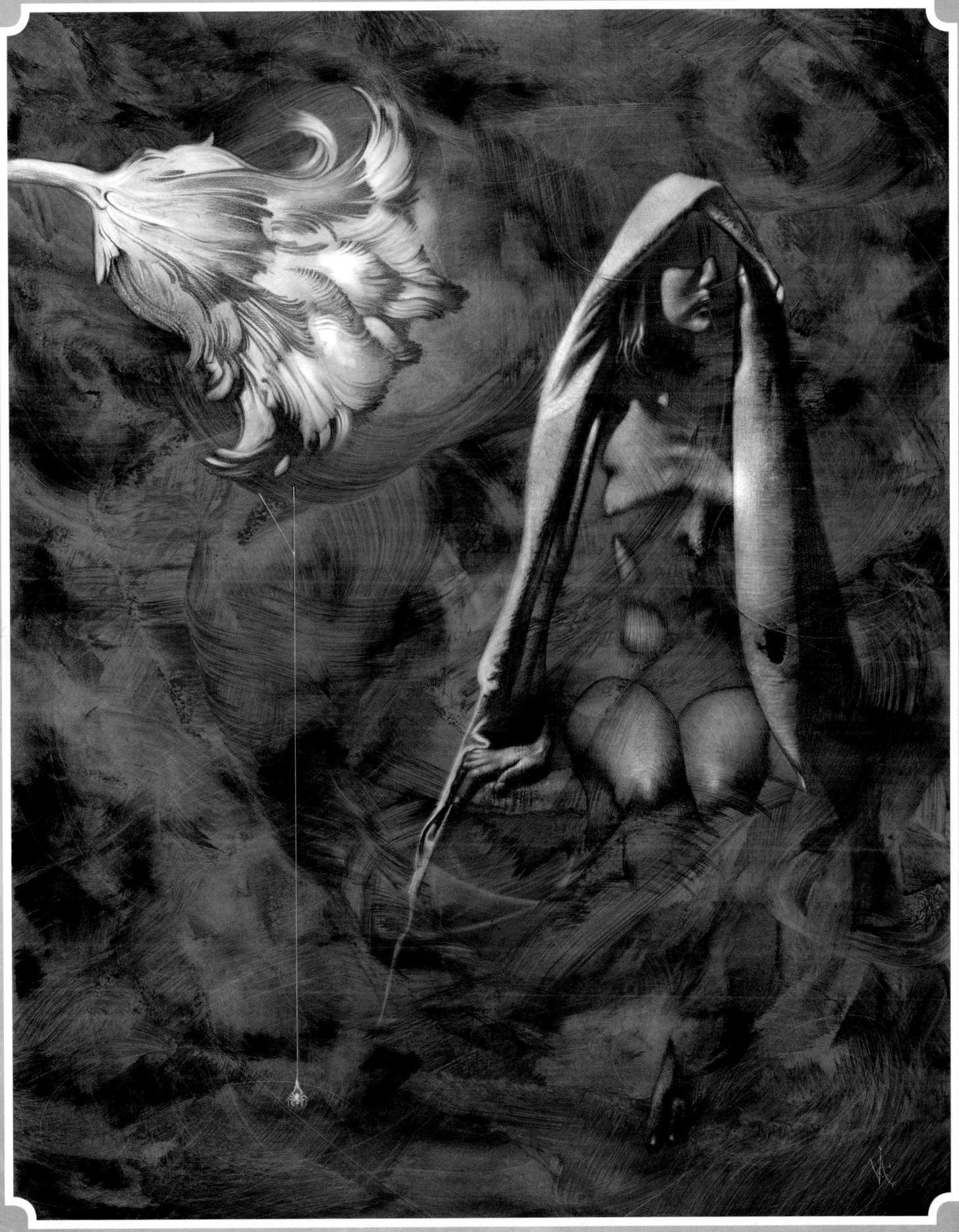

Daughter of the Sea

At night you could hear her
walking around town quietly
singing to herself... that is, until
the wind started blowing from
the ocean side and she would
fall silent, listening.
If you asked her what she heard,
she would look at you strangely
and say, "Can't you hear?
They're calling us home...

but not yet."

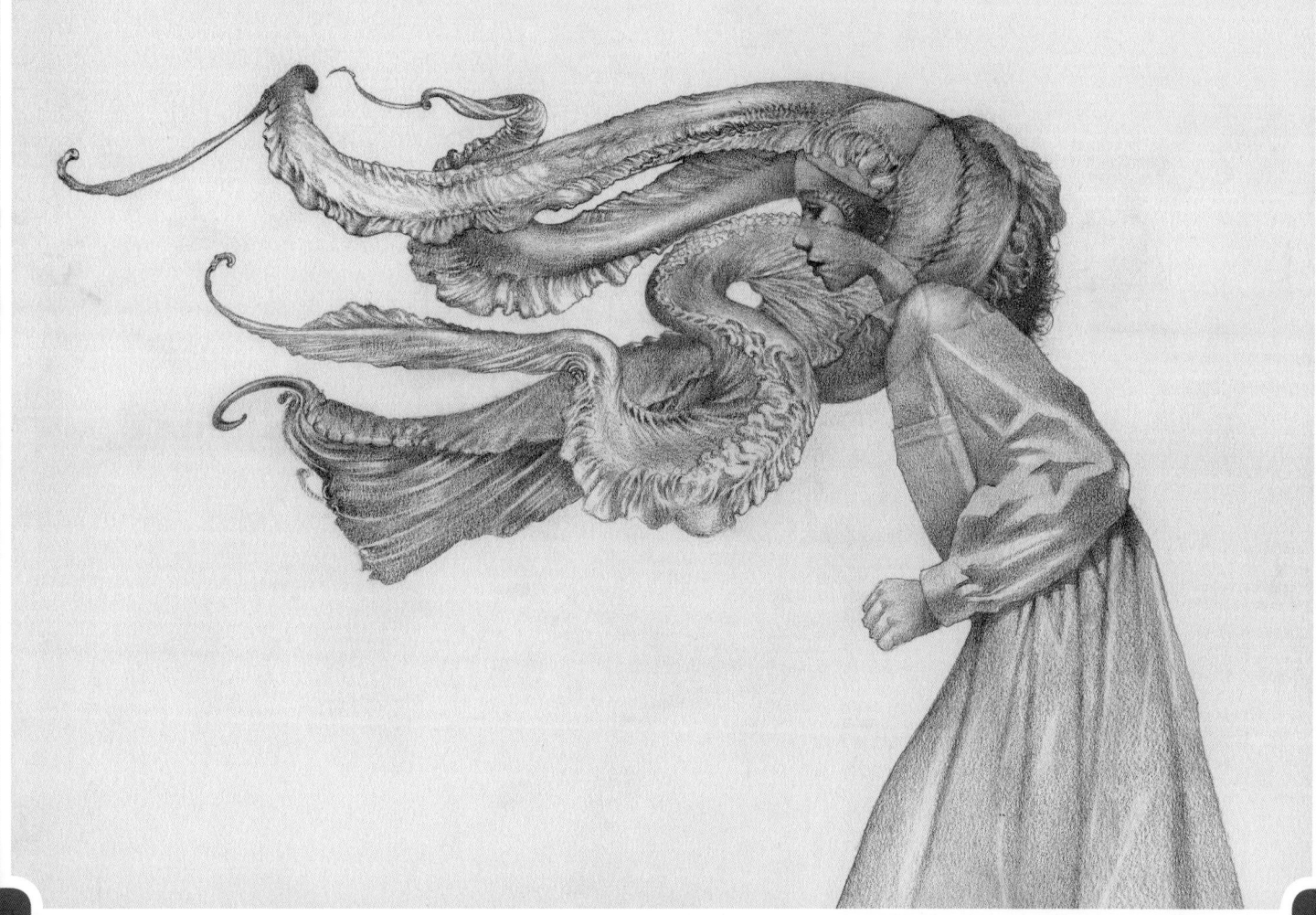

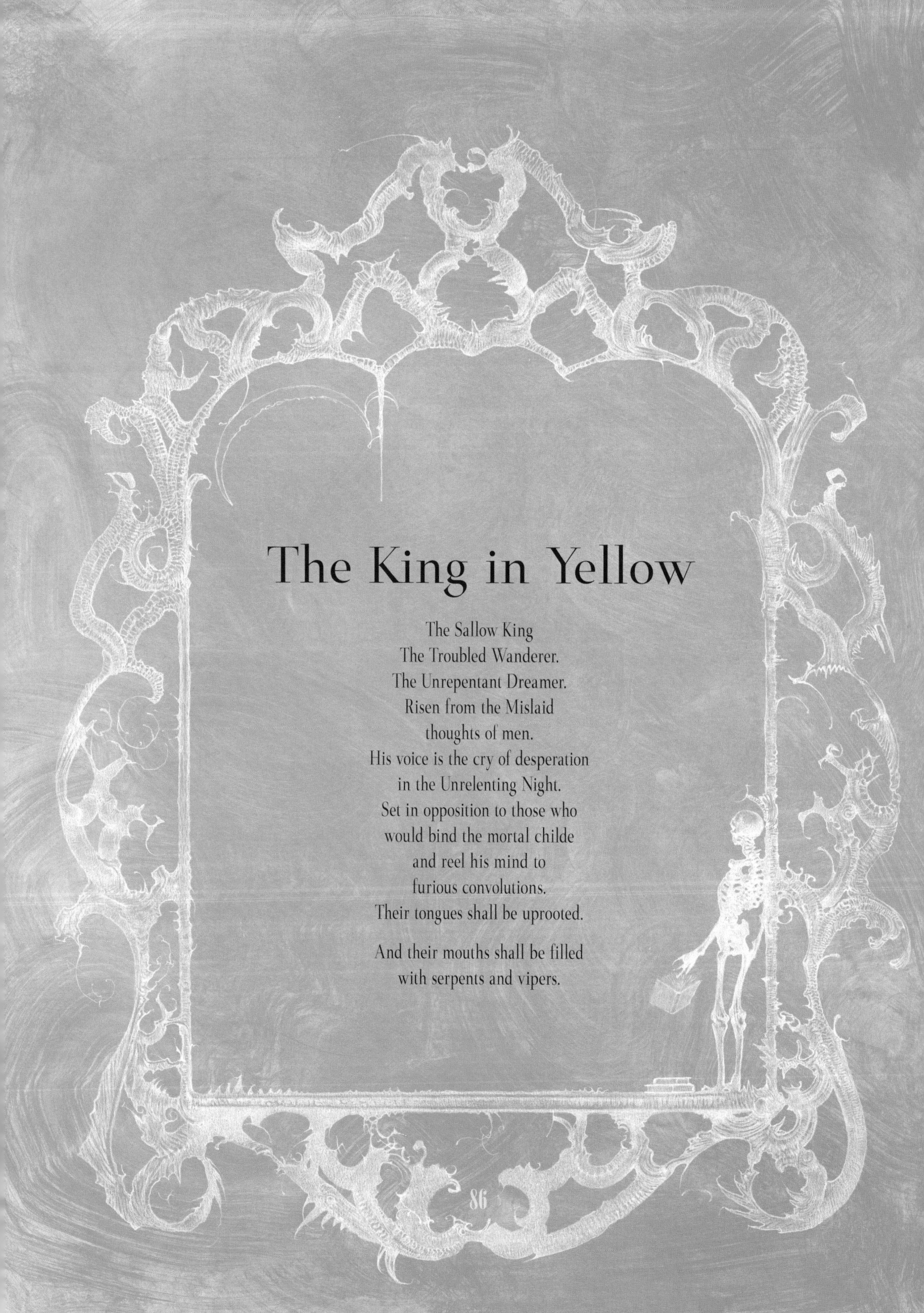

The King in Yellow

The Sallow King
The Troubled Wanderer.
The Unrepentant Dreamer.
Risen from the Mislaid
thoughts of men.
His voice is the cry of desperation
in the Unrelenting Night.
Set in opposition to those who
would bind the mortal childe
and reel his mind to
furious convolutions.
Their tongues shall be uprooted.

And their mouths shall be filled
with serpents and vipers.

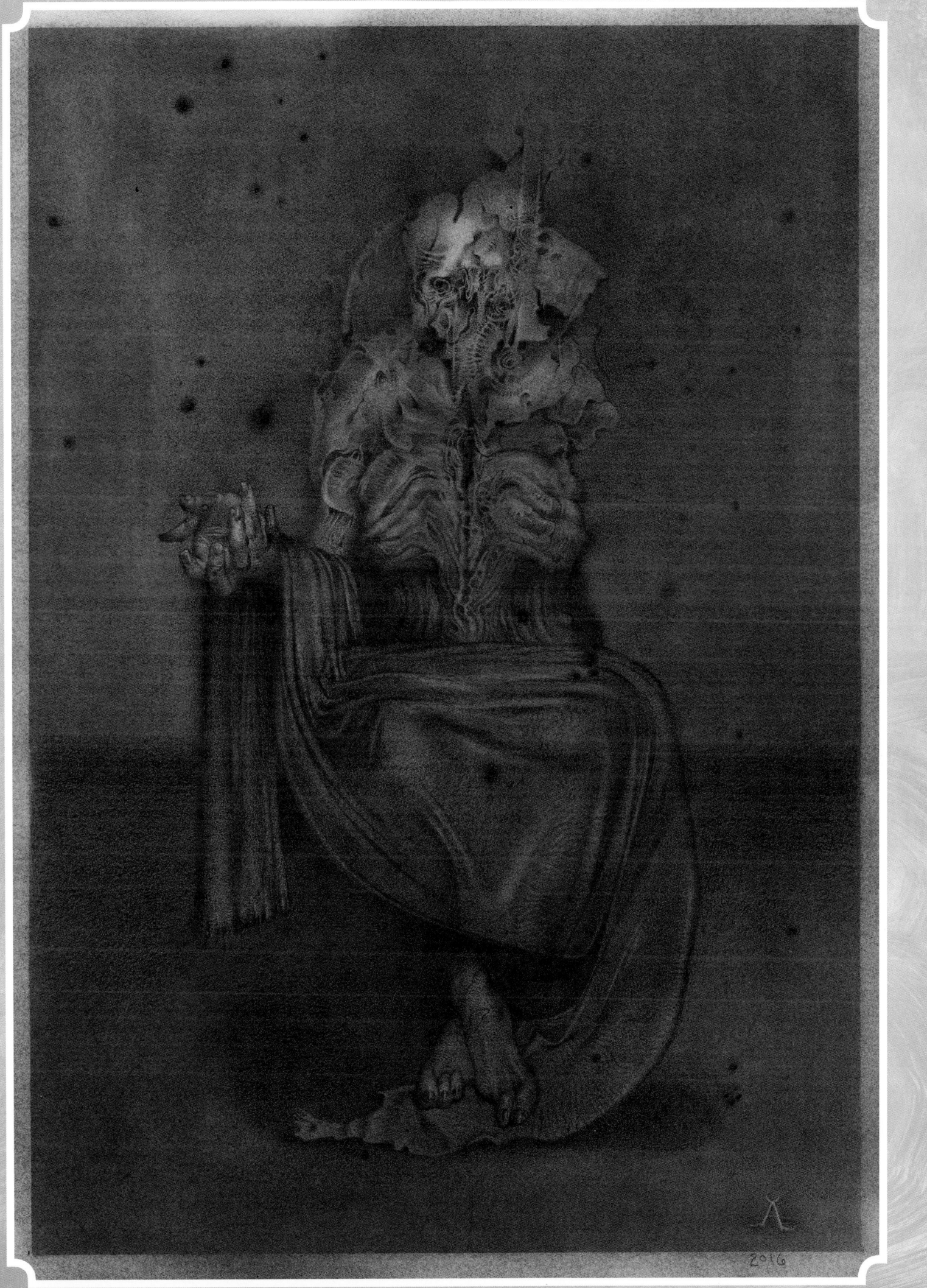

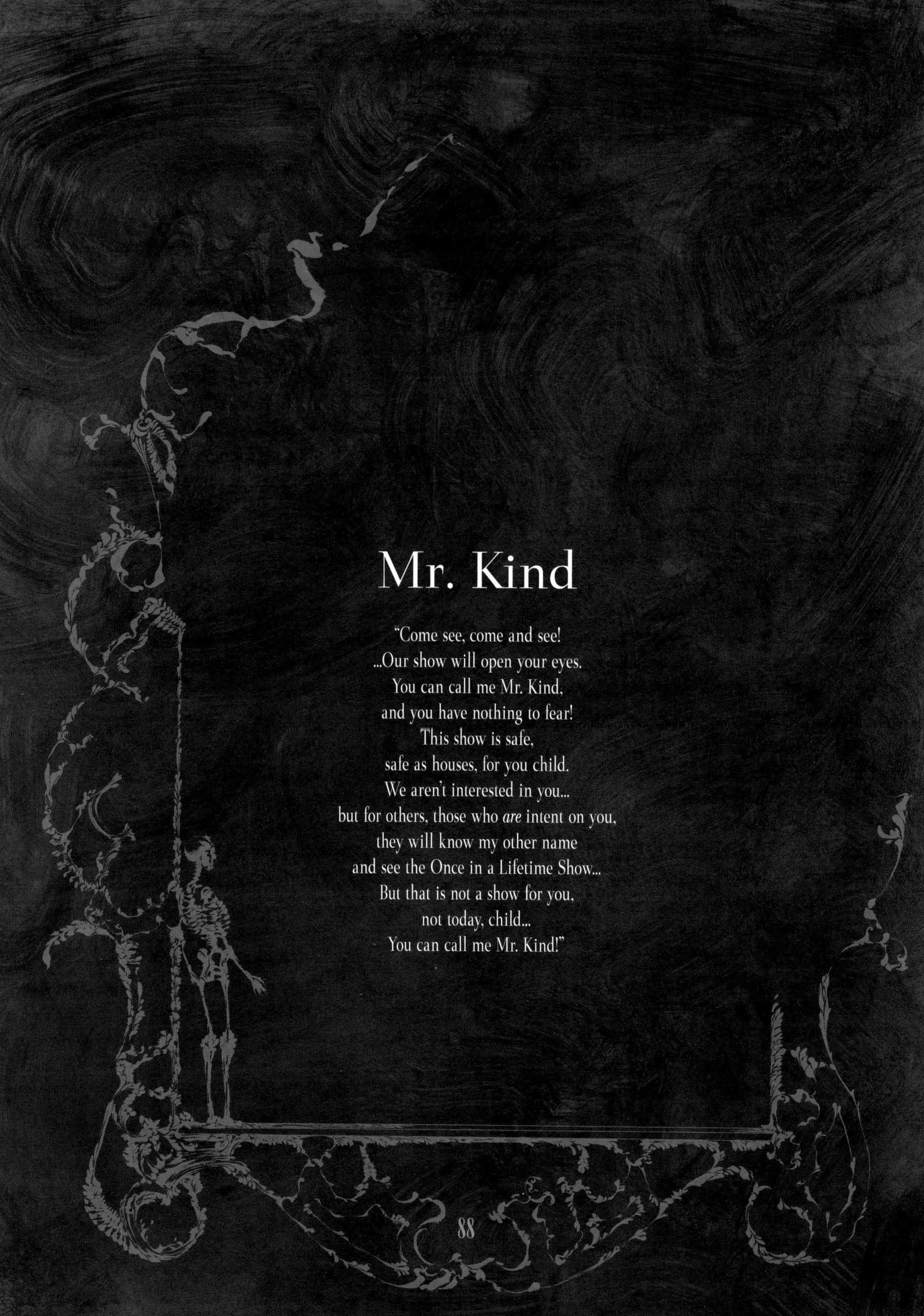

Mr. Kind

"Come see, come and see!
...Our show will open your eyes.
You can call me Mr. Kind,
and you have nothing to fear!
This show is safe,
safe as houses, for you child.
We aren't interested in you...
but for others, those who *are* intent on you,
they will know my other name
and see the Once in a Lifetime Show...
But that is not a show for you,
not today, child...
You can call me Mr. Kind!"

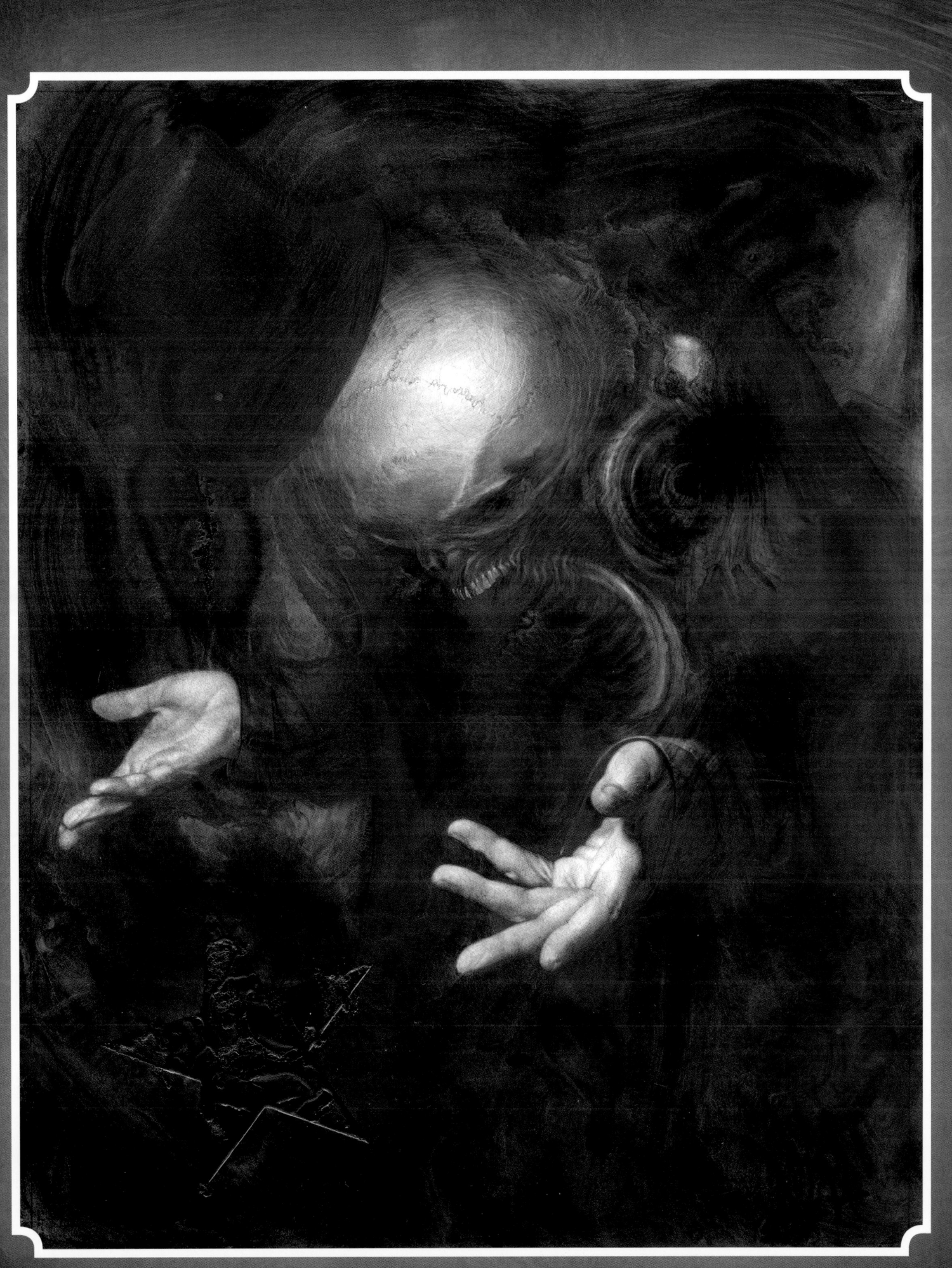

Twisted

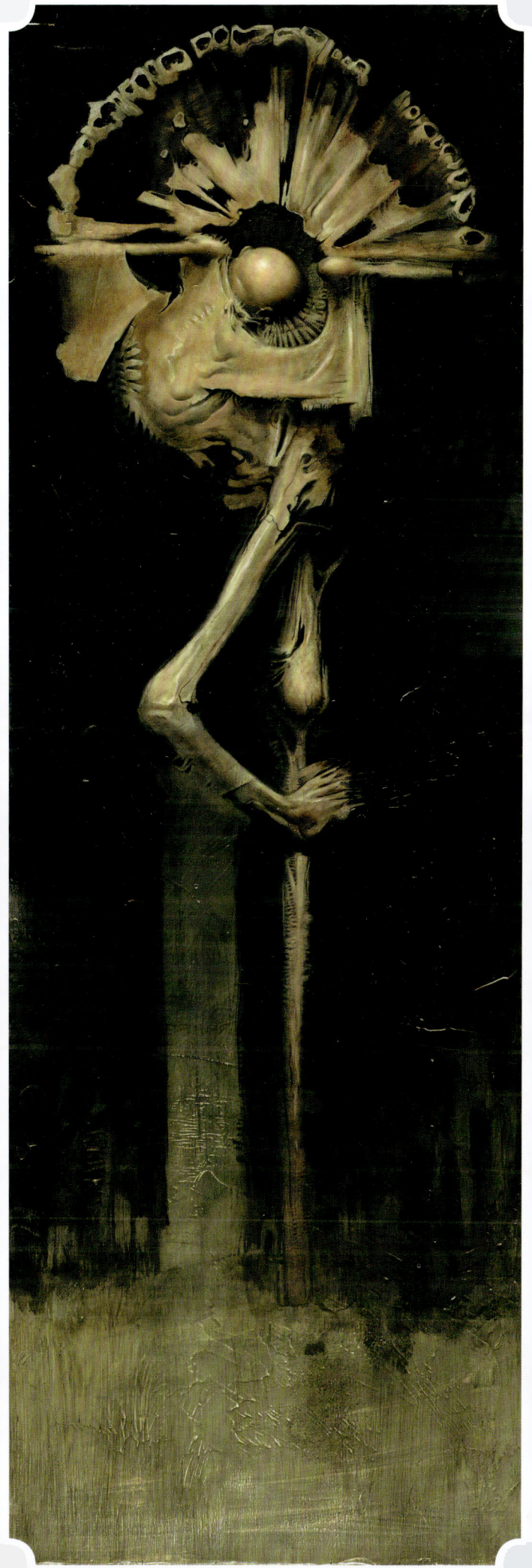

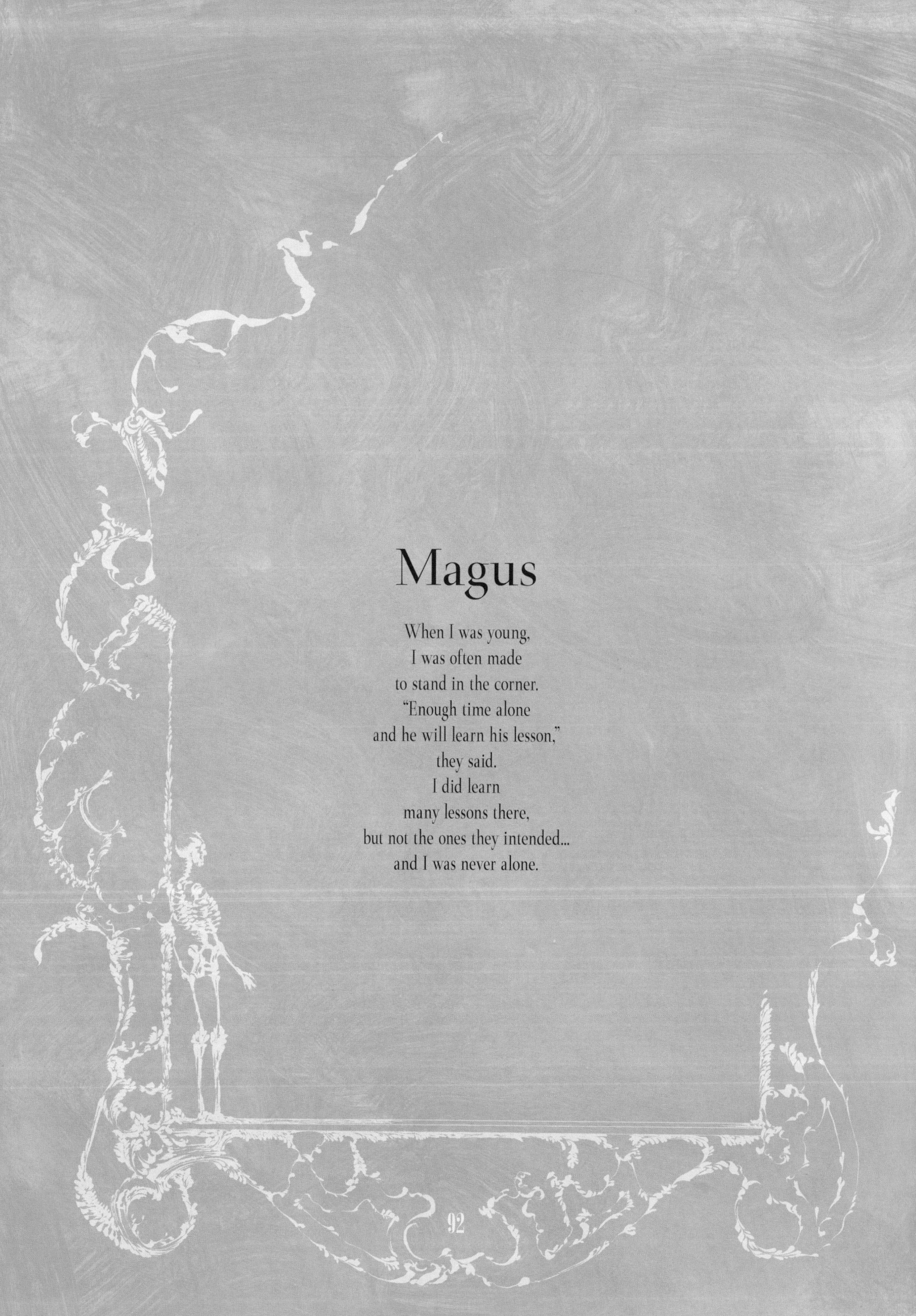

Magus

When I was young,
I was often made
to stand in the corner.
"Enough time alone
and he will learn his lesson,"
they said.
I did learn
many lessons there,
but not the ones they intended...
and I was never alone.

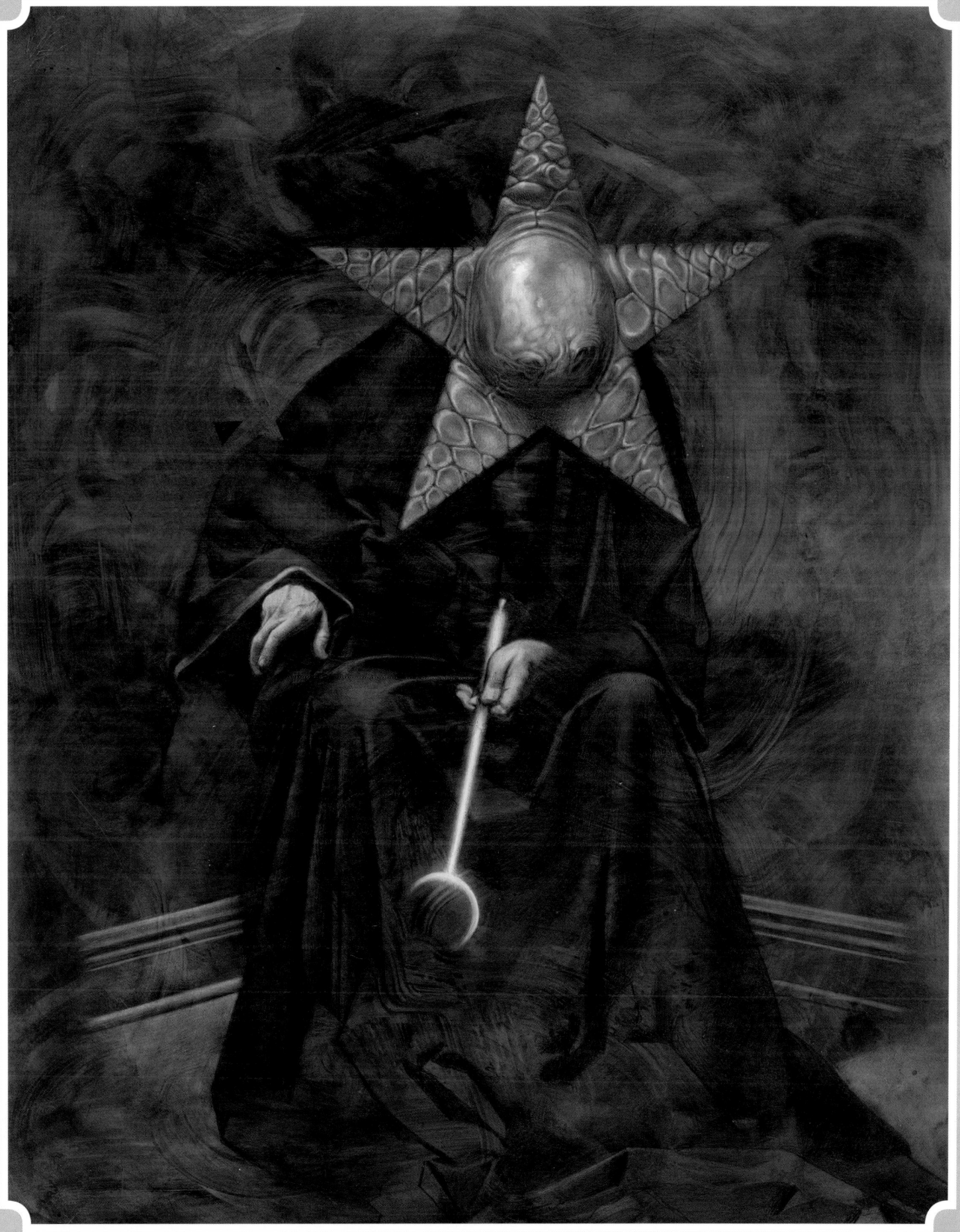

War Study

Into the sleeping World
rode War,
quietly and upon
the Subtle Beast of Fear.
But that is his way,
to enter stealthily
and unseen but leave as a
thrashing, bloody lion.

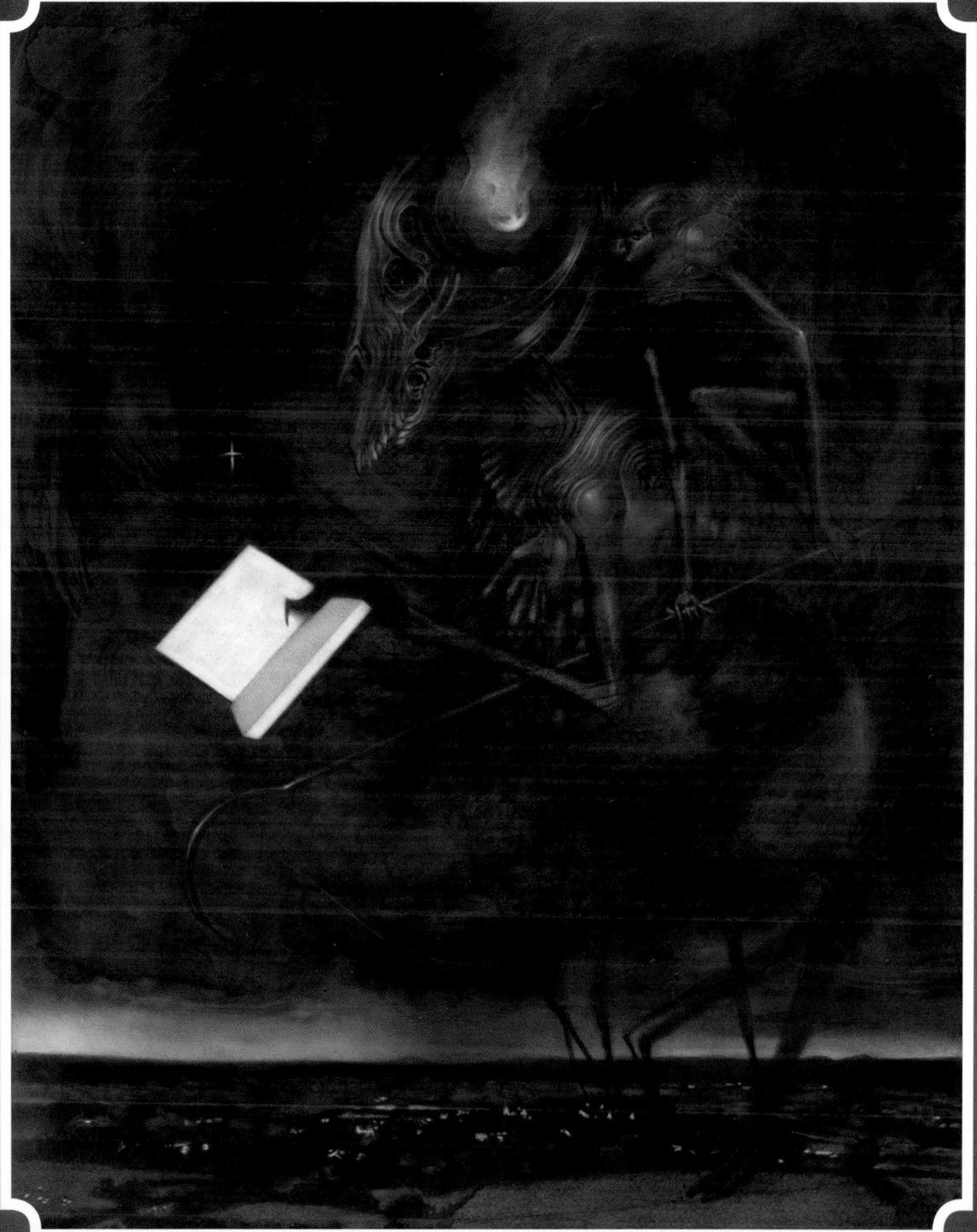

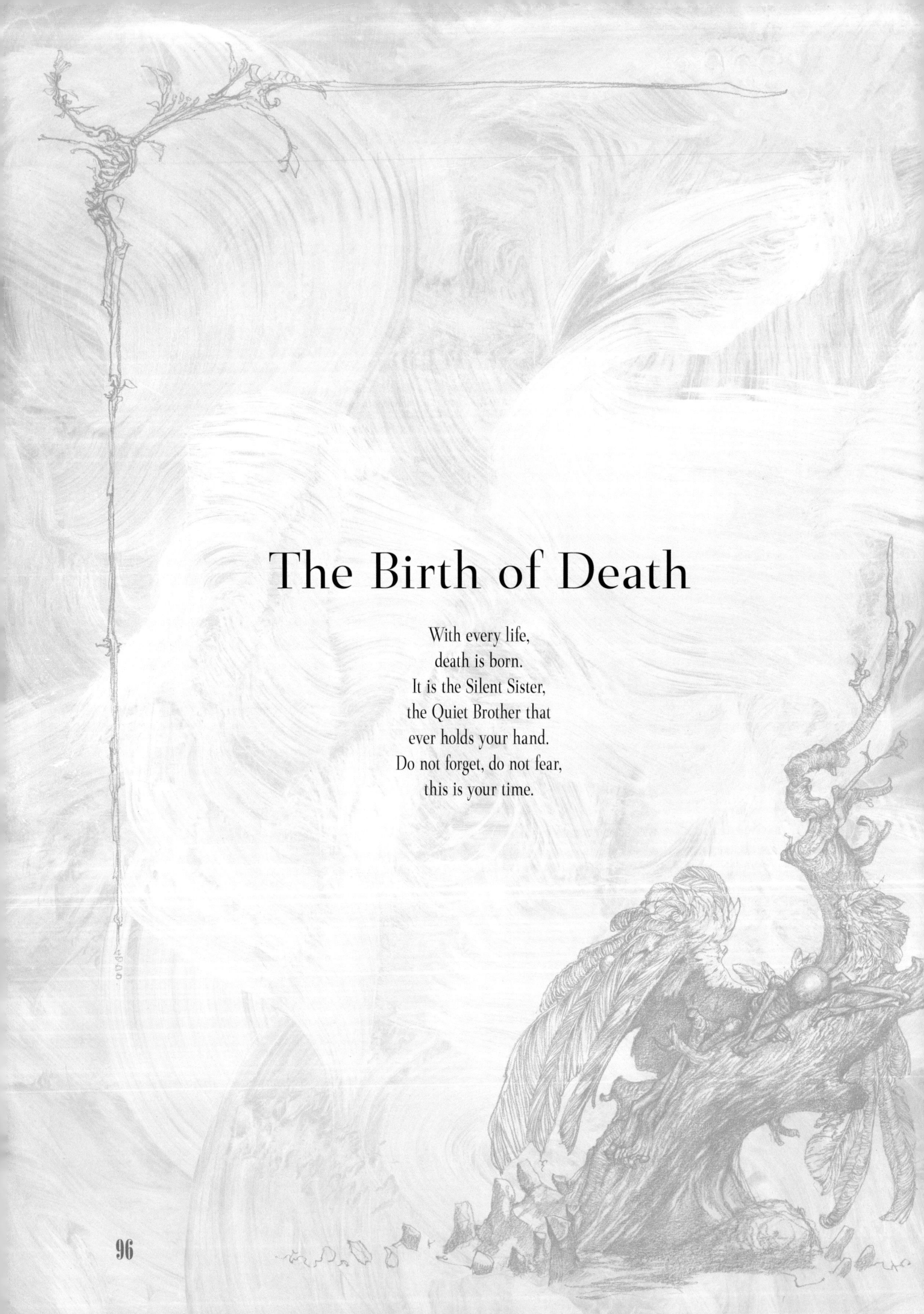

The Birth of Death

With every life,
death is born.
It is the Silent Sister,
the Quiet Brother that
ever holds your hand.
Do not forget, do not fear,
this is your time.

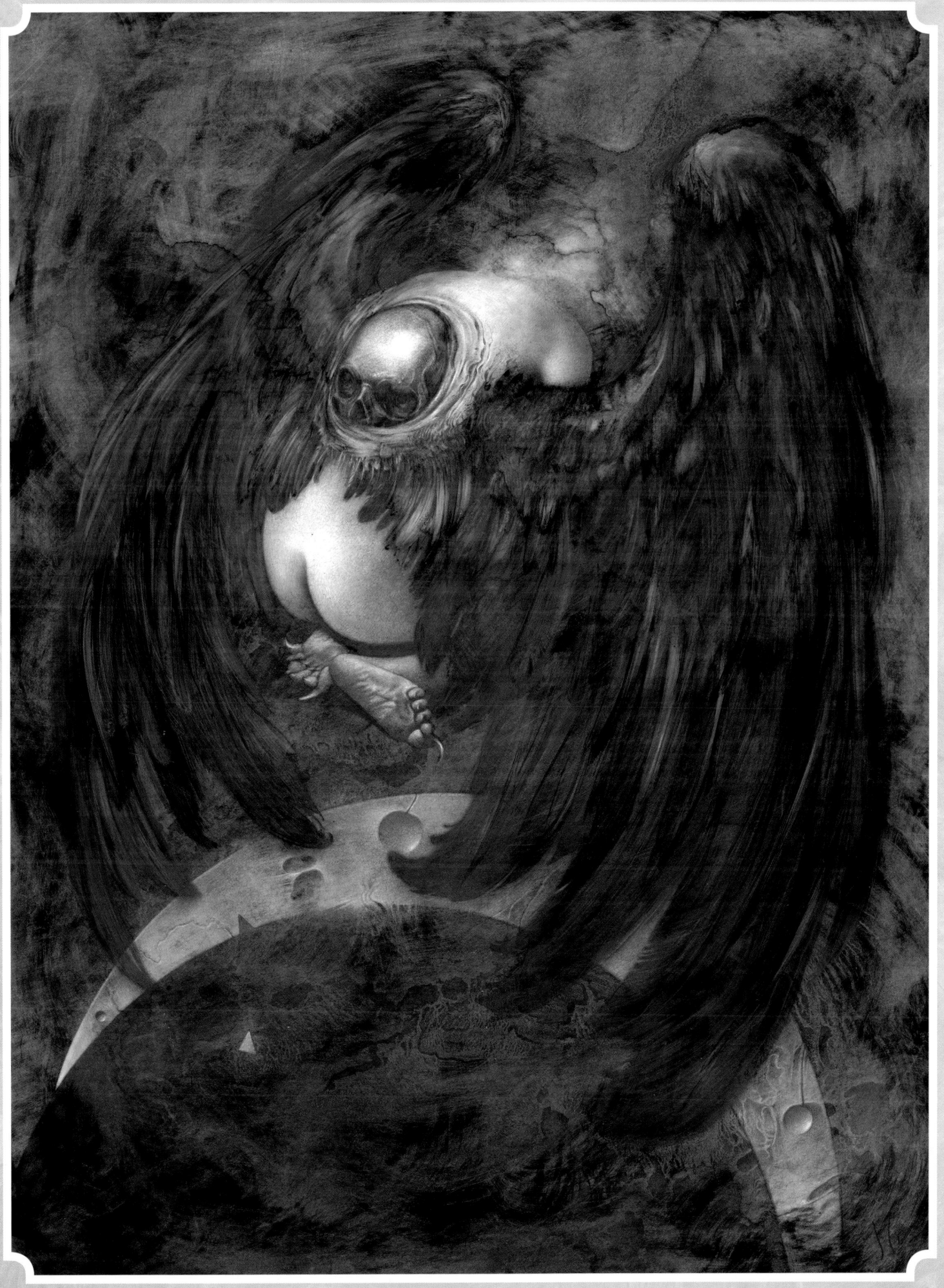

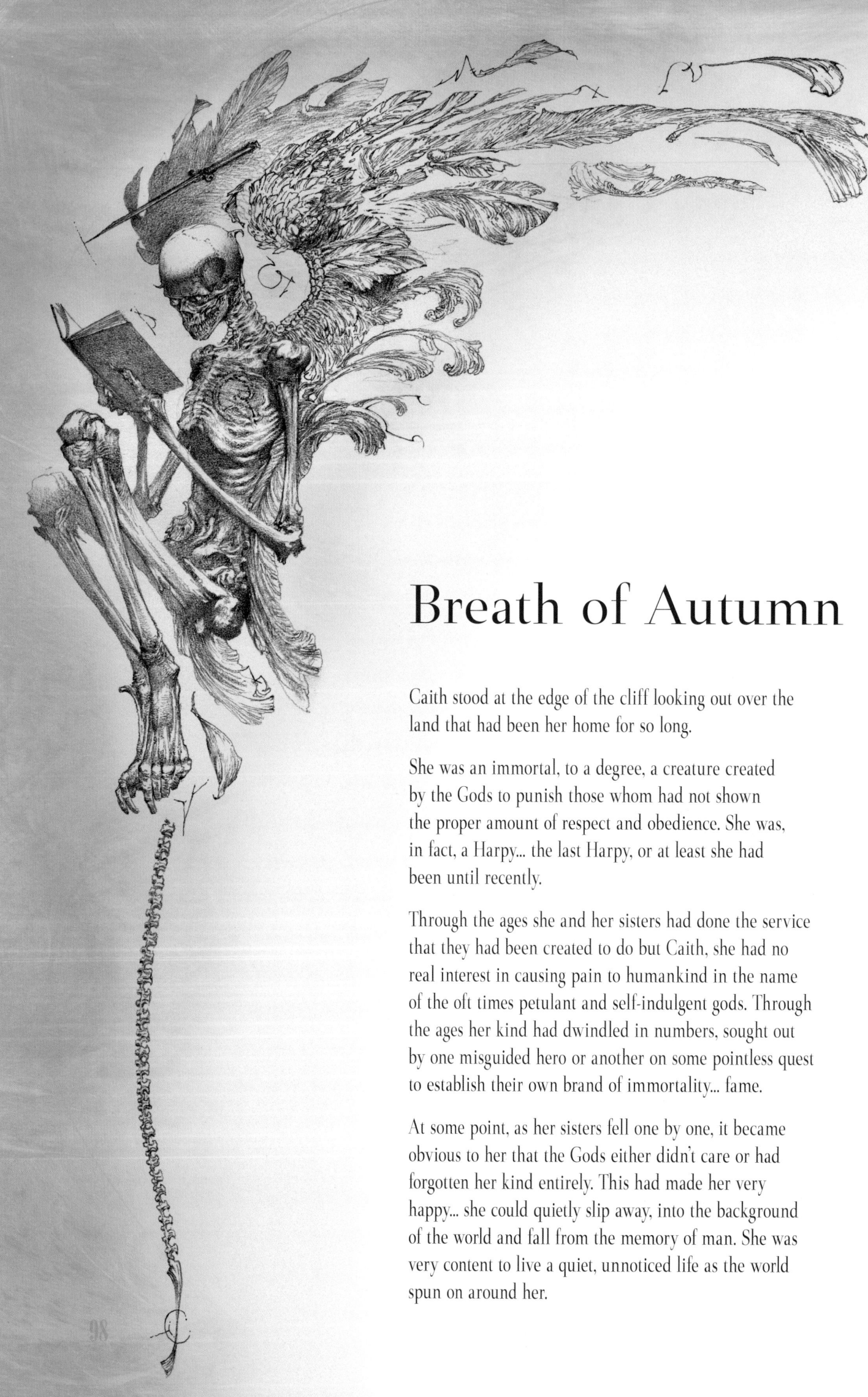

Breath of Autumn

Caith stood at the edge of the cliff looking out over the land that had been her home for so long.

She was an immortal, to a degree, a creature created by the Gods to punish those whom had not shown the proper amount of respect and obedience. She was, in fact, a Harpy... the last Harpy, or at least she had been until recently.

Through the ages she and her sisters had done the service that they had been created to do but Caith, she had no real interest in causing pain to humankind in the name of the oft times petulant and self-indulgent gods. Through the ages her kind had dwindled in numbers, sought out by one misguided hero or another on some pointless quest to establish their own brand of immortality... fame.

At some point, as her sisters fell one by one, it became obvious to her that the Gods either didn't care or had forgotten her kind entirely. This had made her very happy... she could quietly slip away, into the background of the world and fall from the memory of man. She was very content to live a quiet, unnoticed life as the world spun on around her.

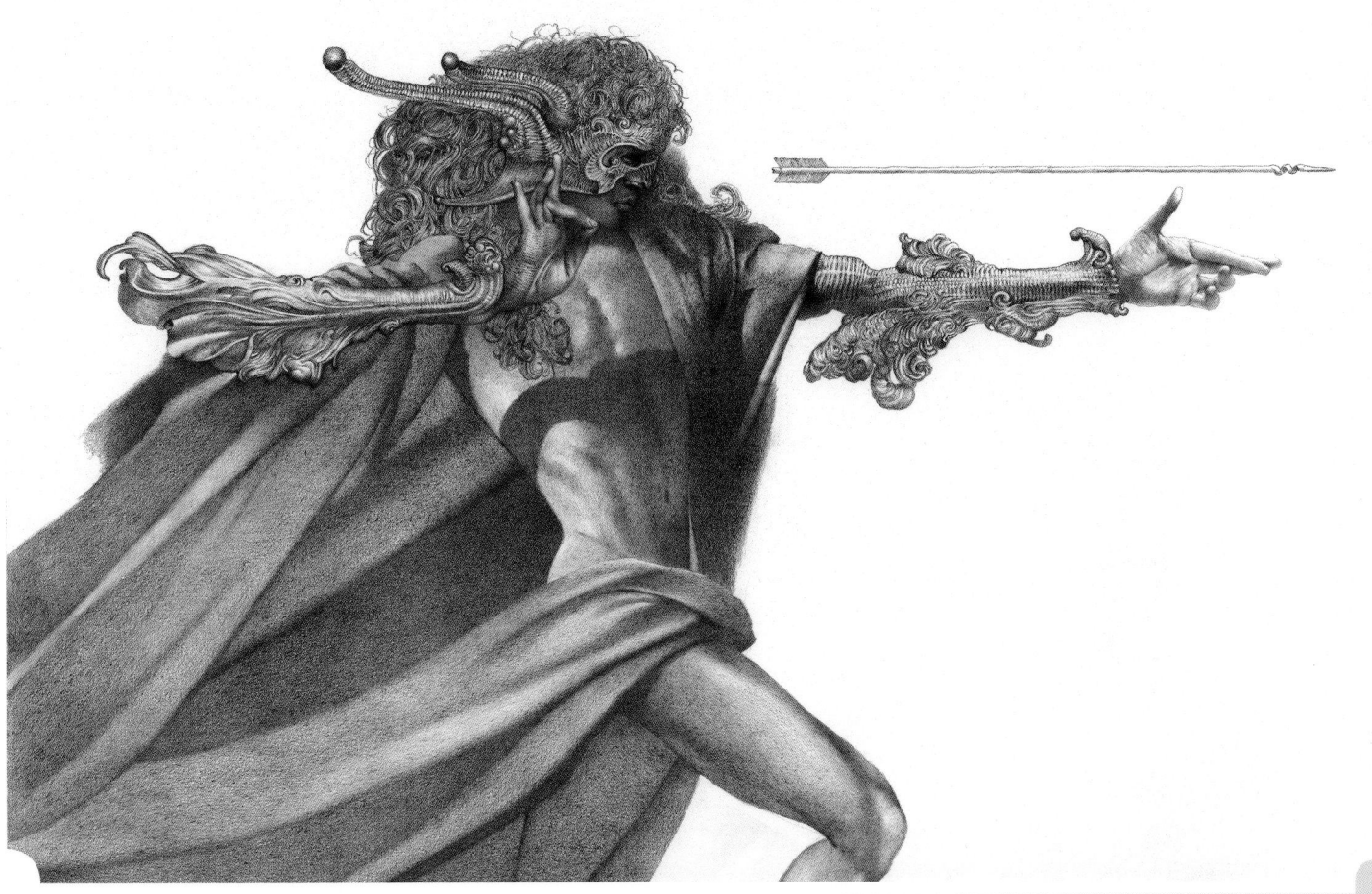

As time passed, occasionally someone would see her and, being the ever-fearful creatures that they were, the humans would try to dispatch her. Thankfully, there were not many left alive that knew how to do such a thing. Immortals, left to their own, could live forever, but if one knew how, they could be killed.

Such a thing happened to Caith. Just three days ago, a young man with a strong bow had sought her out ready to make his name in the world by slaying a Harpy. He had come upon her unawares and had let his arrow fly. The arrow had found its mark in her foot and had stung her, but even if the arrow had pierced her heart it wouldn't have done her in... if it had been merely an arrow.

But it had been coated with sap from a thousand-year oak, and that... that was poison to her. As she began to weaken and die, the young man saw her pain and was filled with great anguish and regret. As it turned out, the young man

was actually a wayward son of one of the old gods, a demigod himself. Likely that was how he had come by the knowledge of how to slay her. He reached out to her but knew he could not save the Harpy from the poison, so he did the one thing he could do. He summoned all of the power of his aspect and the grace of his father and he laid upon her a spell. She began to change, and in but a few moments laying before him was a fully human female.

Now... if this were the tale of a romantic, one would expect that she had been transformed into a beautiful maiden so that the two could then rush off and fall in love. This is not that tale.

Athas, his name was, stood before the very old and decrepit woman who lay at his feet. He spread his cloak about her to give her warmth and a degree of modesty. She opened her eyes and looked upon his face. He had never in his life seen such sorrow in a person's eyes as this. He could not bear its weight upon him.

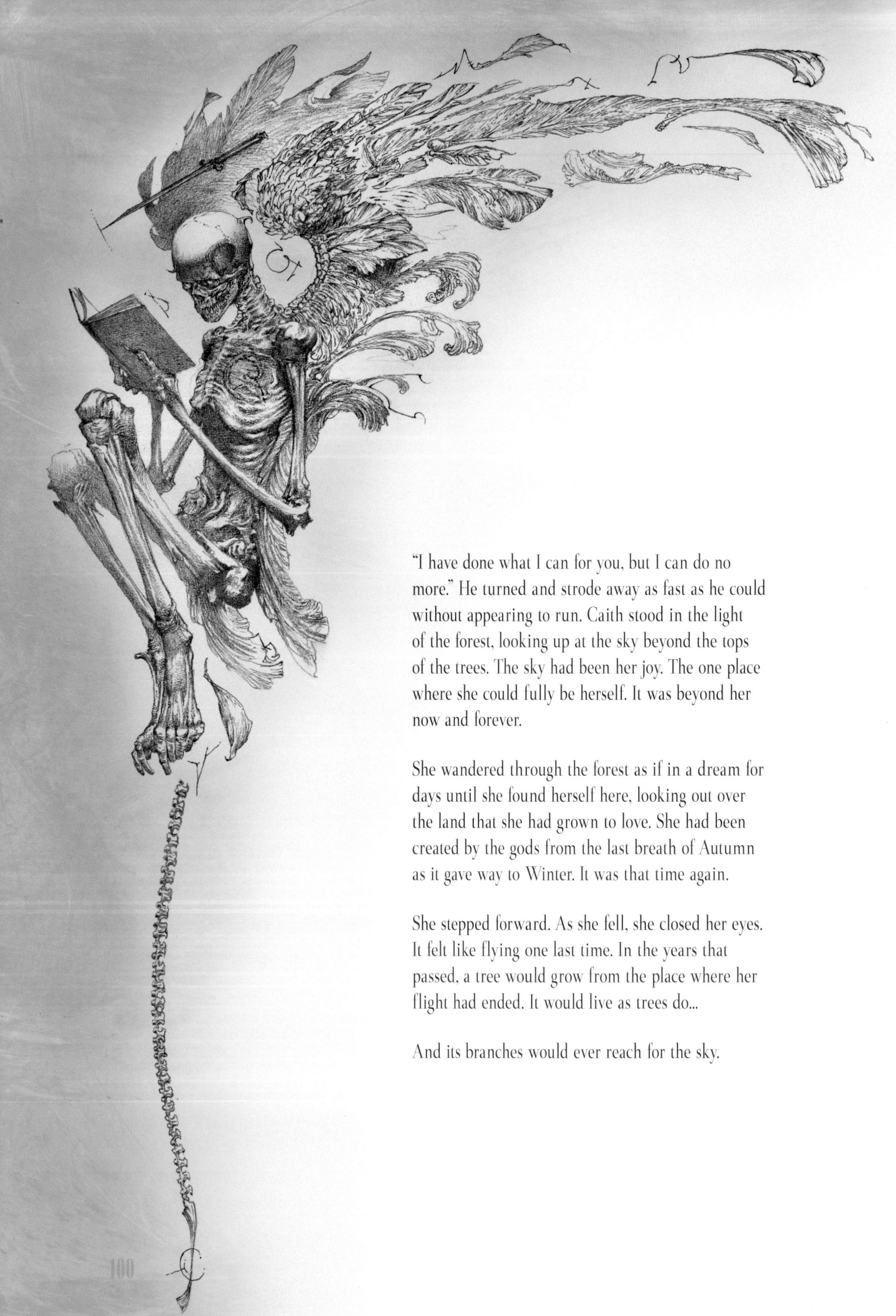

"I have done what I can for you, but I can do no more." He turned and strode away as fast as he could without appearing to run. Caith stood in the light of the forest, looking up at the sky beyond the tops of the trees. The sky had been her joy. The one place where she could fully be herself. It was beyond her now and forever.

She wandered through the forest as if in a dream for days until she found herself here, looking out over the land that she had grown to love. She had been created by the gods from the last breath of Autumn as it gave way to Winter. It was that time again.

She stepped forward. As she fell, she closed her eyes. It felt like flying one last time. In the years that passed, a tree would grow from the place where her flight had ended. It would live as trees do...

And its branches would ever reach for the sky.

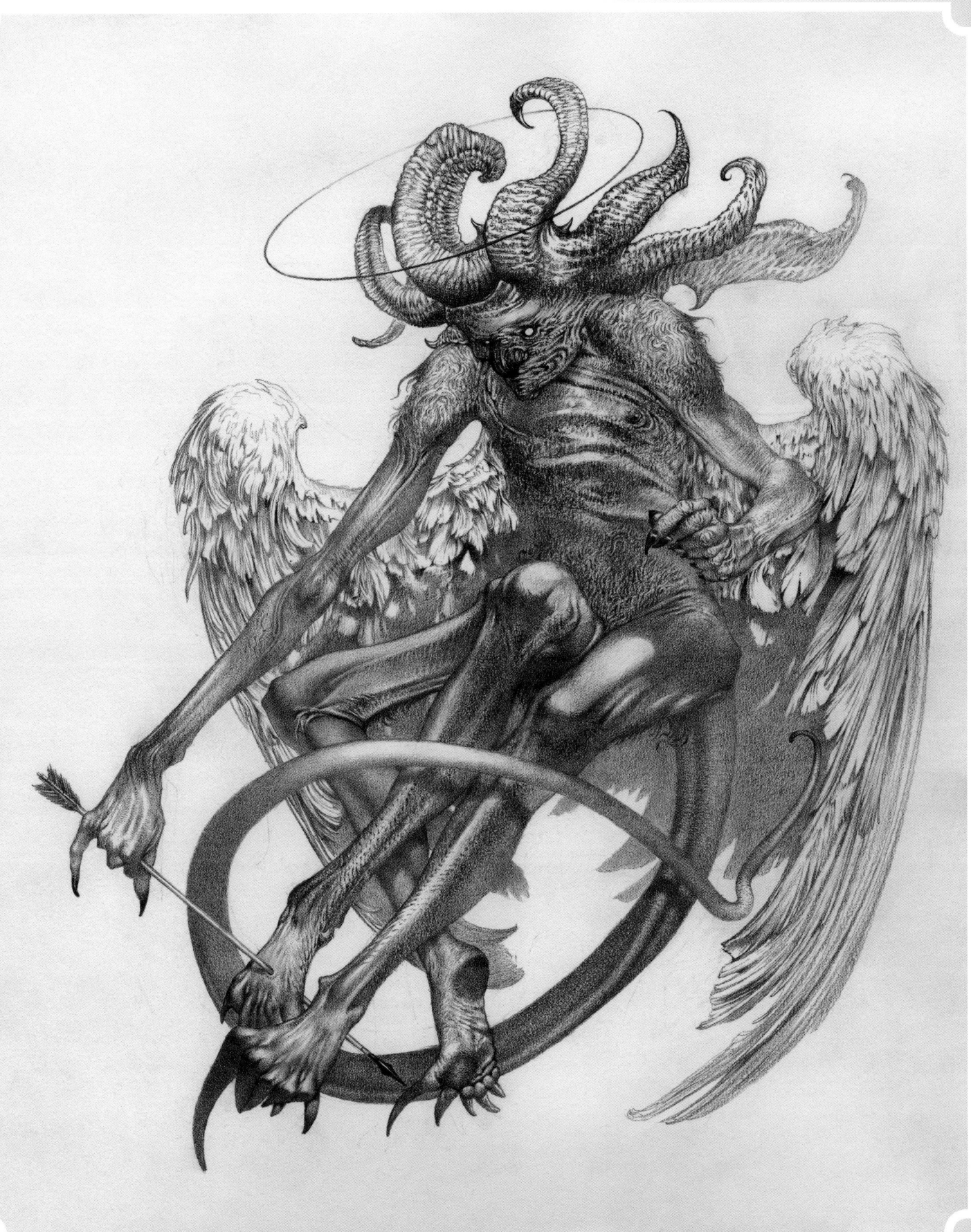

Dis

"...and as it happened,
I found myself
to be in the deep woods
of my spirit on Modraniht,
and there I came upon
the Dis,
who would teach me
a different way."

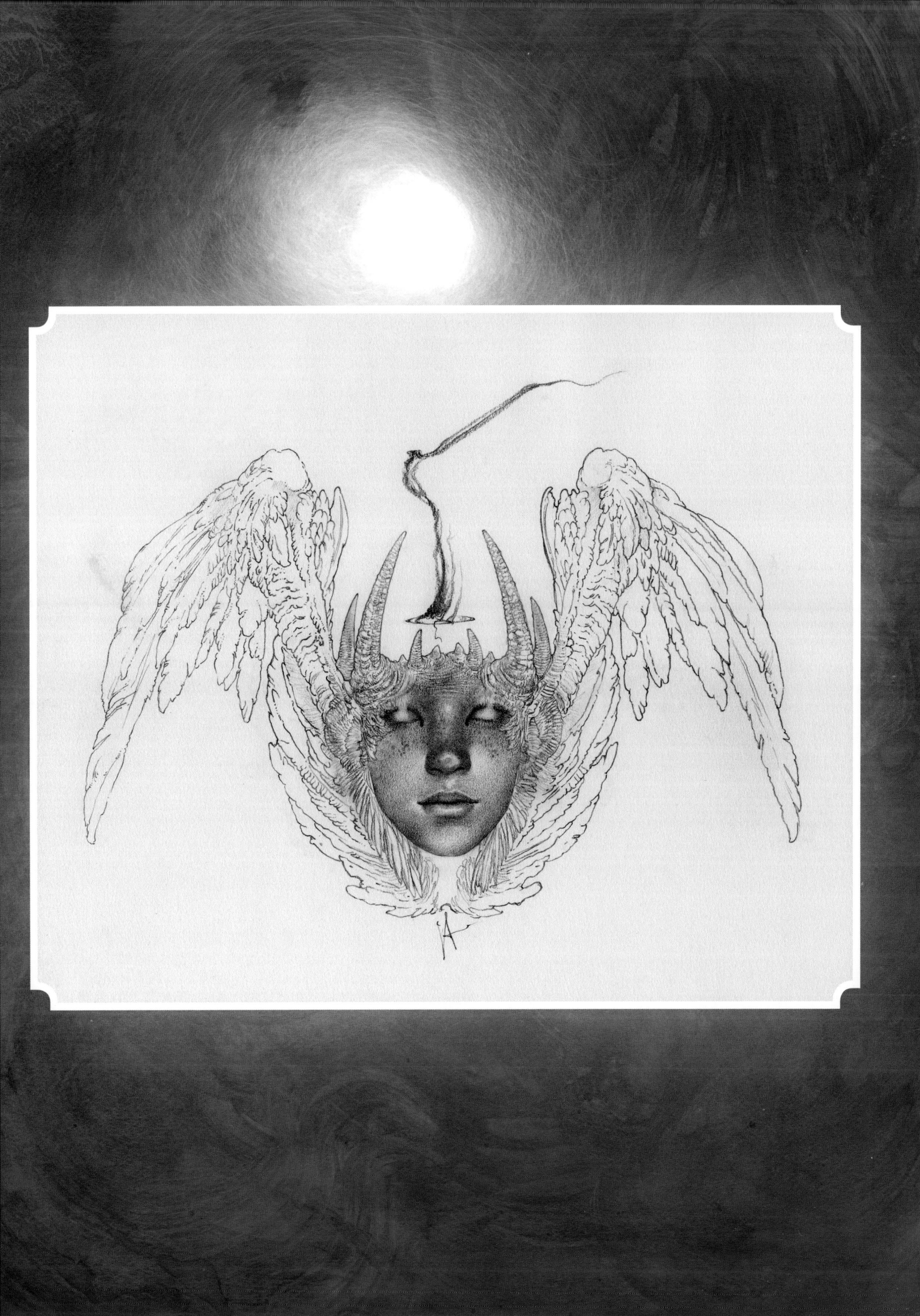

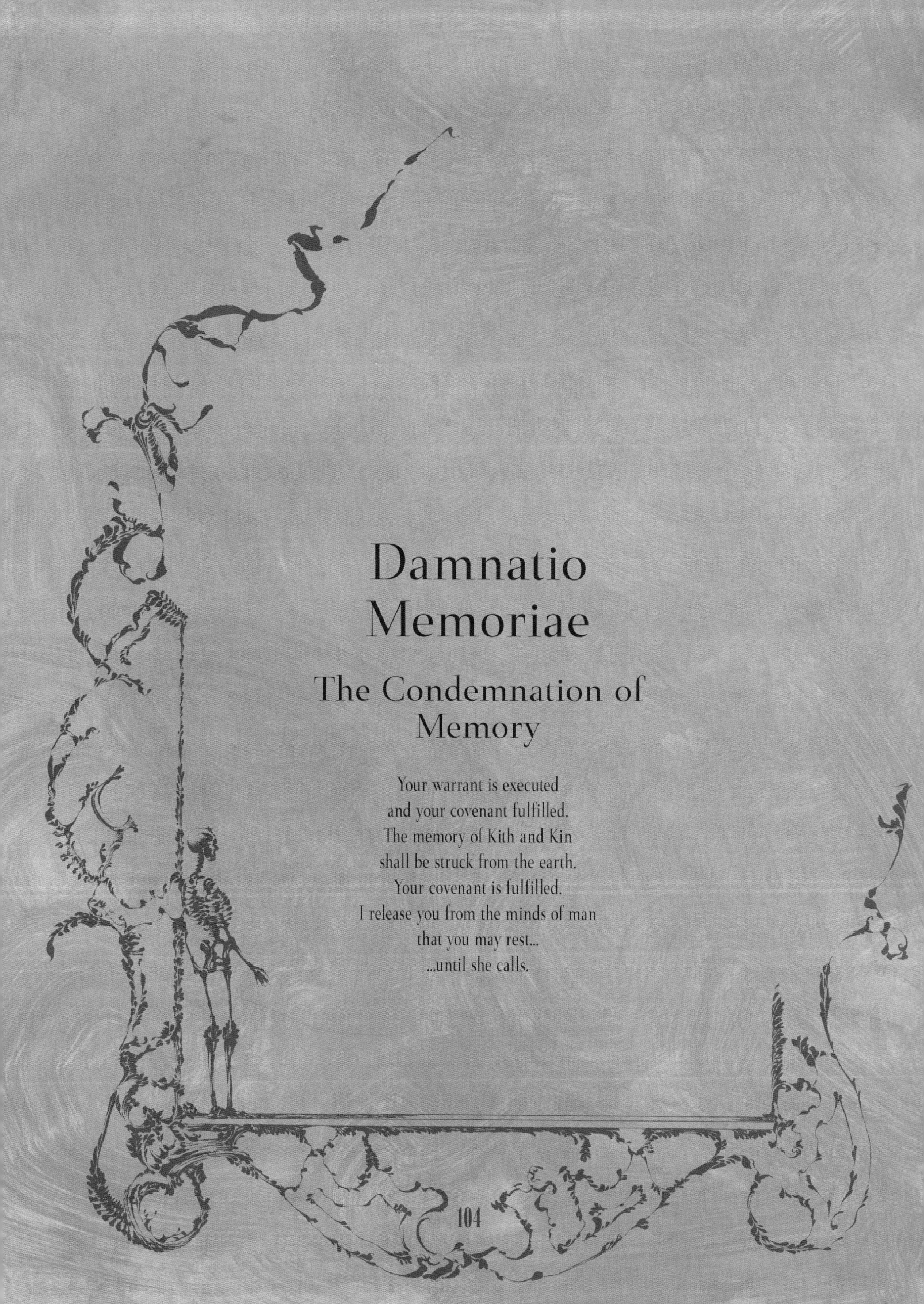

Damnatio Memoriae

The Condemnation of Memory

Your warrant is executed
and your covenant fulfilled.
The memory of Kith and Kin
shall be struck from the earth.
Your covenant is fulfilled.
I release you from the minds of man
that you may rest...
...until she calls.

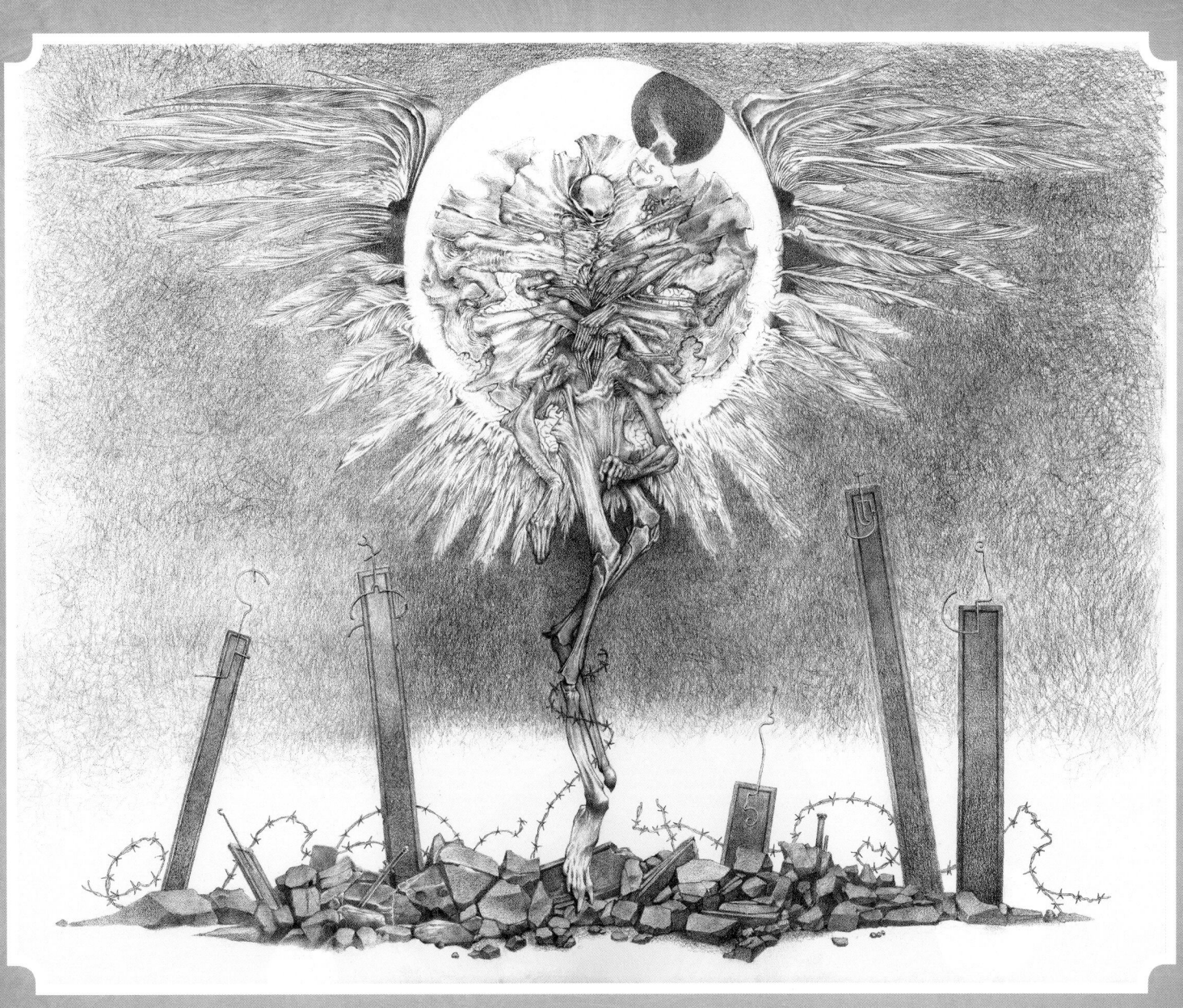

The Throne

"Whyfor do you manifest
to me as such,
with such a terrifying visage?"
I asked.

In answer to my question,
the entity posed its own.

"Do you truly think the Divine cares,
even notices how you have been assembled?
You, who have been Earth and Star, Man and Woman,
Wolf and Child, Nothing and Everything."

"When last did you love
without looking?"

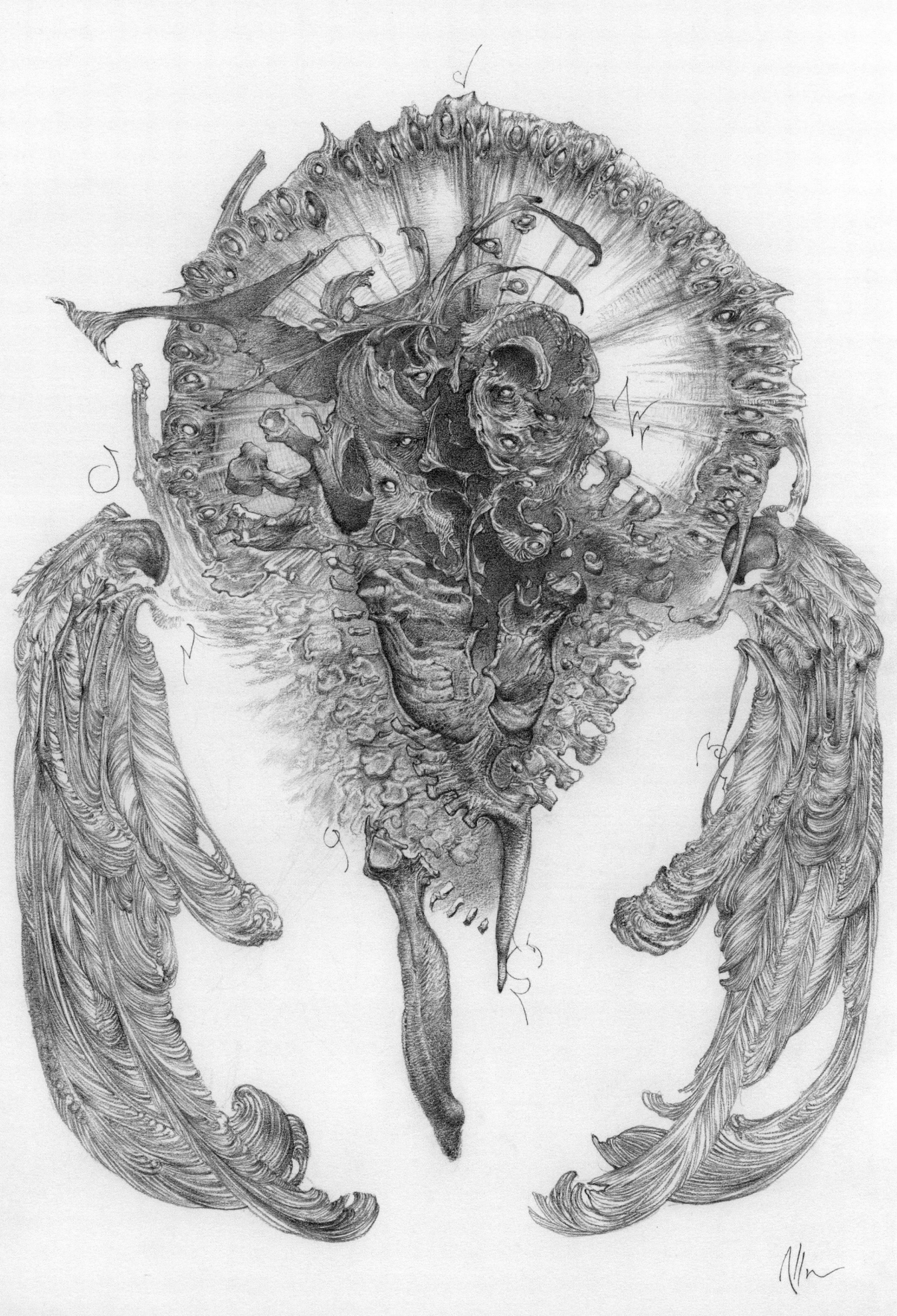

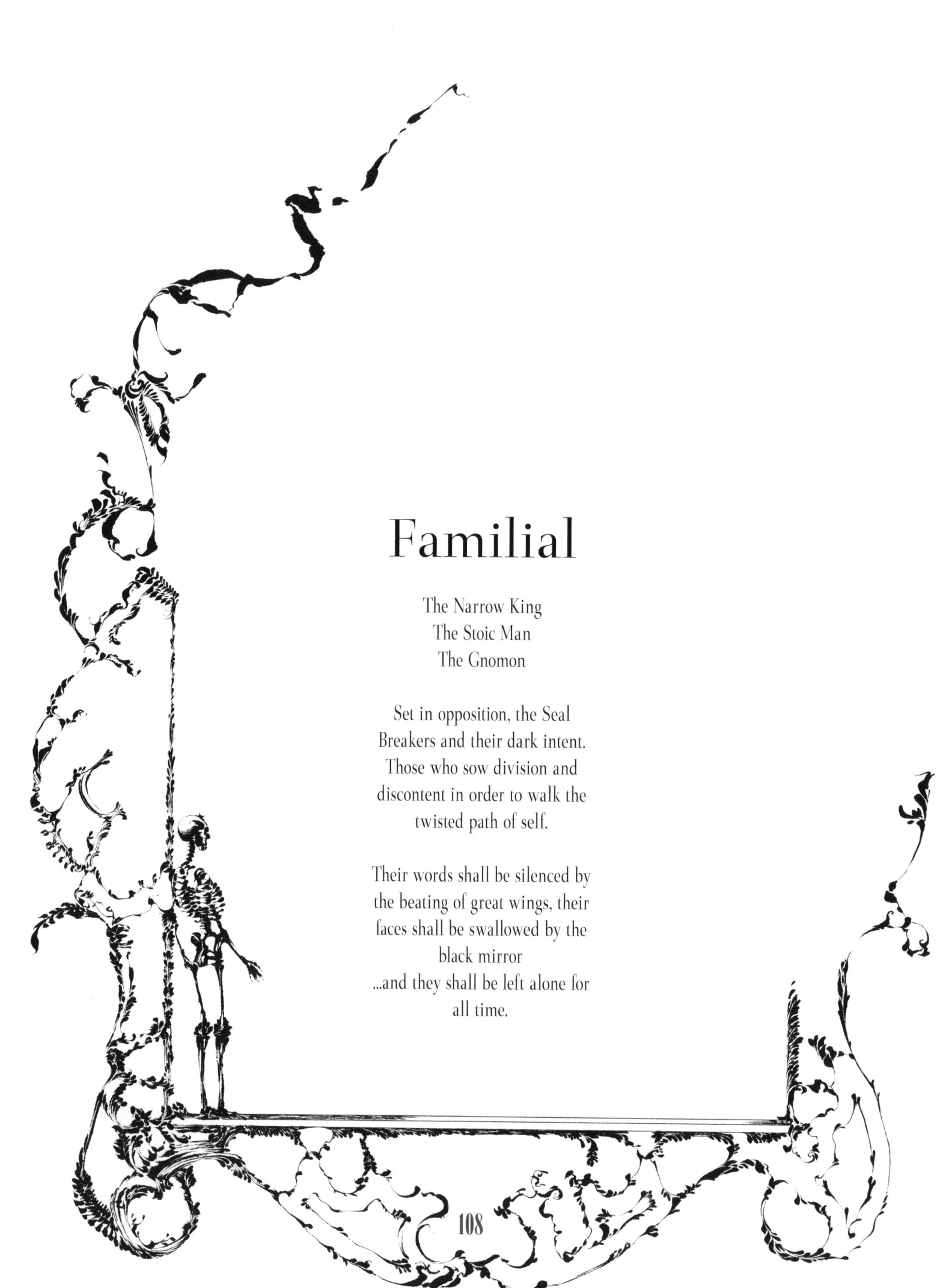

Familial

The Narrow King
The Stoic Man
The Gnomon

Set in opposition, the Seal
Breakers and their dark intent.
Those who sow division and
discontent in order to walk the
twisted path of self.

Their words shall be silenced by
the beating of great wings, their
faces shall be swallowed by the
black mirror
...and they shall be left alone for
all time.

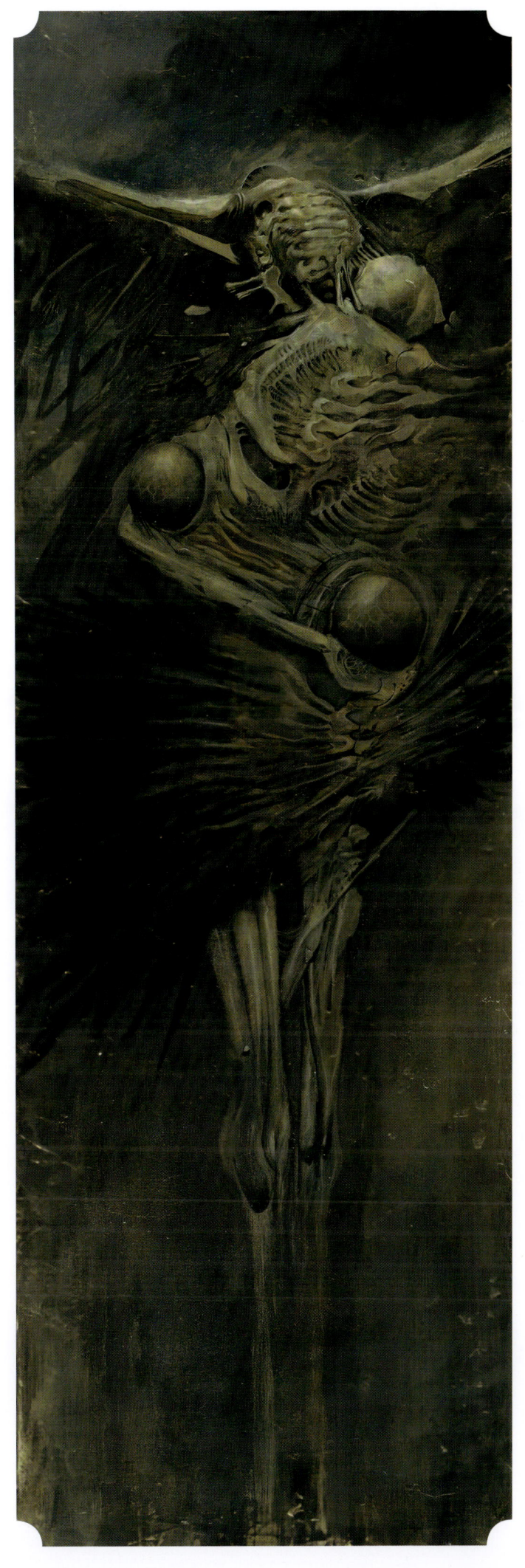

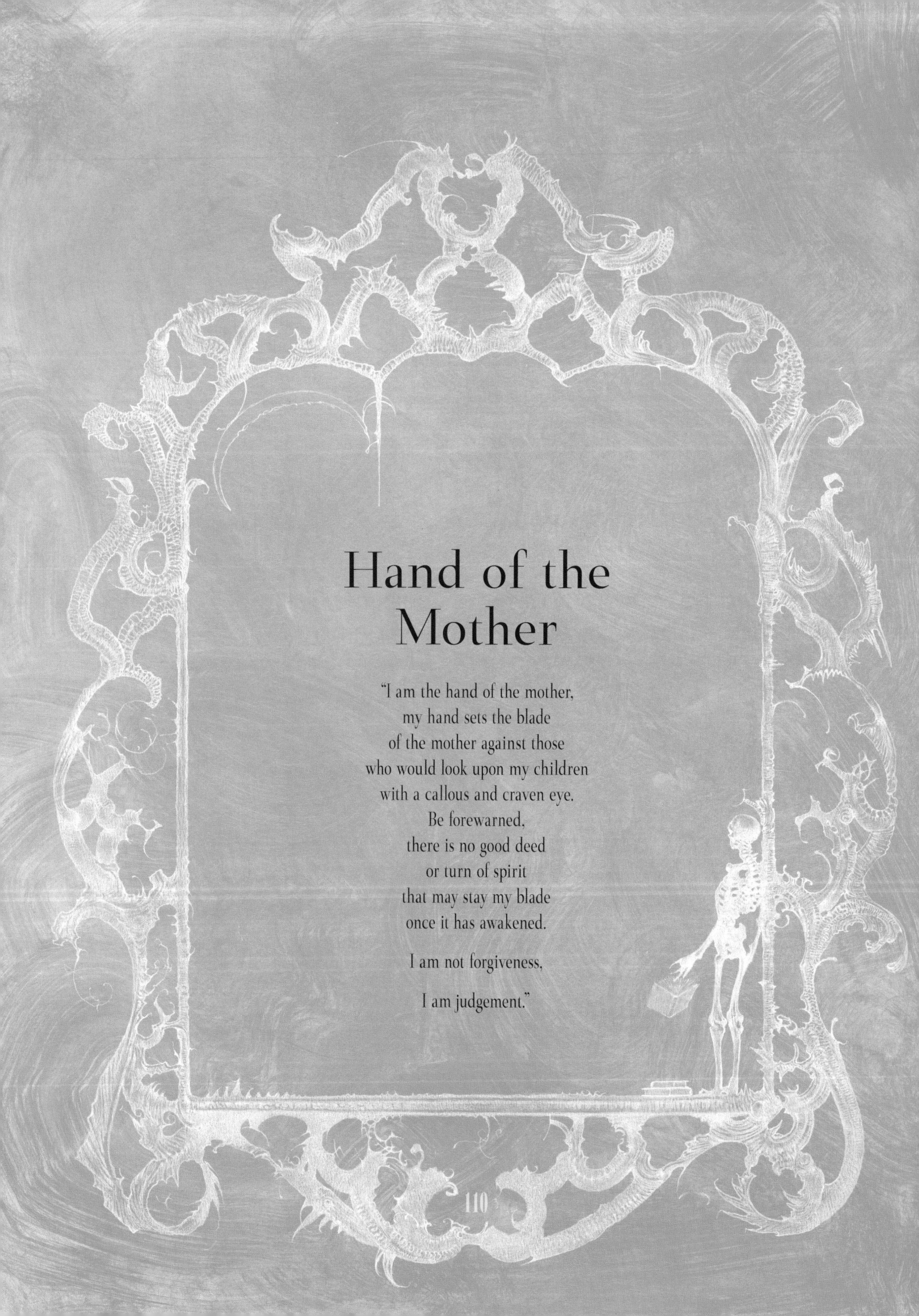

Hand of the Mother

"I am the hand of the mother,
my hand sets the blade
of the mother against those
who would look upon my children
with a callous and craven eye.
Be forewarned,
there is no good deed
or turn of spirit
that may stay my blade
once it has awakened.

I am not forgiveness,

I am judgement."

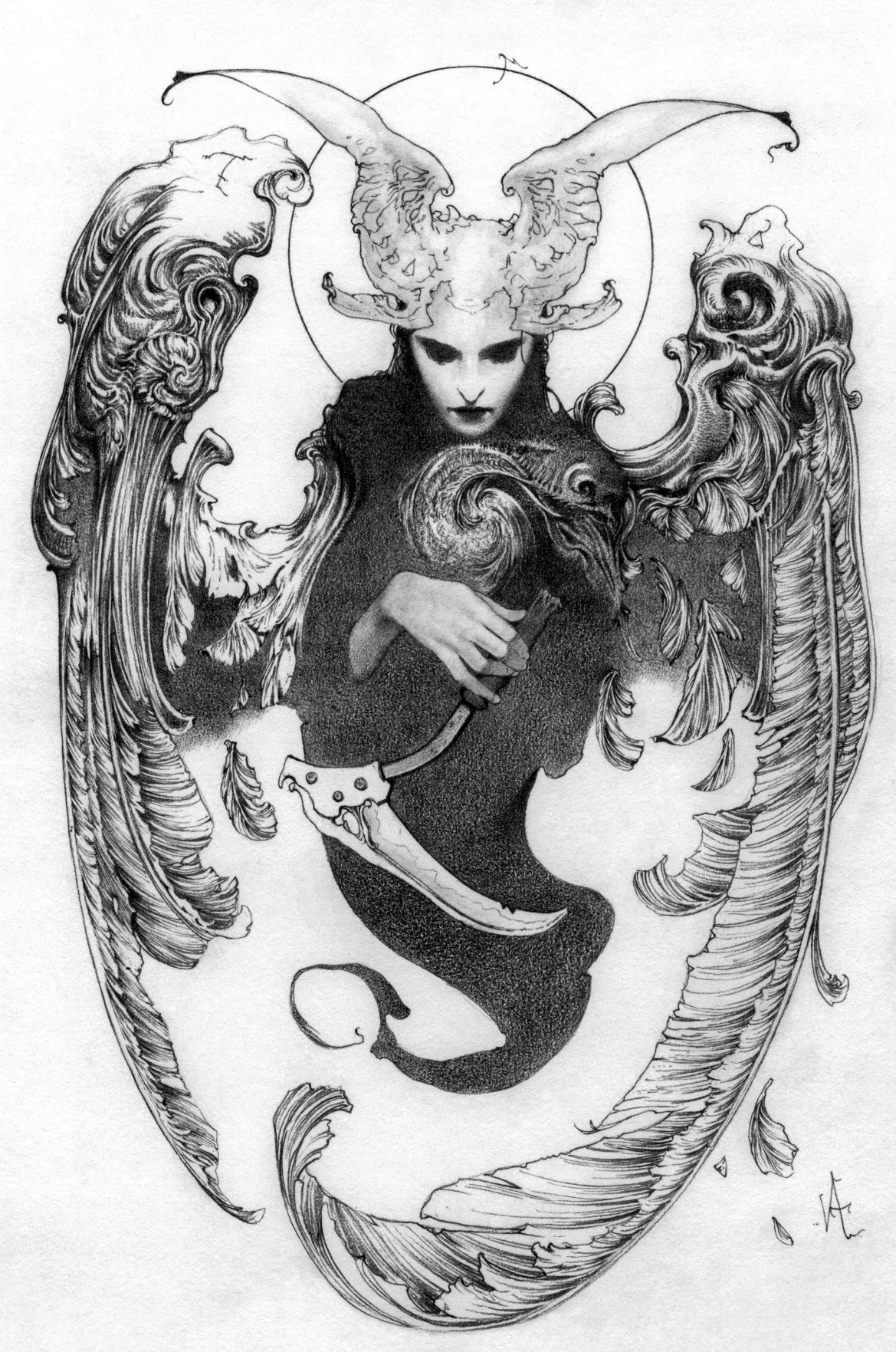

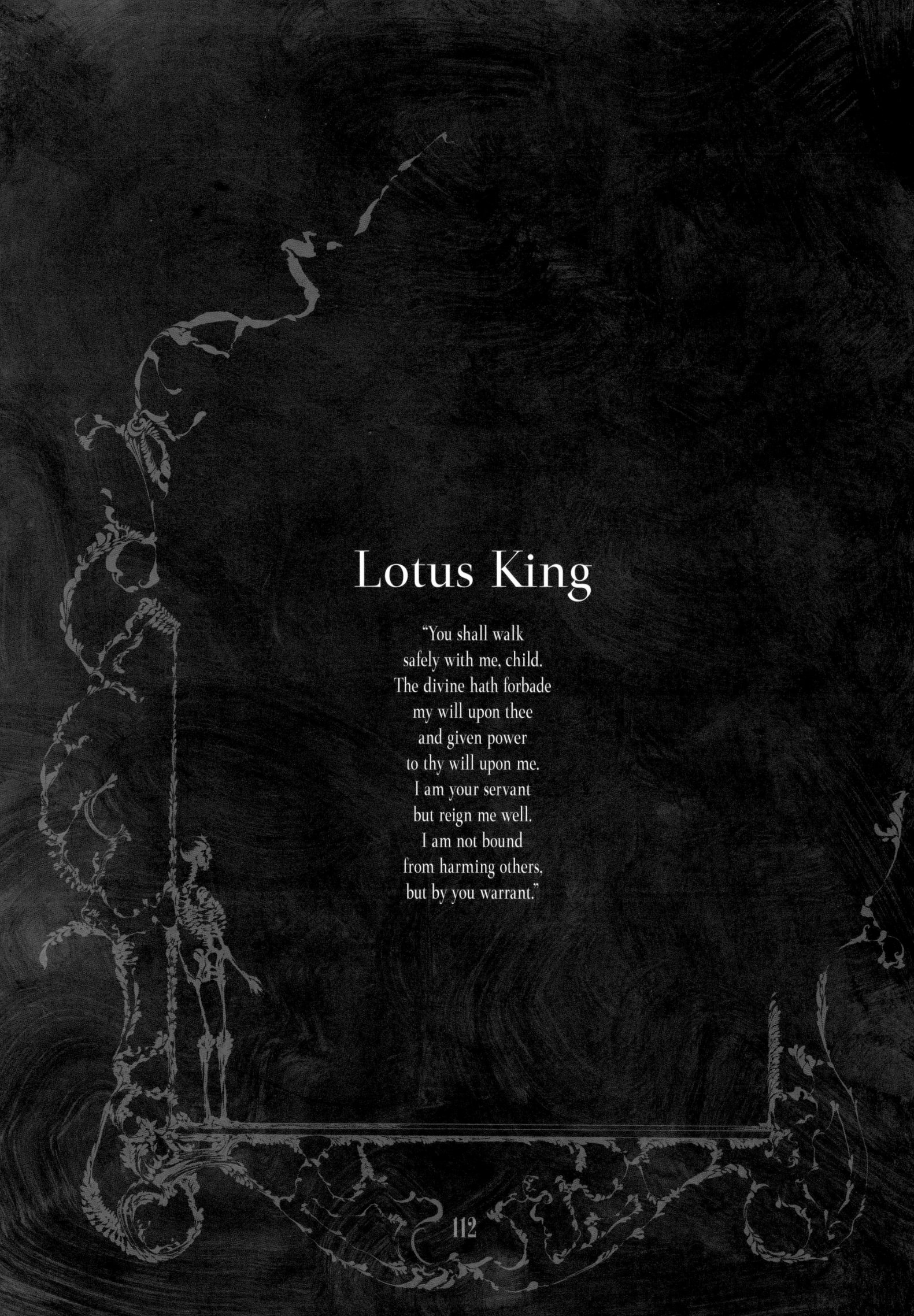

Lotus King

"You shall walk
safely with me, child.
The divine hath forbade
my will upon thee
and given power
to thy will upon me.
I am your servant
but reign me well.
I am not bound
from harming others,
but by you warrant."

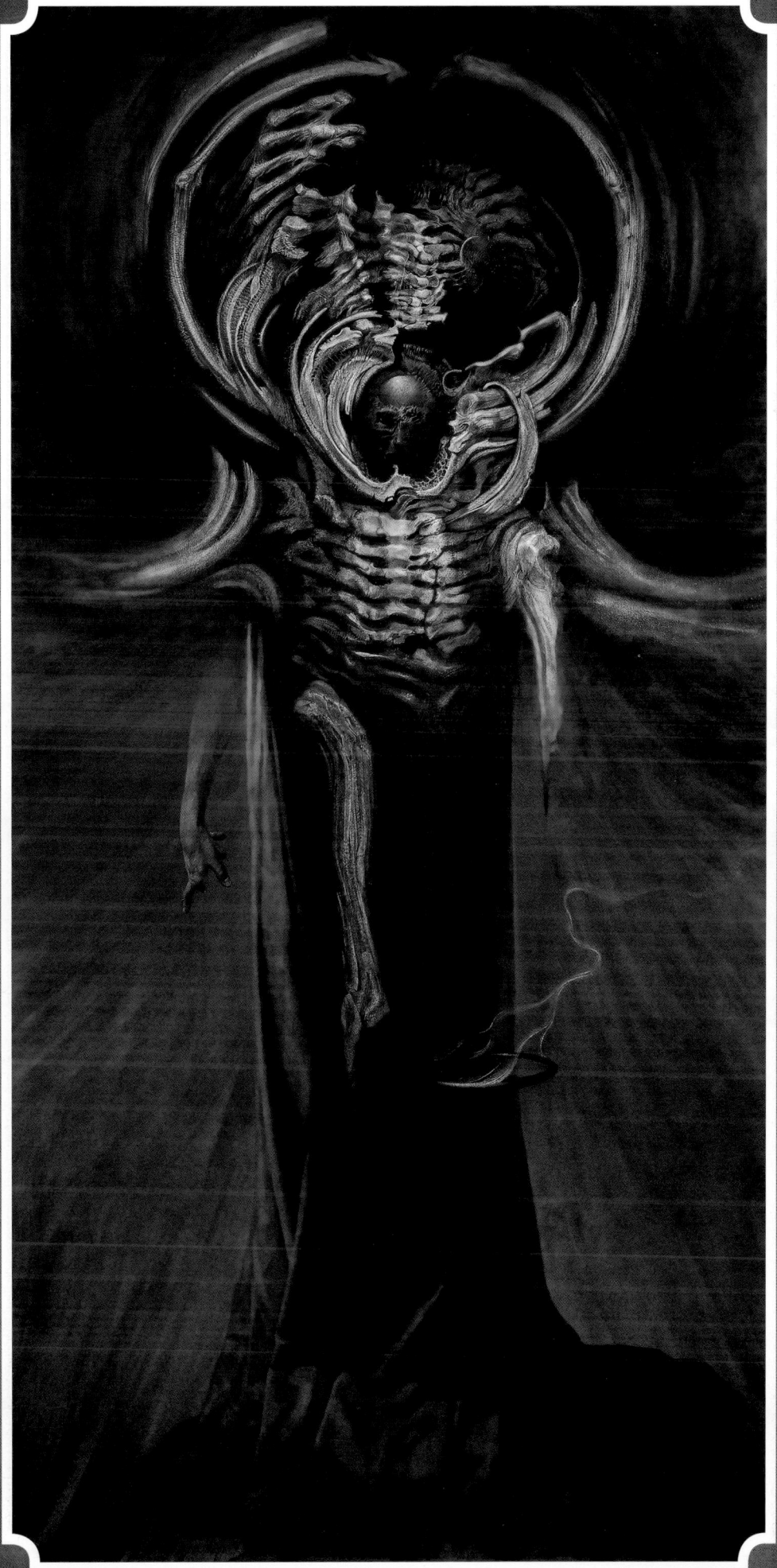

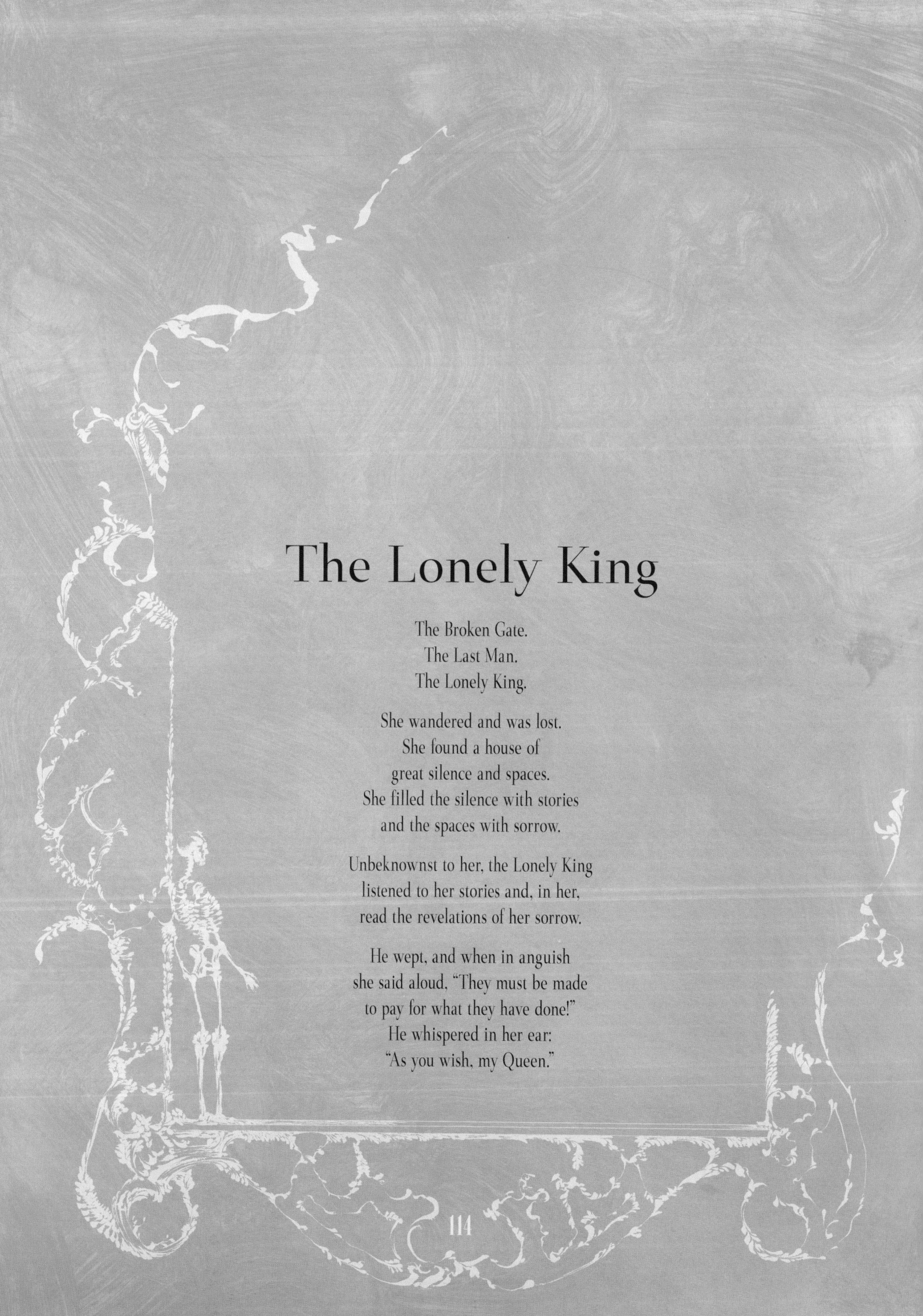

The Lonely King

The Broken Gate.
The Last Man.
The Lonely King.

She wandered and was lost.
She found a house of
great silence and spaces.
She filled the silence with stories
and the spaces with sorrow.

Unbeknownst to her, the Lonely King
listened to her stories and, in her,
read the revelations of her sorrow.

He wept, and when in anguish
she said aloud, "They must be made
to pay for what they have done!"
He whispered in her ear:
"As you wish, my Queen."

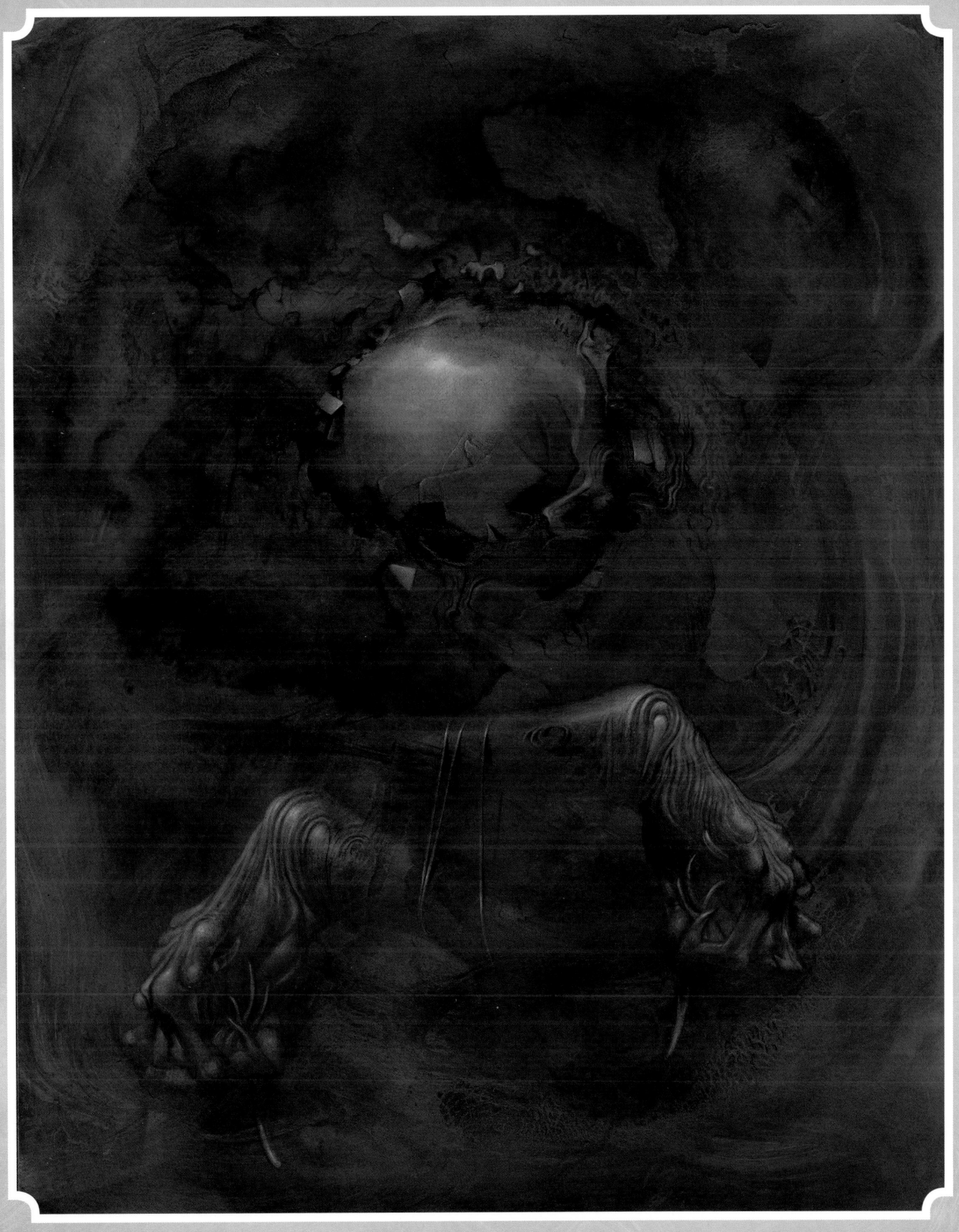

Mounted War

...and War was brought
upon the world of man,
summoned by man,
borne on a beast both bloated,
obese yet desperately starving.
Governed by the headless angel,
divine yet unseeing
and uncaring.

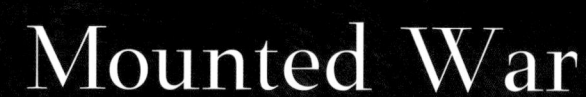

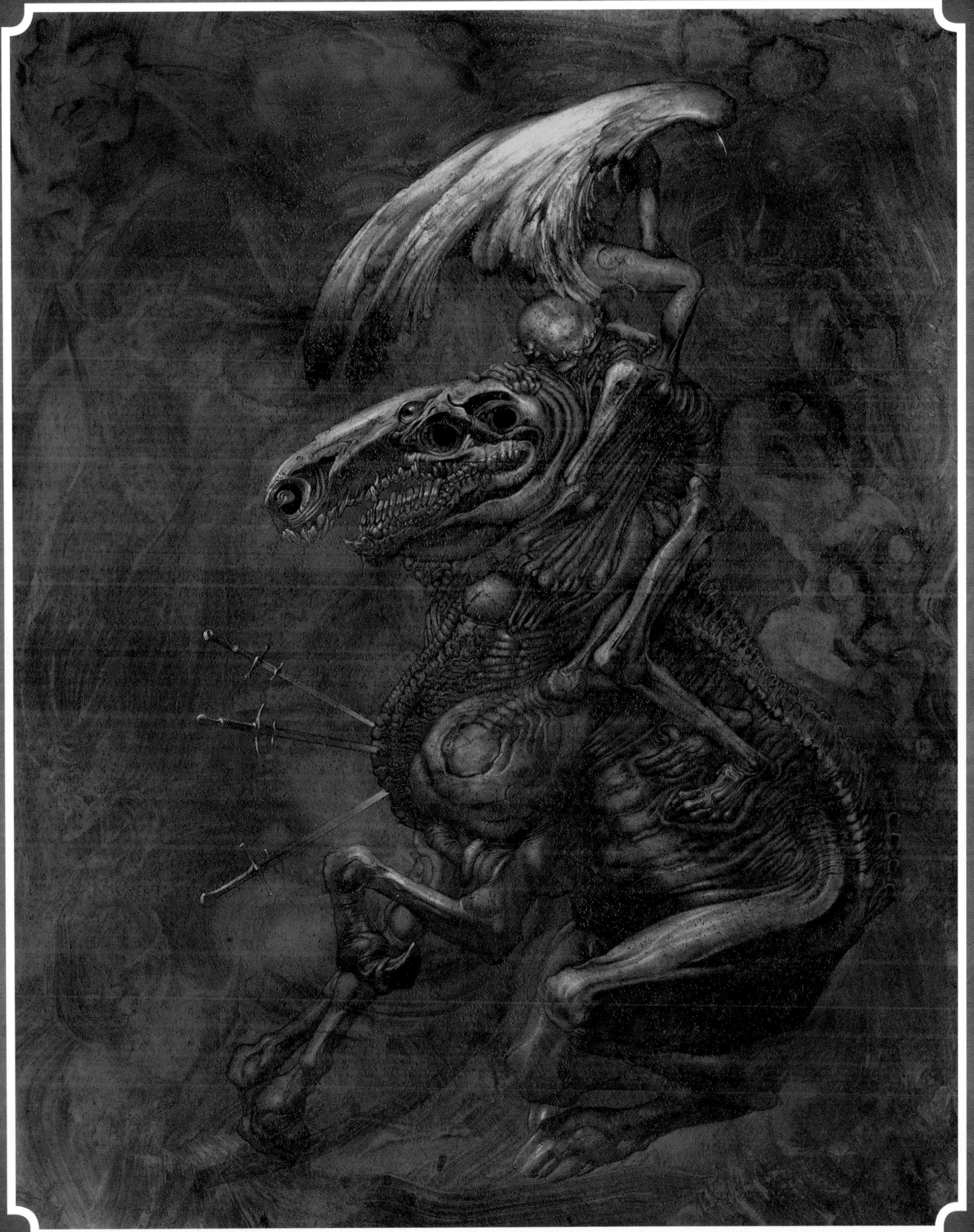

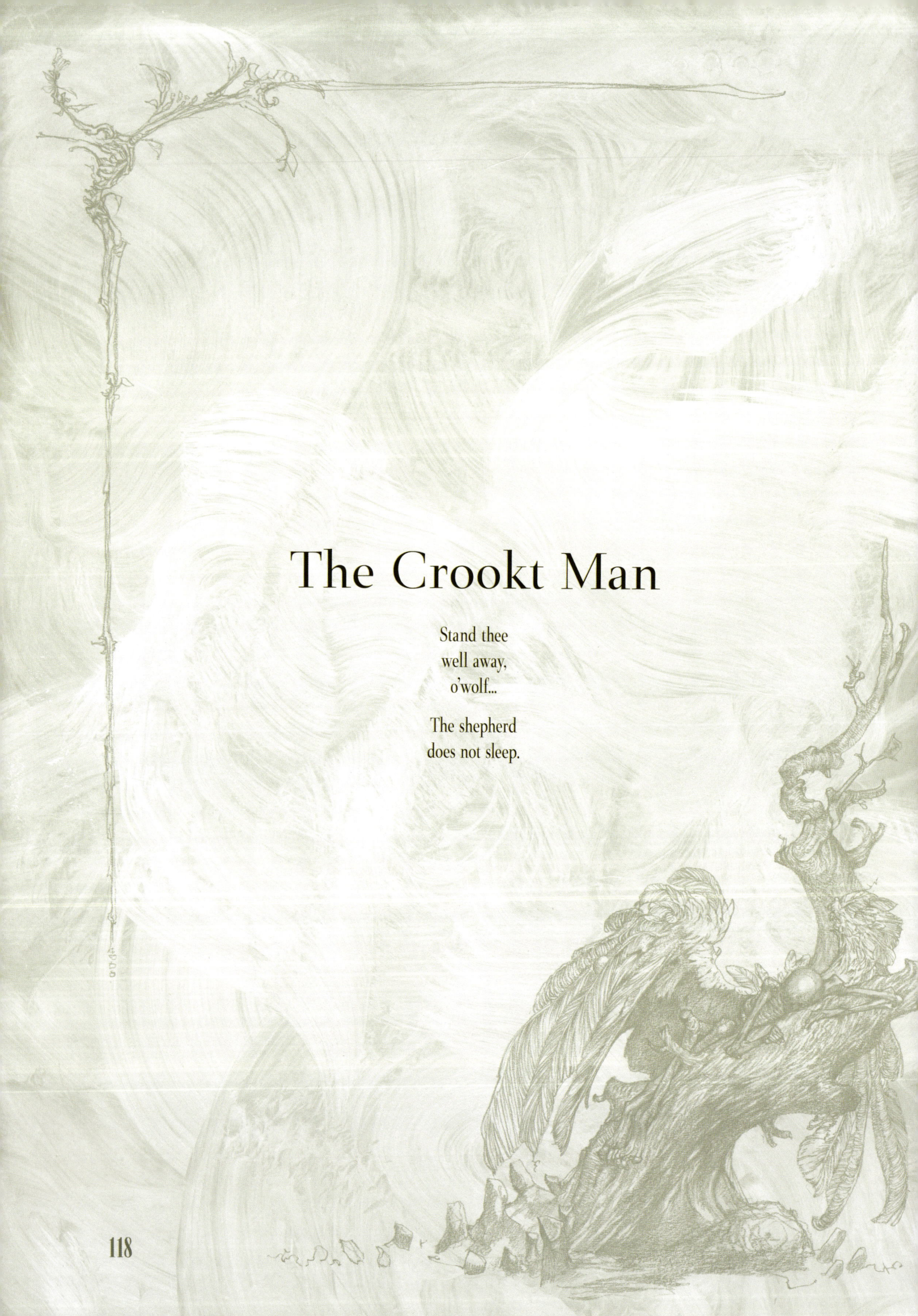

The Crookt Man

Stand thee
well away,
o'wolf...

The shepherd
does not sleep.

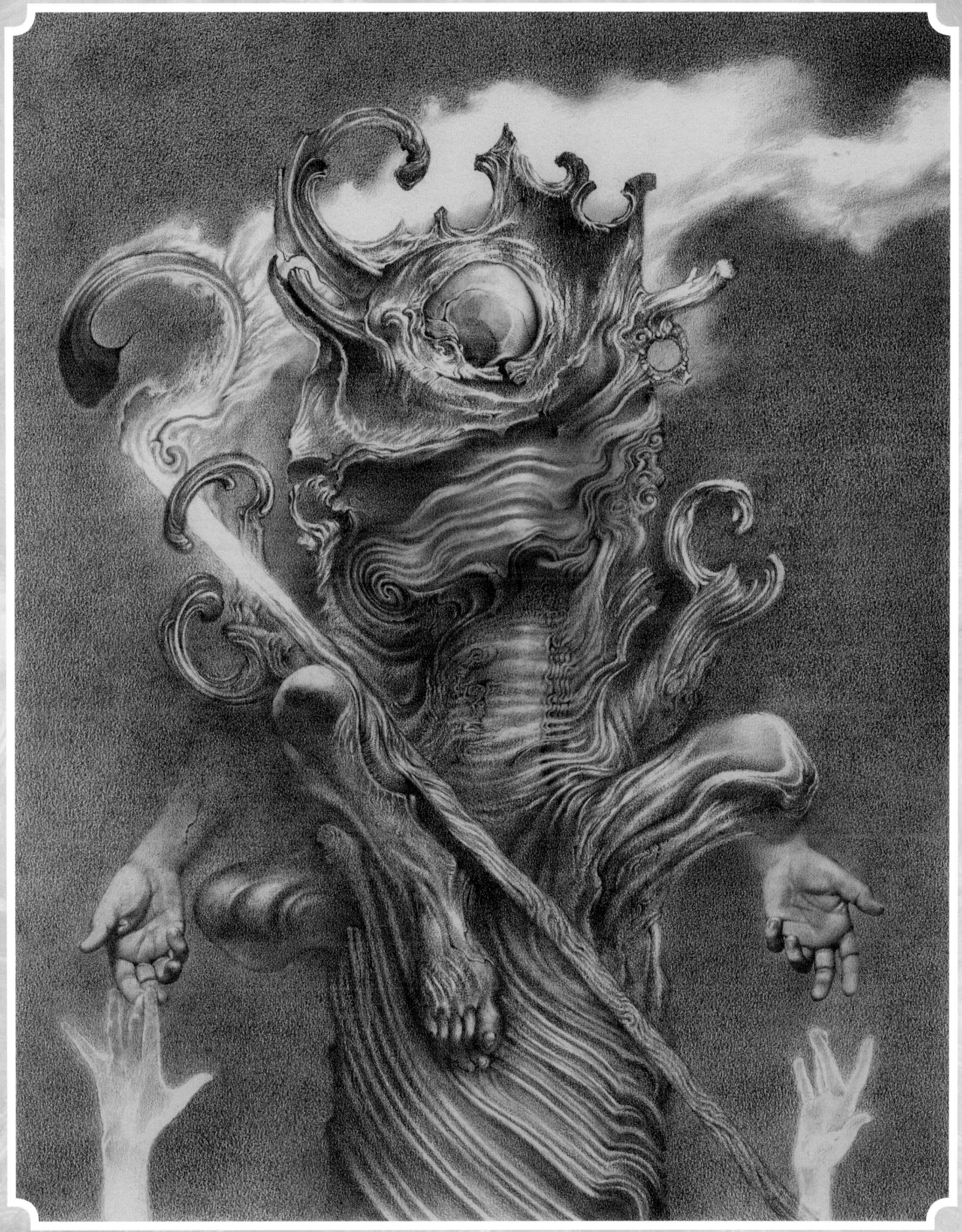

The Cathedral

The Headless King awaits,
and there is no laughter
in his court.

Set against those
who extol the beautiful
and condemn the grotesque
without the weighing
of their virtue.

His hand is as iron
against his foe,
unbiased and unswaying
by the distractions
of the mortal coil.

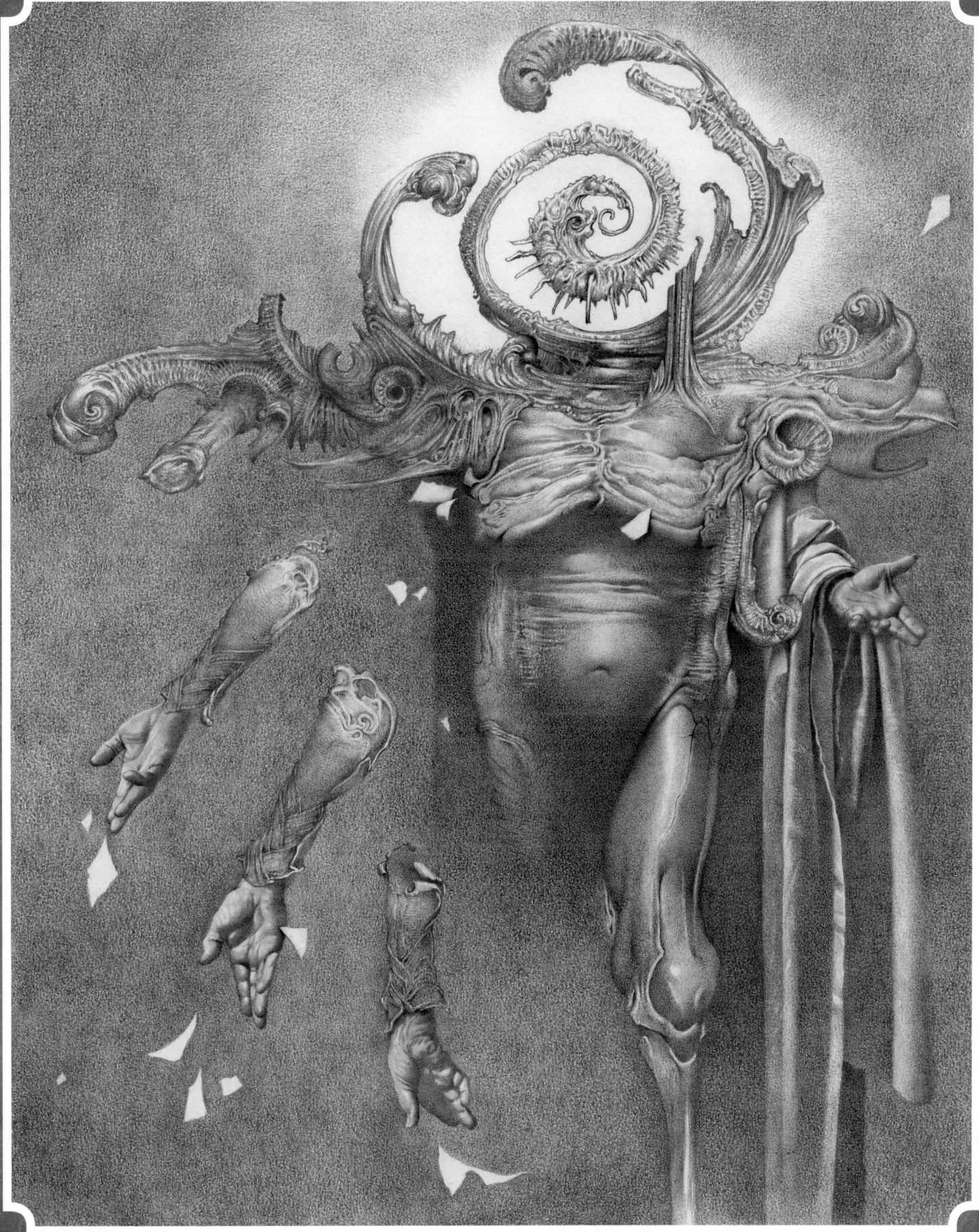

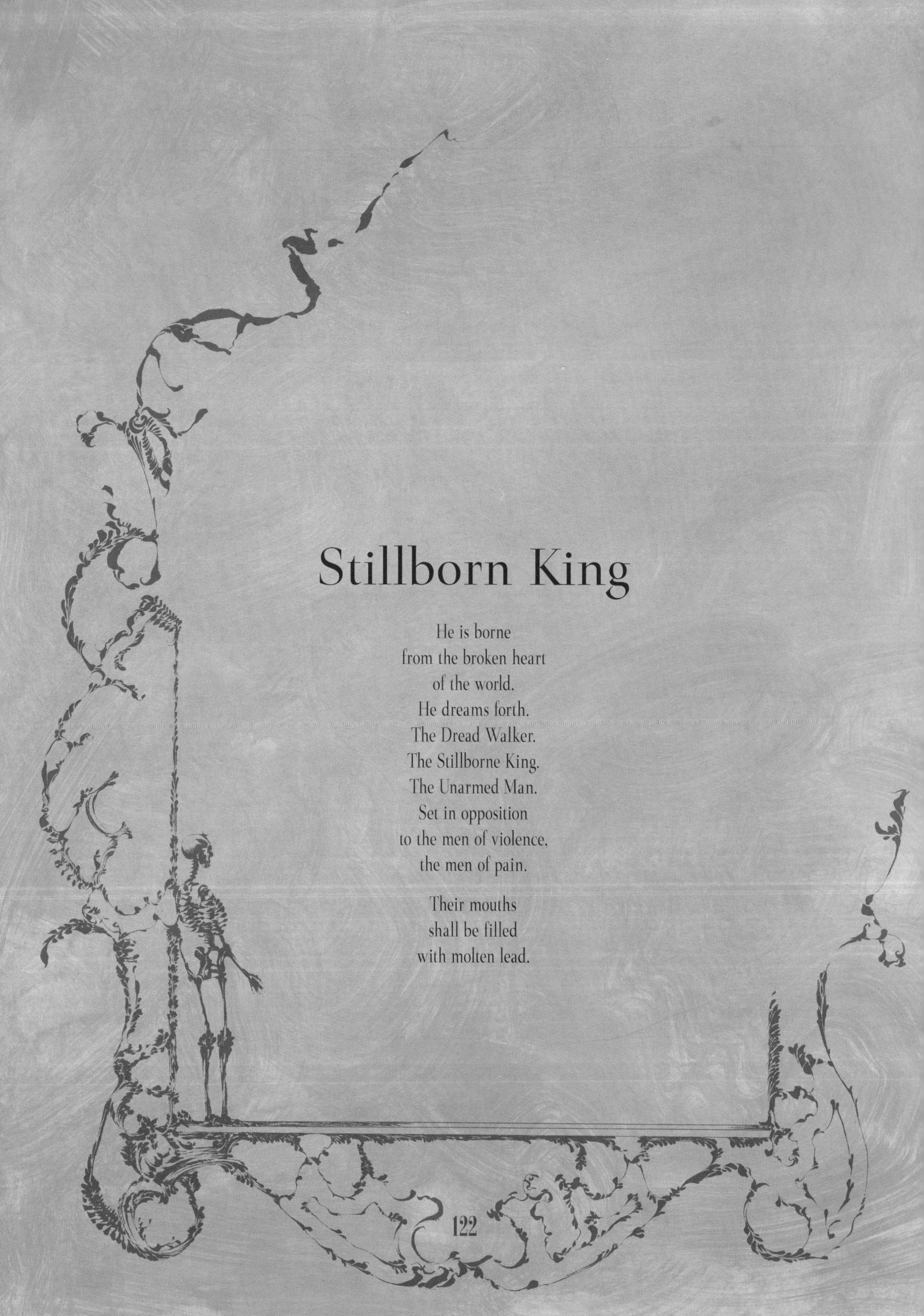

Stillborn King

He is borne
from the broken heart
of the world.
He dreams forth.
The Dread Walker.
The Stillborne King.
The Unarmed Man.
Set in opposition
to the men of violence,
the men of pain.

Their mouths
shall be filled
with molten lead.

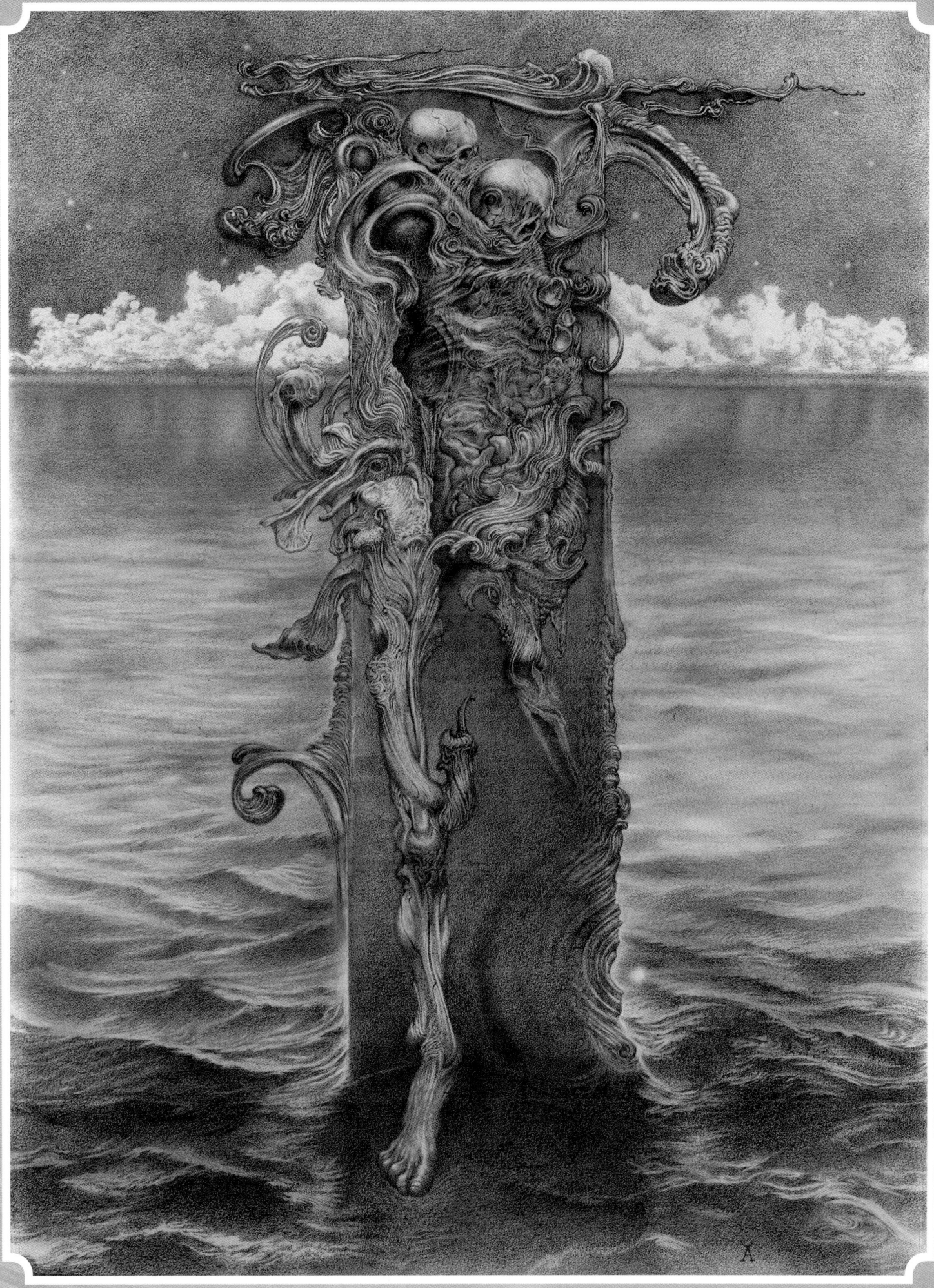

The Mortal Coil

He is the Truth borne
in the pause
between their lies.
The Still point
of the coming storm
The Quiet Man
The Veiled King
The Unspoken Word
In opposition to the
men of deceptions,
set against the
King of High Places
His silence shall fall
as thunder to their ears
And their mouths shall be
filled with thorns.

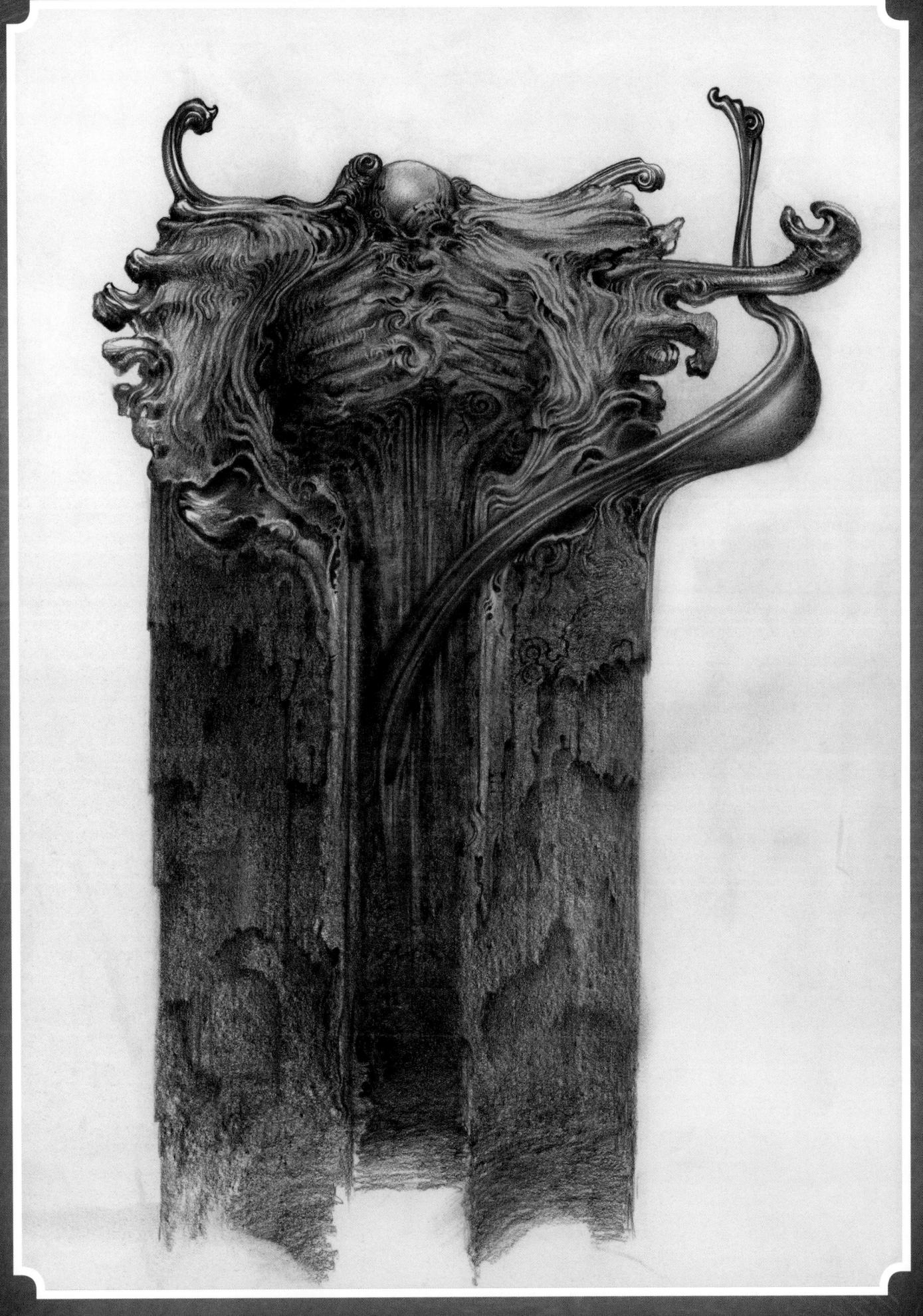

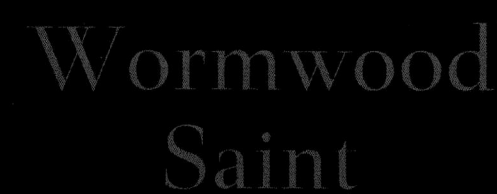

Wormwood
Saint

It is often
in desolate spaces
that the spirit
may find
stillness.
Amidst sadness
and decay
therein is healing.

Your pain
is not a sin.

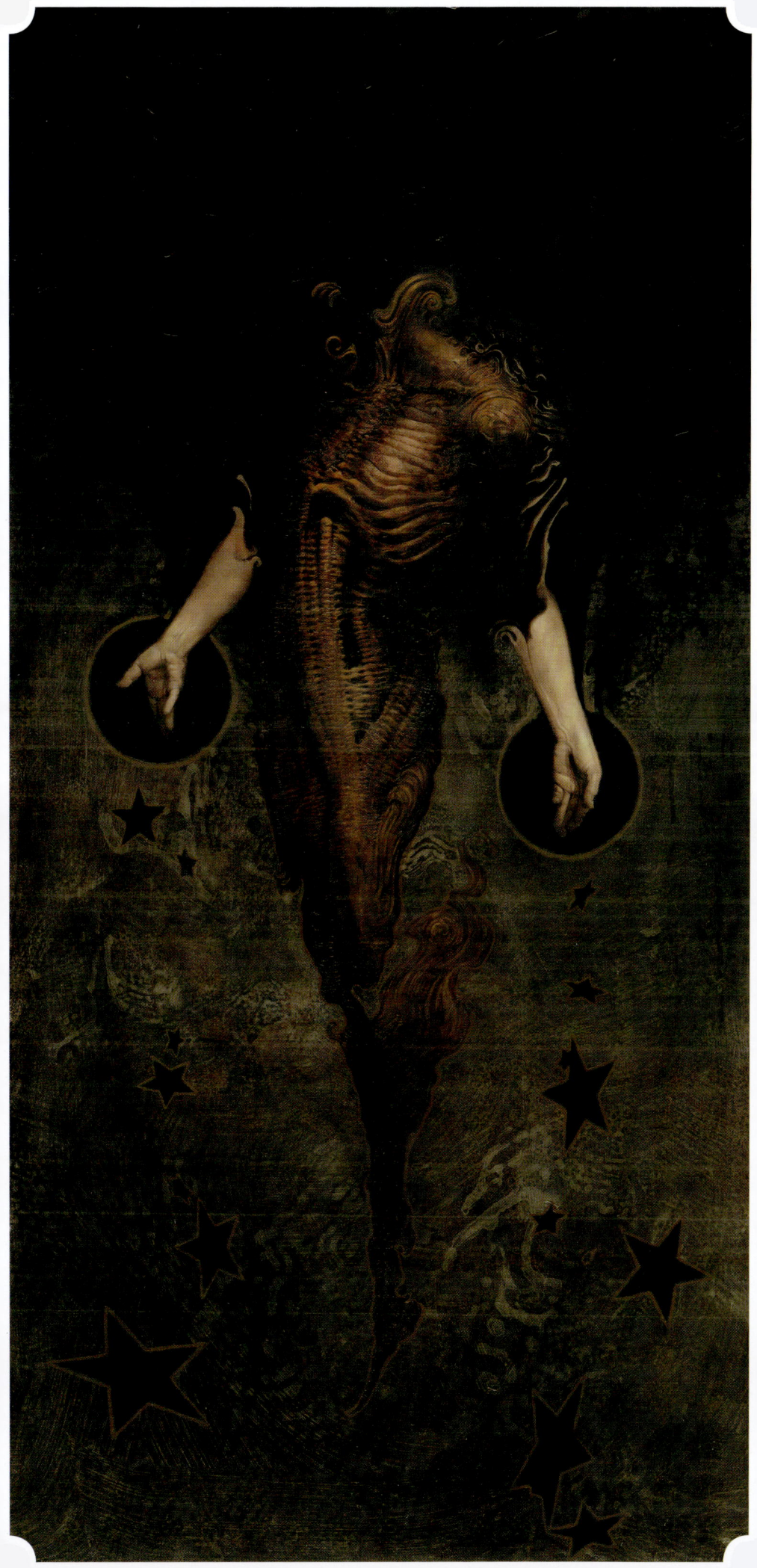

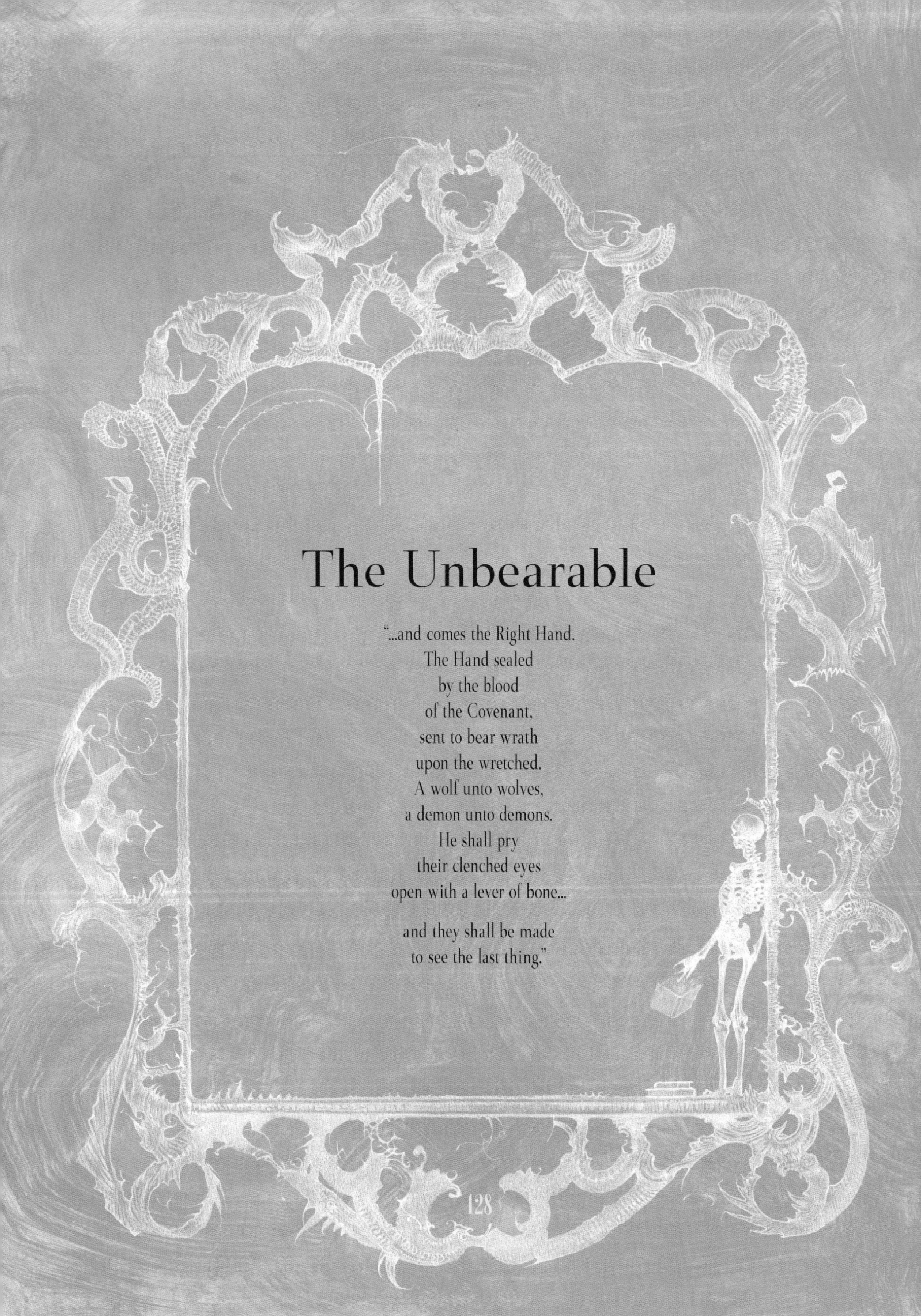

The Unbearable

"...and comes the Right Hand.
The Hand sealed
by the blood
of the Covenant,
sent to bear wrath
upon the wretched.
A wolf unto wolves,
a demon unto demons.
He shall pry
their clenched eyes
open with a lever of bone...

and they shall be made
to see the last thing."

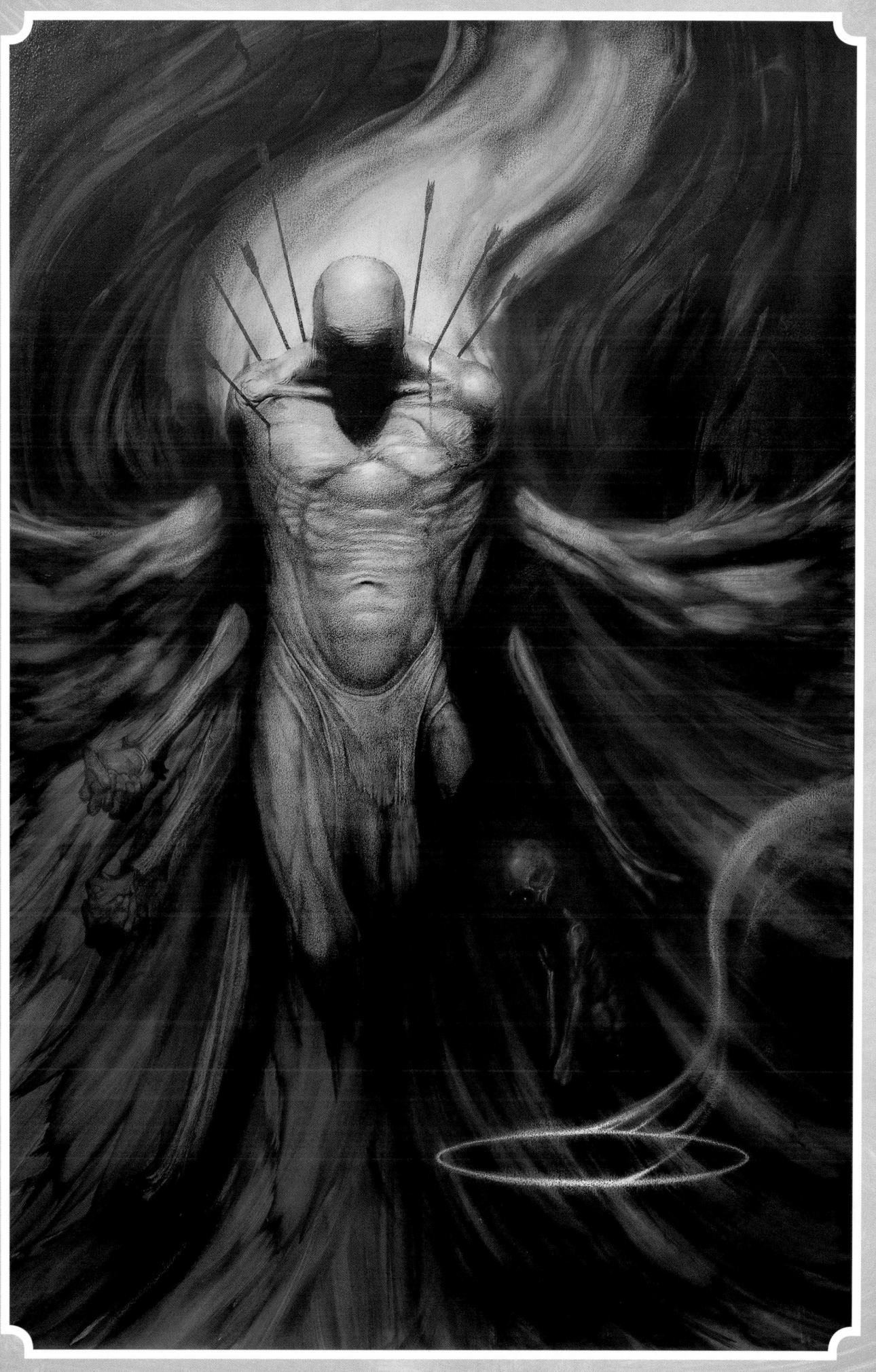

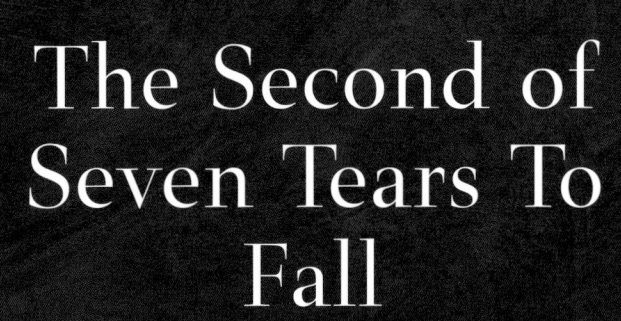

The Second of Seven Tears To Fall

From the House of Seven Stars
Fell the Second Tear of the Divine
...and set itself against the false kings
and their prophets.
"Bear witness. It is your doors
that shall be darkened, your tongues
that shall be charred and your crowns that
shall be broken. I fall from afar and I shall fall,
burning and brightly upon thee.
I, the First Sword
The Sword of Many Names
The Claiomh Solais
Nomorrodnegār
Asi."

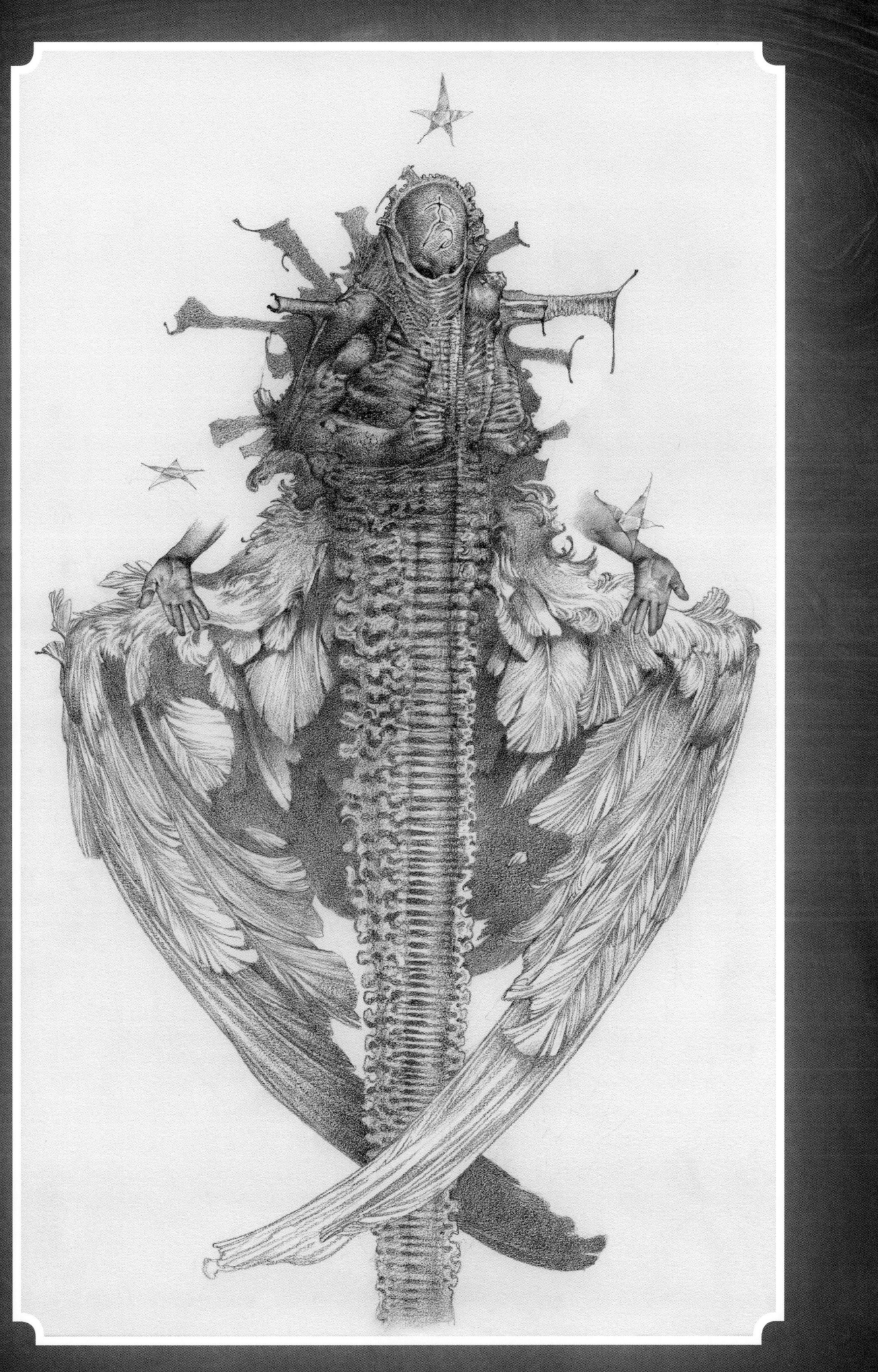

Wormwood Prince

"I was born in the heart
of the fire that made the sun...
all suns.
I am present in this moment
and all moments,
but in this moment
I am a warning.
Cease this destruction,
deconstruction of humanity.
Cease or suffer the plagues of your issue
to be visited upon your own house.
Cease, cease and be done...

While the Chains of Solomon
remain Unbroken."

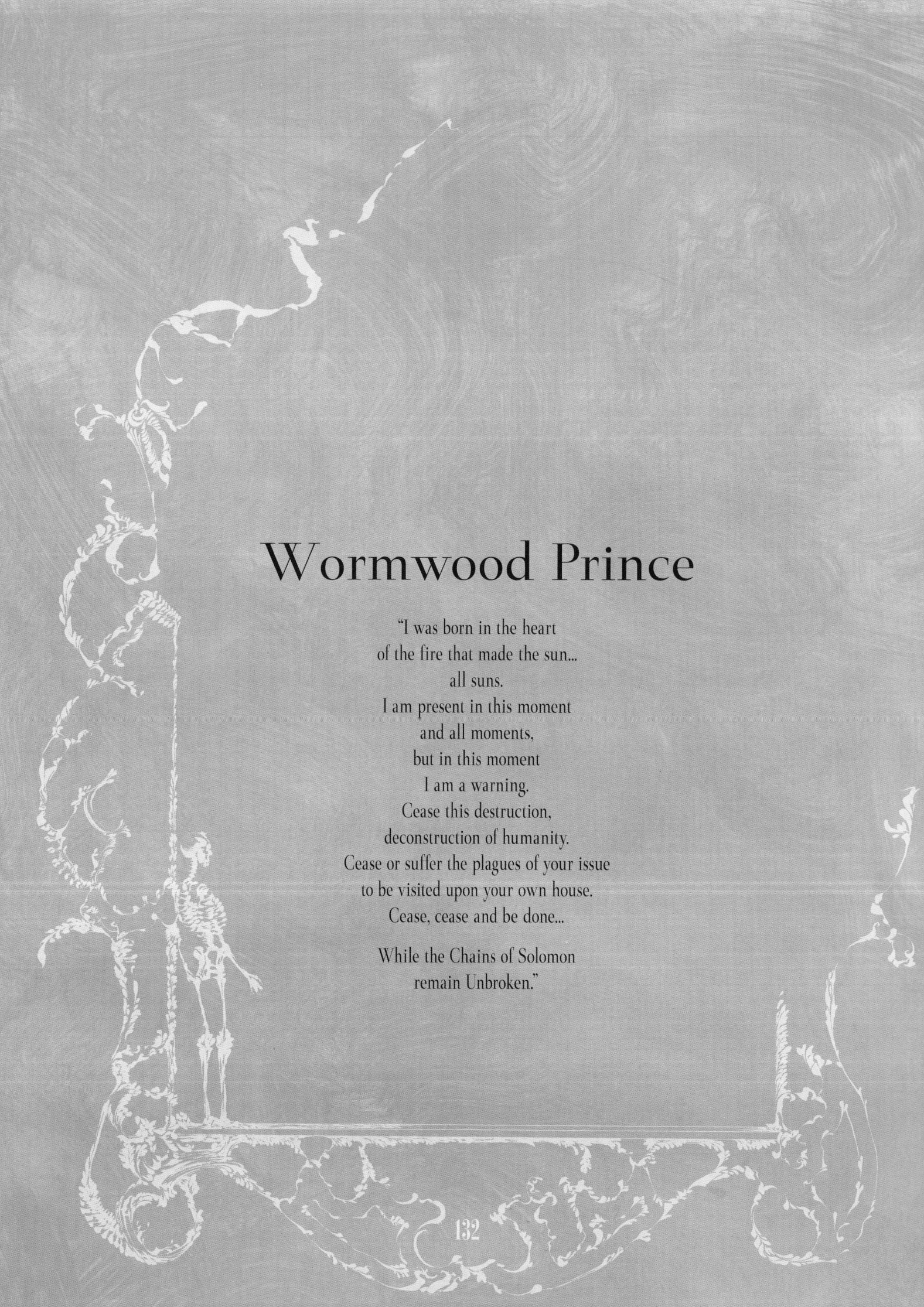

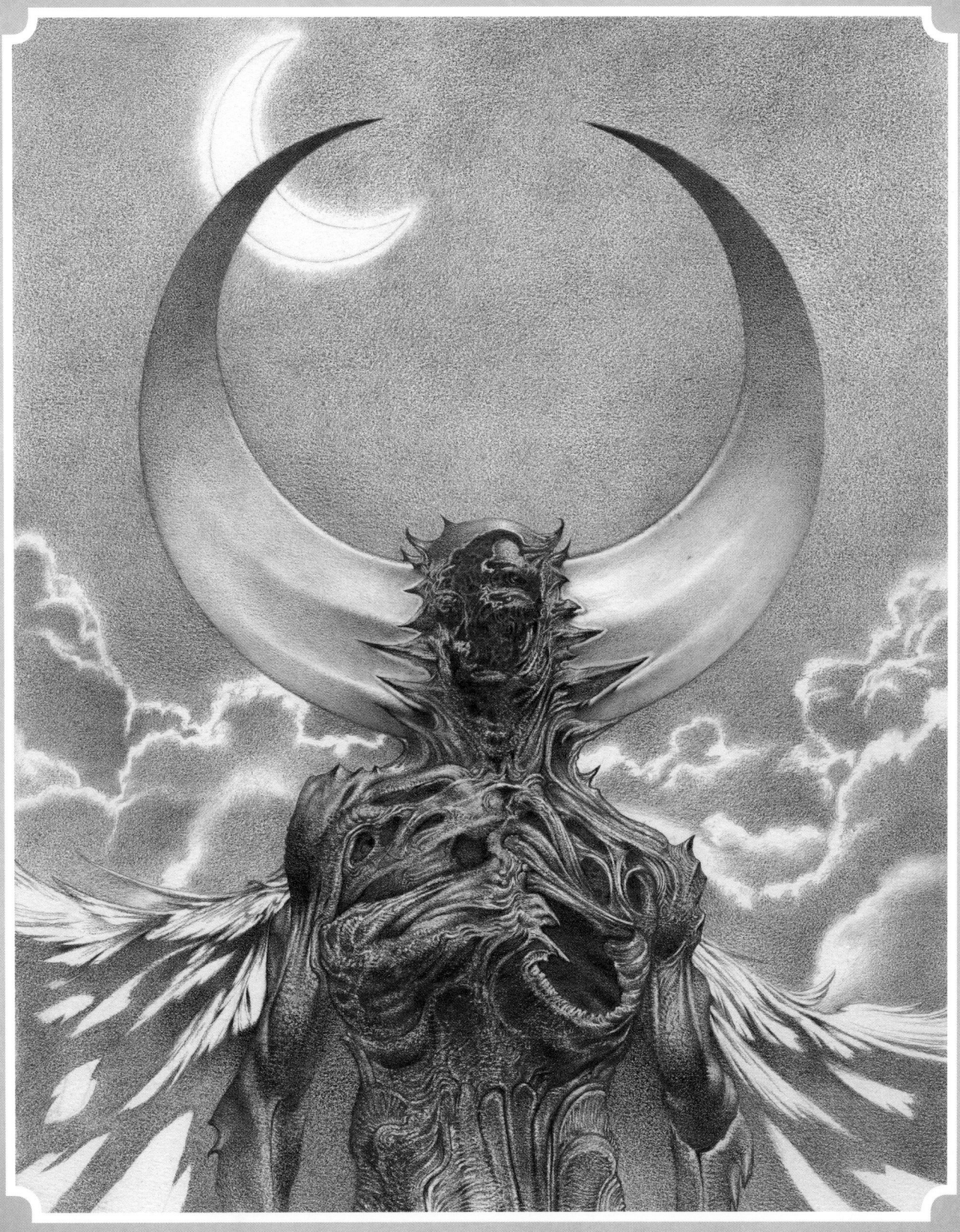

The Good Dog

The three stood close. The humans' remains were draped between them, strung about their appendages like ribbons decorating a tree. They reveled in his destruction, took glory from it.

They spread his blood and offal about them like a sacred anointing. This was the closest thing they felt to gratification—the rending of human flesh was orgasmic to them. When there was nothing left to tear, eat or wear, they turned to look for another victim, and this was how they spent every hour of the day and night... consuming mankind.

As they turned, seeking, they paused their eye-like organs—"seeing" something different, something new. In the distance, on the hood of an abandoned car, stood a great white dog. It was perfectly still. This was surprising to them. Since their ascendance, the animals of Earth had been unseen. They had all disappeared on the very day the demons had fully manifested.

The three moved in unison toward the dog, which stood as if made of stone. Instantly, there were dozens upon dozens of dogs standing on the hoods and roofs of all the cars. But not just dogs. Cats, wolves, coyotes, cougars, lions, tigers, even bears were everywhere as far as the eye could see. The three paused, not understanding, not knowing enough to be afraid. They had subjugated man, their kind. Nothing could stand against them... It was known.

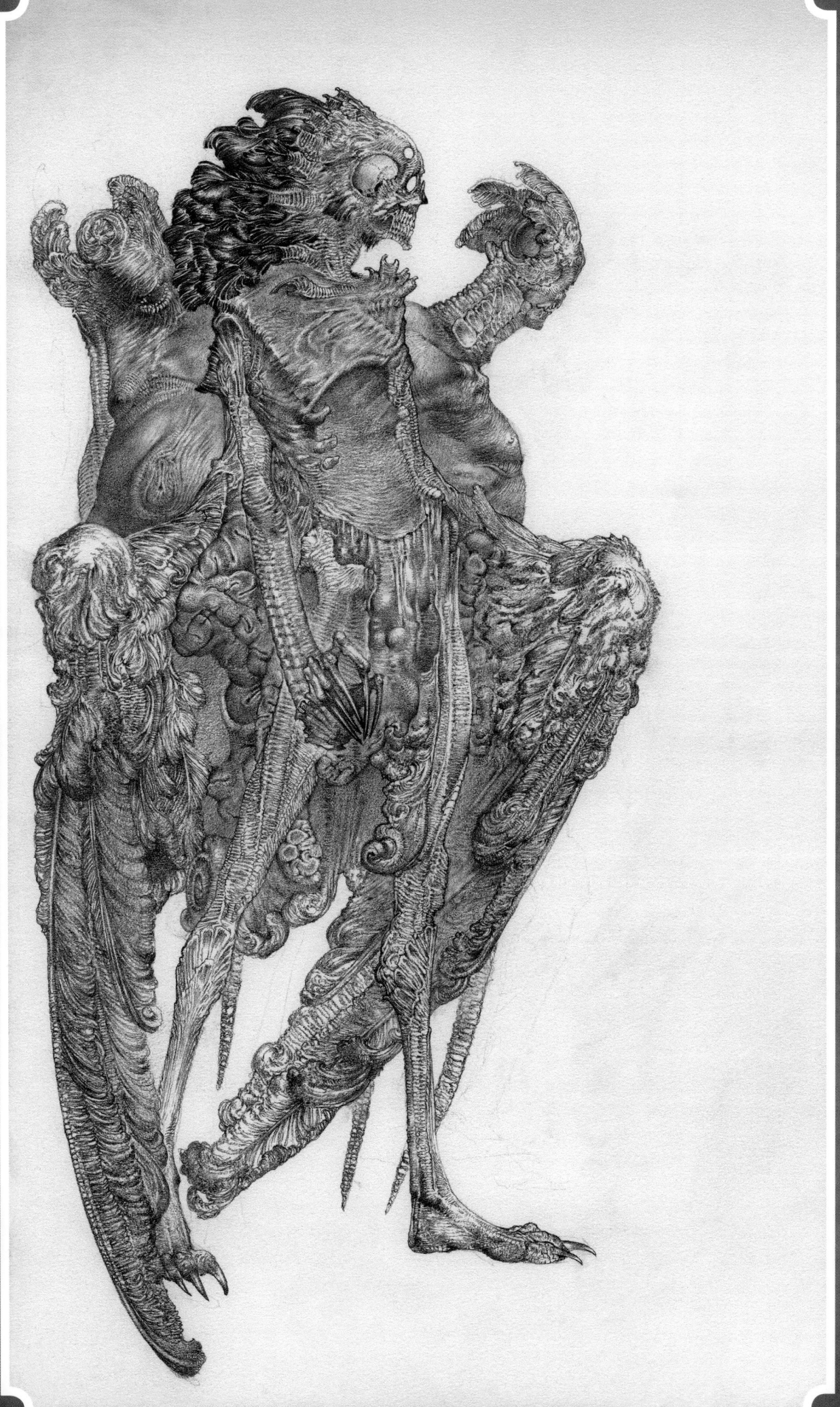

A low, growling sound began to build as all the animals at once opened their mouths. Seemingly from every crack, from every corner and shadow, the rats came. The rats—the creatures that had brought plague after plague upon man, not to destroy him but to prepare him for this last final real plague.

The demons began to bellow and howl as the rats rolled like a wave upon the three and began to bite and tear and rend and consume. Their eyes were bloodshot and feverish, and their small bodies were wickedly hot as they consumed the three, uncaring of the screams and shrieks. In but a moment, they were done. There was nothing left, and the rats were gone as quickly as they had appeared.

They were all gone, except for the dog, who stood surveying the field of this first battle. The first battle... but there would be many, many more.

He chuffed once in approval and sat for a moment. He looked around in that hopeful way that dogs do, for someone to play with, his tail wagging slightly. A short, gentle bark escaped his lips, and he stood. No one to play with, not yet, but he would be patient. He was, after all, a very good dog.

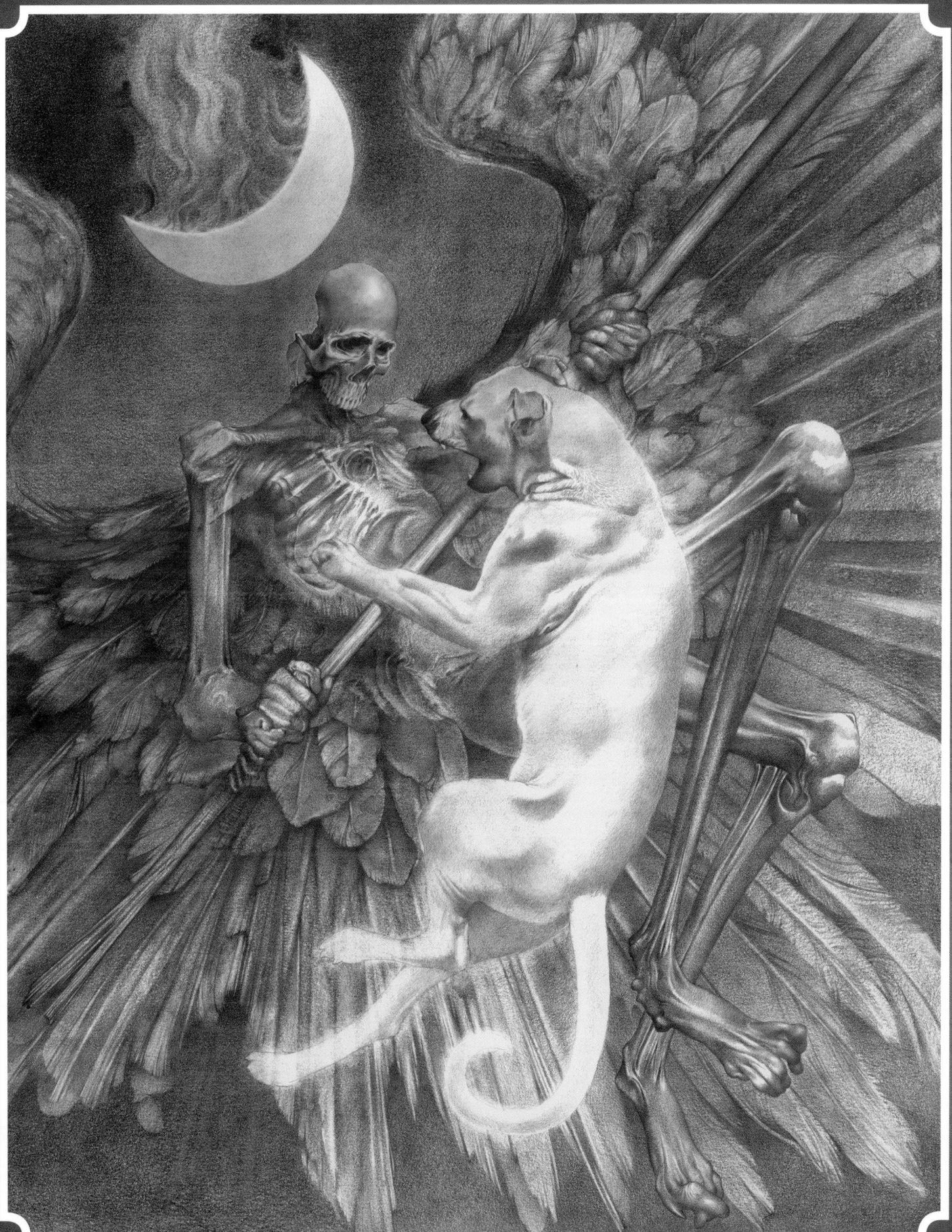

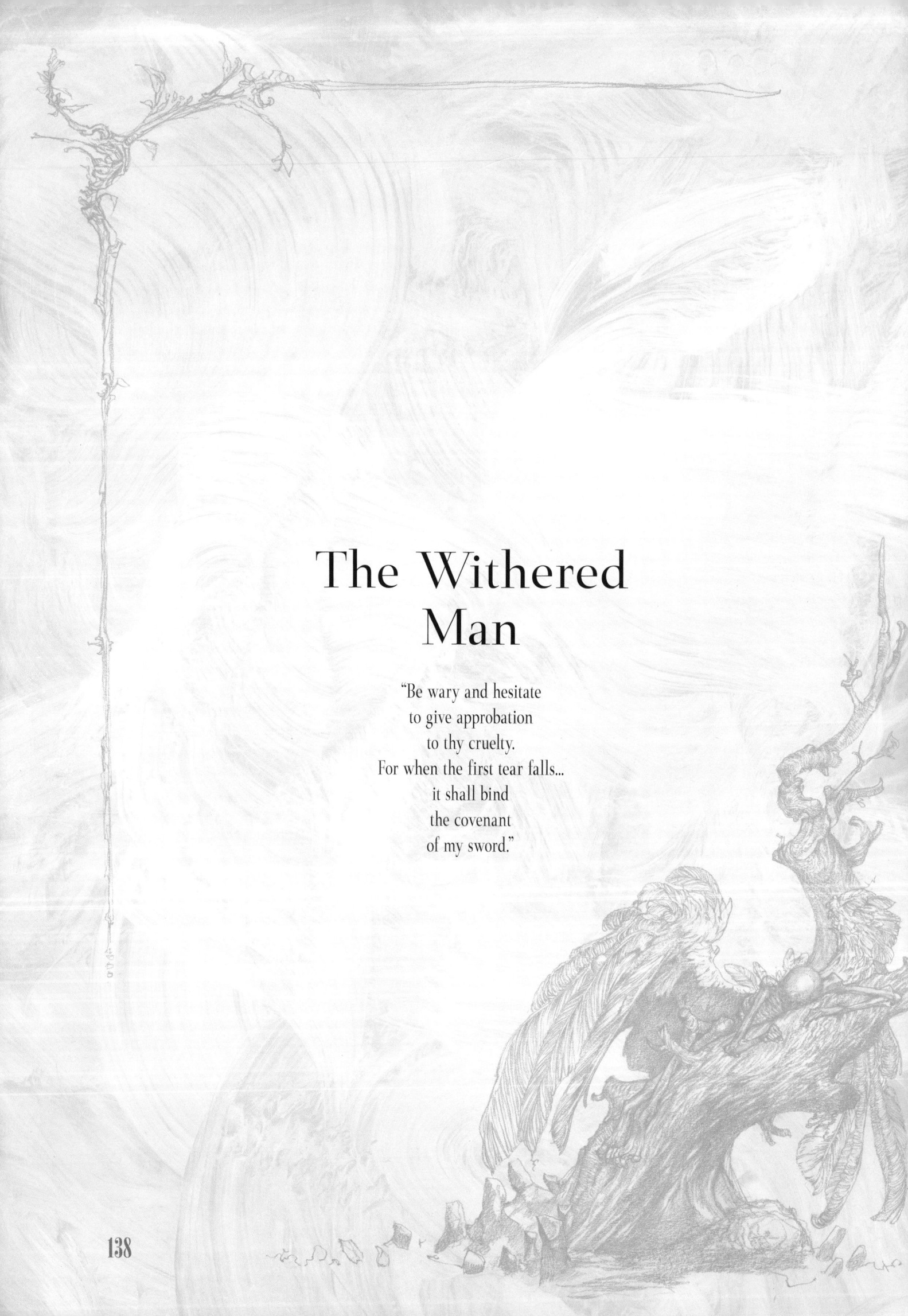

The Withered Man

"Be wary and hesitate
to give approbation
to thy cruelty.
For when the first tear falls...
it shall bind
the covenant
of my sword."

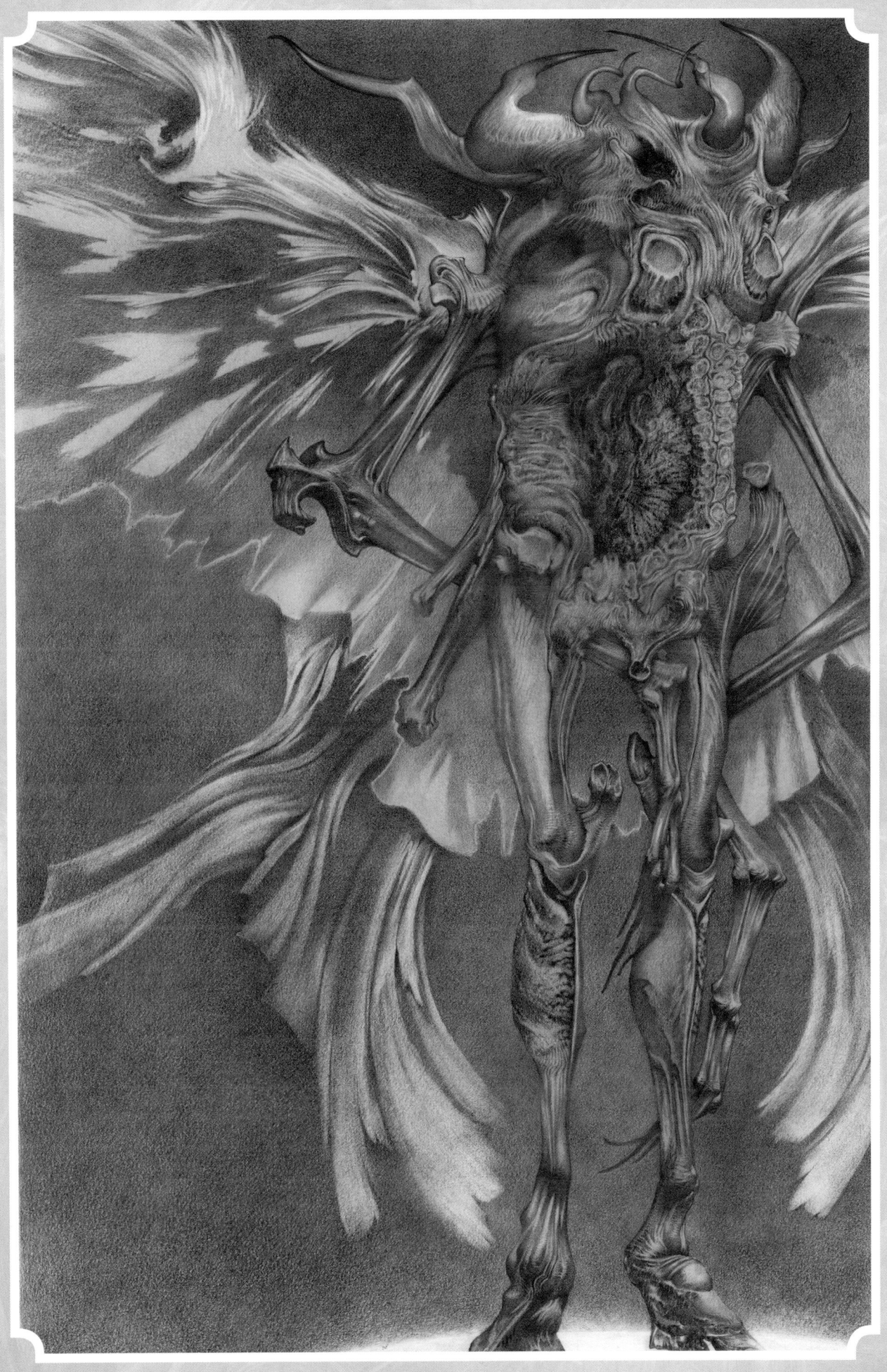

Foregone Kings

The Unheard
The Silent Kings
The Forgone
Their Wrath, in Silence, Falls.

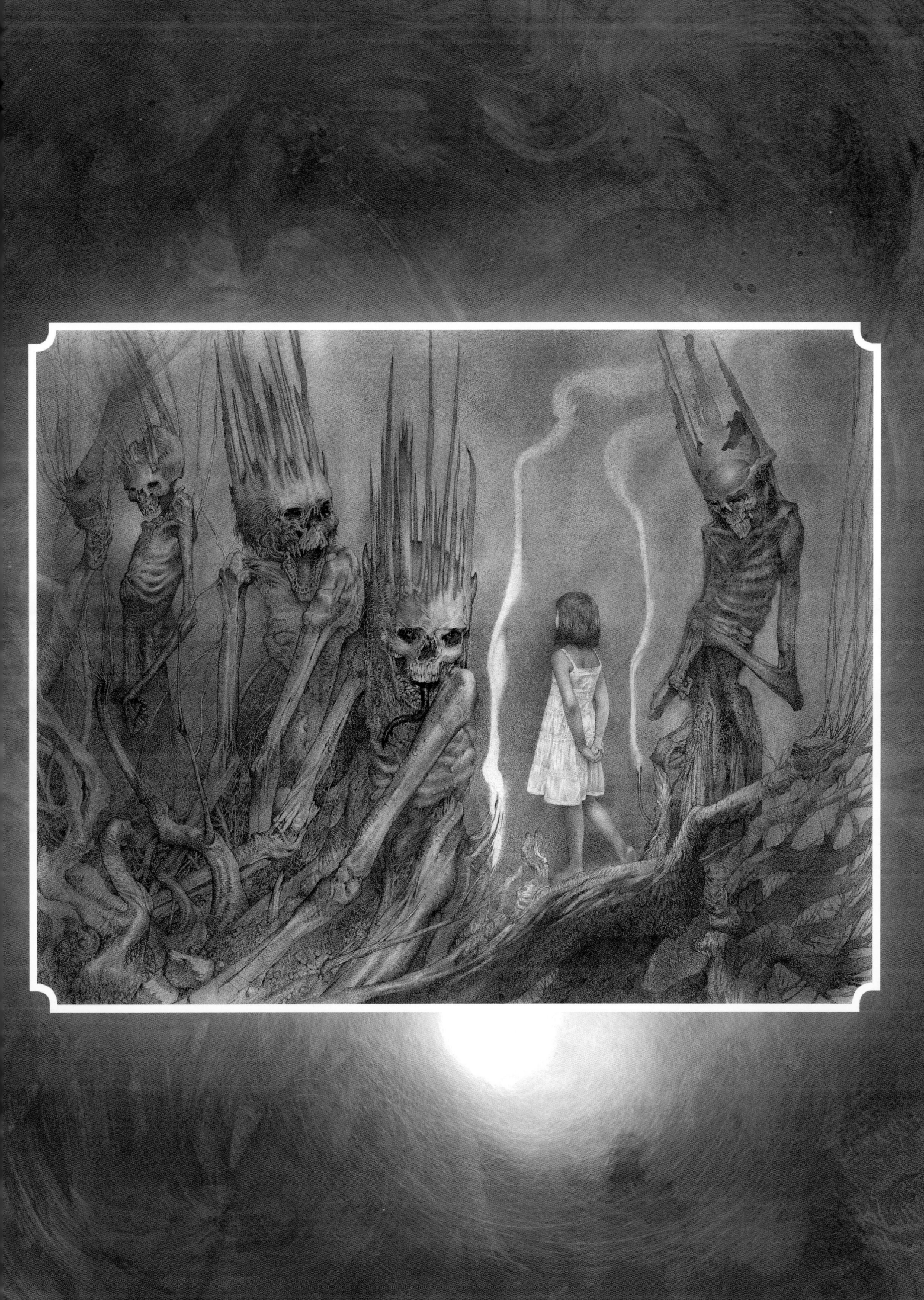

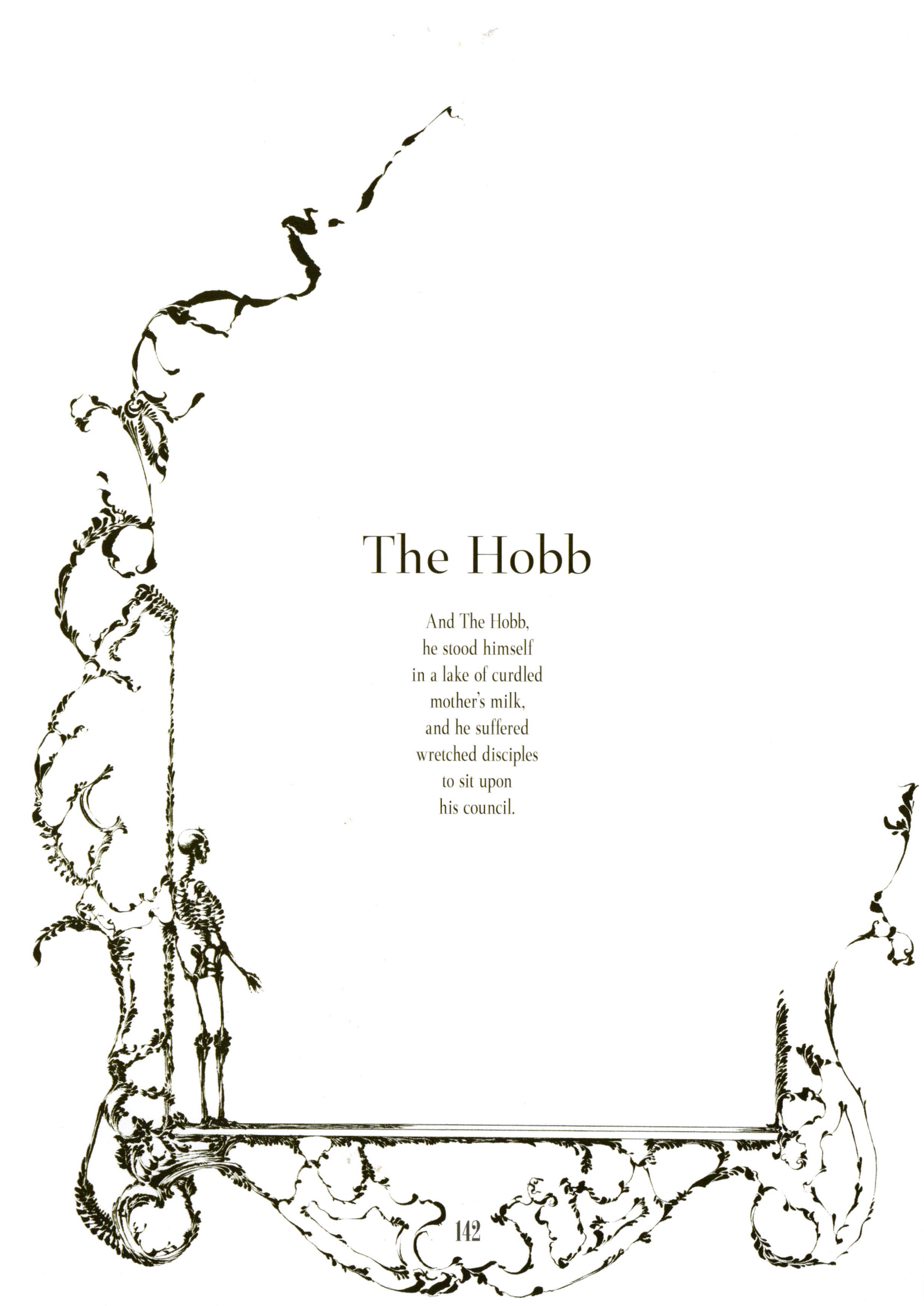

The Hobb

And The Hobb,
he stood himself
in a lake of curdled
mother's milk,
and he suffered
wretched disciples
to sit upon
his council.

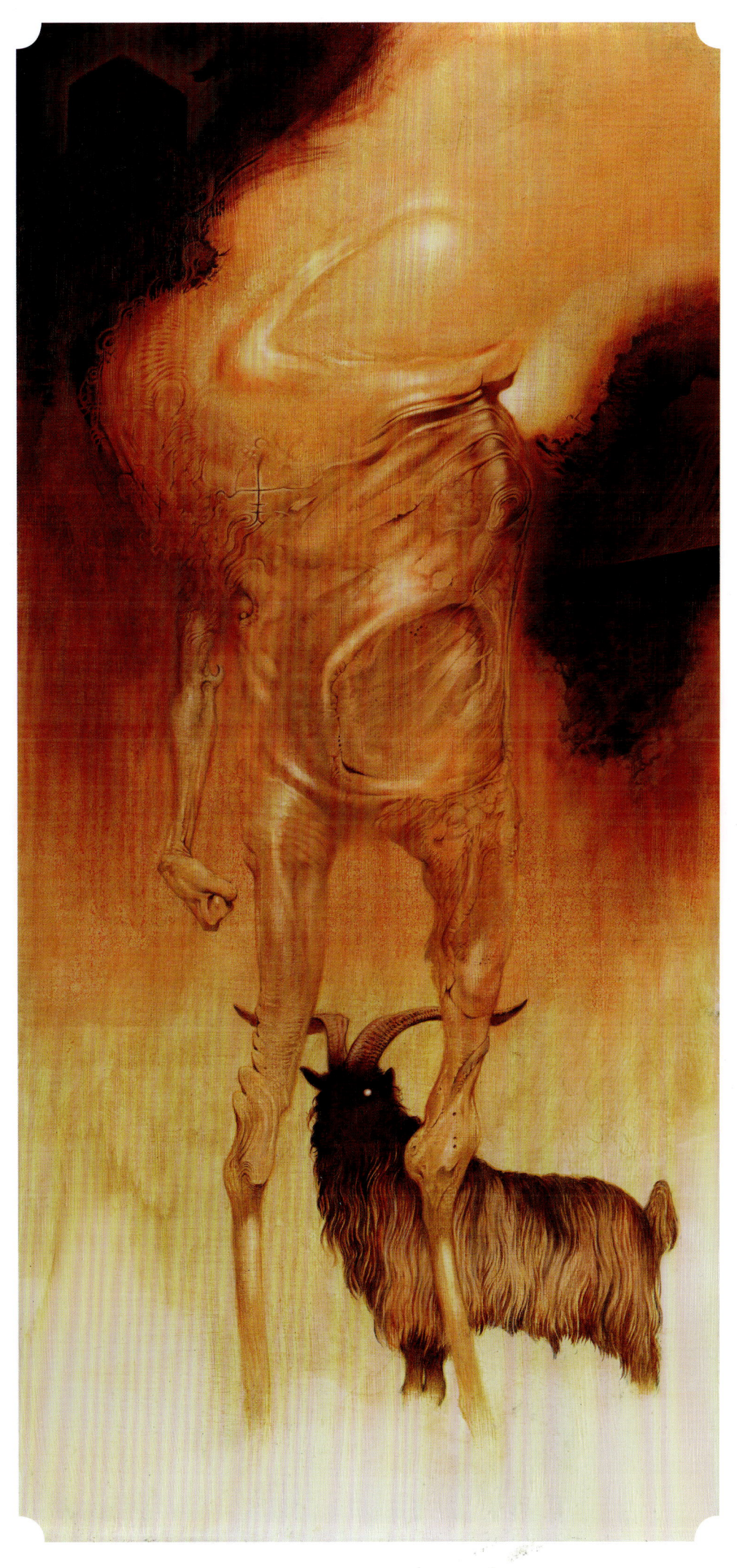

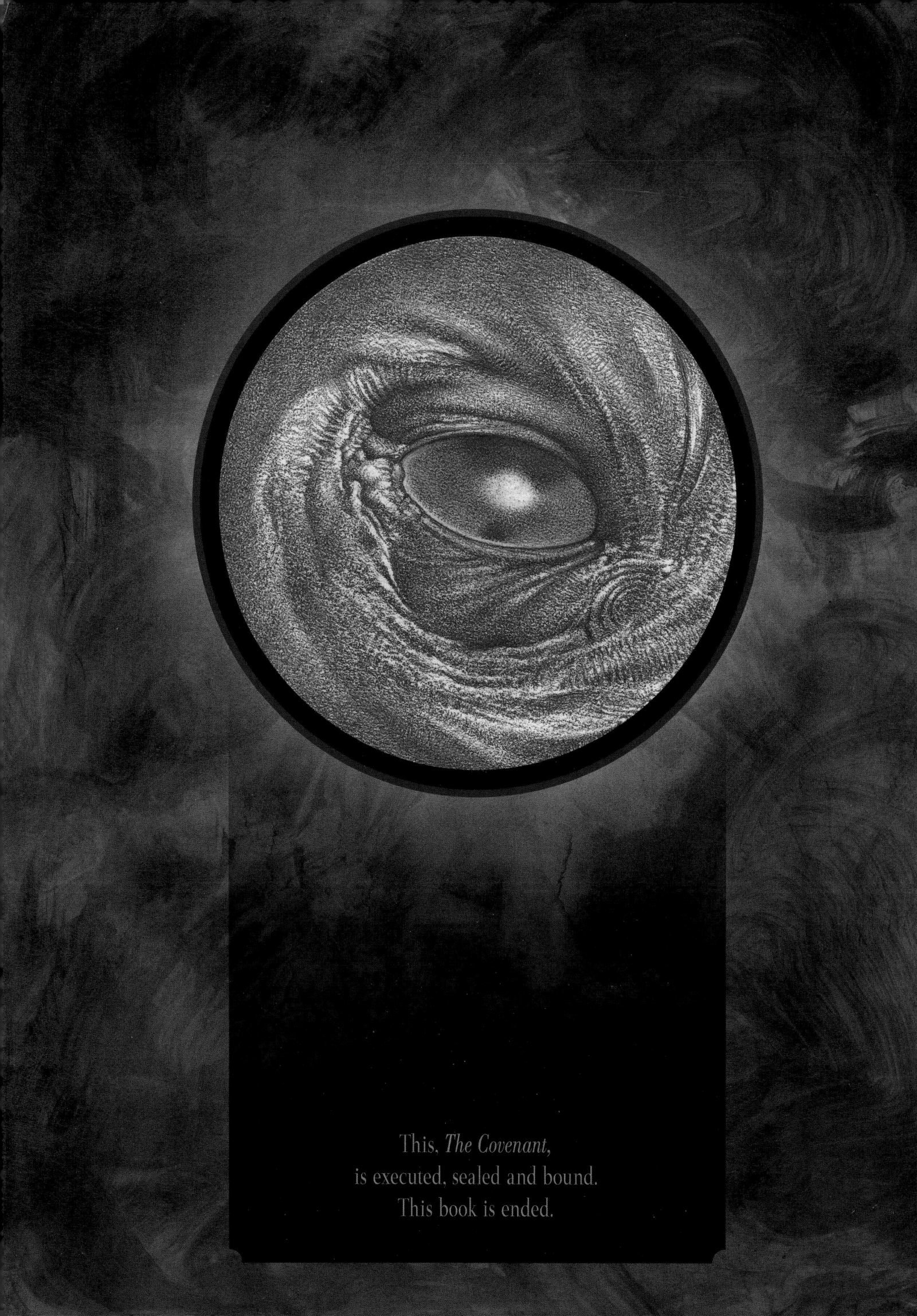

This, *The Covenant*,
is executed, sealed and bound.
This book is ended.